"Pastor Anthony Thompson's wife, Myra, was brutally ..... at Emanuel AME Church in Charleston along with eight others on June 17, 2015. The nation was shocked by this racially motivated hate crime. No one could have anticipated what would happen next. Pastor Thompson stood in front of the killer, forgave him, and then offered him the hope of the gospel in Jesus Christ. That moment, broadcast worldwide, inspired the entire city to act on grace rather than revenge and hatred. *Called to Forgive* offers the backstory, the heart-wrenching story, while celebrating and challenging the reader to experience the greatest force known to humanity, God's grace. As his colleague and friend, I commend Pastor Thompson to you. Every word written herein is authenticated by his life. If you long to understand forgiveness, meet Anthony Thompson."

—Marshall Blalock, pastor, First Baptist Church of Charleston;
president, South Carolina Baptist Convention (2018)

"Anthony Thompson has led the way in how to respond to those who wound and hurt us, even in the midst of awful tragedy. *Called to Forgive* inspires greater understanding in how to forgive as Christ has forgiven us (Ephesians 4:32) and how to be released from the slavery of unforgiveness."

—Foley Beach, archbishop and primate,
Anglican Church in North America

"In a world where there is so much negative rhetoric, hatred, and division, the words contained in this book will inspire you to forgive, heal, and grow. I am truly thankful for Anthony and his willingness to be open with his pain, struggles, and road to forgiveness. His testimony will change your life!"

—Eric S.C. Manning, pastor, Mother Emanuel AME Church,
Charleston, South Carolina

"In June 2015 I experienced two most unthinkable acts. The first was the killing of nine devout church members at Bible study, based solely on their race by a hateful bigot. Then just two days later, devastated family members showing an extreme act of grace by telling the murderer they forgive him. This beautiful book encourages and challenges the reader to see the powerful and healing act of forgiveness in the face of hate."

—Joseph P. Riley Jr., former mayor
of Charleston, South Carolina

"A powerful, compelling story of forgiveness. Rev. Thompson was prepared, ready for God's call. Through this amazing example of God's compassion and forgiveness, the citizens of Charleston will forever affirm that Love Is Stronger Than Hate. Thank you, Rev. Thompson—we love you!"

—John Tecklenburg, mayor of Charleston, South Carolina

"Part memoir, part guidebook for the soul, *Called to Forgive* tells the deeper story of Rev. Anthony Thompson's decision to publicly forgive his wife's murderer. Full of empathy and deep wisdom, Thompson explains the complexities behind his decision to forgive and the power it exerts in his life. This is a story that can change the world."

—Marjory Wentworth, coauthor, *We Are Charleston:
Tragedy and Triumph at Mother Emanuel*

CALLED TO
FORGIVE

CALLED TO
FORGIVE

THE CHARLESTON CHURCH SHOOTING,
A VICTIM'S HUSBAND, *and the*
PATH TO HEALING AND PEACE

ANTHONY B. THOMPSON
WITH DENISE GEORGE

BETHANYHOUSE
a division of Baker Publishing Group
Minneapolis, Minnesota

© 2019 by Anthony Thompson

Published by Bethany House Publishers
11400 Hampshire Avenue South
Bloomington, Minnesota 55438
www.bethanyhouse.com

Bethany House Publishers is a division of
Baker Publishing Group, Grand Rapids, Michigan

Printed in the United States of America

Library of Congress Cataloging-in-Publication Data
Names: Thompson, Anthony B., author. | George, Denise, author.
Title: Called to forgive : the Charleston church shooting, a victim's husband, and
    the path to healing and peace / Anthony B. Thompson with Denise George.
Description: Bloomington, Minnesota : Bethany House Publishers, [2019] | Includes
    bibliographical references.
Identifiers: LCCN 2018053534| ISBN 9780764232985 (trade paper : alk. paper) |
    ISBN 9781493418718 (e-book)
Subjects: LCSH: Thompson, Anthony B.—Family. | Emanuel AME Church
    (Charleston, S.C.) | Mass shootings—South Carolina—Charleston. | Murder
    victims' families—South Carolina—Charleston. | Hate crimes—South
    Carolina—Charleston. | Forgiveness.
Classification: LCC HV6534.C34 T46 2019 | DDC 241/.4—dc23
LC record available at https://lccn.loc.gov/2018053534

Unless otherwise indicated, Scripture quotations are from the HOLY BIBLE, NEW INTERNATIONAL VERSION®. Copyright © 1973, 1978, 1984 Biblica. Used by permission of Zondervan. All rights reserved.

Scripture quotations identified NKJV are from the New King James Version®. Copyright © 1982 by Thomas Nelson. Used by permission. All rights reserved.

Scripture quotations identified NRSV are from the New Revised Standard Version of the Bible, copyright © 1989 National Council of the Churches of Christ in the United States of America. Used by permission. All rights reserved.

Scripture quotations identified KJV are from the King James Version of the Bible.

This book recounts events in the life of Anthony Thompson according to the author's recollection and information from the author's perspective.

Cover design by LOOK Design Studio
Cover photography by Nathan Bell, Richard Bell Photography

Authors are represented by WordServe Literary Agency.

19 20 21 22 23 24 25   7 6 5 4 3 2 1

I dedicate this book to the memory of my wife,
the late Myra Quarles-Singleton Thompson,
who is *the sparkle in my eyes*.
Her love, giving spirit,
and dedication to education and ministry
for the Lord are my greatest inspiration.

I also extend a special dedication to the memory of the Emanuel Nine victims: Myra Quarles-Singleton Thompson, Sharonda Coleman-Singleton, Cynthia Graham Hurd, Susie Jackson, Ethel Lance, Depayne Middleton Doctor, Clementa Carlos Pinckney, Tywanza Sanders, and Daniel L. Simmons Sr.

A very special dedication to the survivors of the Emanuel Nine Tragedy, who are our **Voices of Hope and Reflection**: Although we find ourselves in a broken world—a world in which hurting people far too often hurt other people—we come longing for healing. We gather to pray for peace. Not only that, but we also come pledging to reverse the conditions that have produced such violence and destructive behavior that have torn at the fabric of our families and our communities.

For Jennifer and Malana Pinckney, Felicia Sanders and her grand-daughter, and Polly Sheppard.

Contents

Acknowledgments

"I am the vine, ye are the branches: He that abideth in me, and I in him, the same bringeth forth much fruit: for without me ye can do nothing" (John 15:5 KJV).

To God be the glory, the honor, and the praise. For He and He alone is worthy to be praised!

God brought good out of the Emanuel Nine tragedy. God gave me the peace that "passeth all understanding" in the most tragic and lonely time of my life. He simultaneously assigned me the mission to preach the gospel of forgiveness so that the "peace" may be imparted to our families, churches, cities, states, and nation.

God prepared the way before me by placing His chosen people in my path to successfully implement His mission through this book, *Called to Forgive: The Charleston Church Shooting, a Victim's Husband, and the Path to Healing and Peace.* And it is with great honor that I thank each and every one of them.

Many thanks to my agent, Greg Johnson; to my editor, Andy McGuire; and to the staff of Bethany House.

To Eugene Smith, a lifelong friend who reminded me of the time when we attended Benedict College and God placed the desire in my heart to write a book.

To R. Marshall Blalock, pastor of First Baptist Church in Charleston, South Carolina—a friend who encouraged me with an invitation to begin my mission in a sermon at First Baptist Church on "The Healing Power of Forgiveness."

To Mrs. Cathy Powell Blalock, who through the guidance of the Holy Spirit ignited the flame in my heart to spread the gospel of forgiveness through the writing of this book—a finely tuned instrument of God who enabled me and Denise George to form a harmonious relationship for the spreading of the gospel of forgiveness.

To Denise George, a friend and mentor who worked diligently on this mission. Her expertise, professionalism, insight, and ideas enlightened my mind and assured me of the God-given commonality we have in spreading the gospel of forgiveness.

To Jeanette Jordan, pastor of the Church House of Ministries Worldwide in Ladson, South Carolina, who encouraged and prayed for me every day, every step of the way.

And a special thank-you to my children: Kevin, Anthony, and Denise, whose love and respect for God, and whose act of forgiveness toward Dylann Roof, brought more peace in my life than they could ever imagine.

Introduction

Dear Reader:

On a warm June evening in Charleston, South Carolina, fourteen people were in the basement of the historic Emanuel African Methodist Episcopal Church, twelve of them sitting ready to participate in the Wednesday evening Bible study led by my wife, newly licensed AME minister Myra Thompson. That evening I was unable to go with Myra, assuming the Wednesday evening responsibilities at the church where I serve as pastor, the nearby Holy Trinity Reformed Episcopal Church.

A few minutes after 8 p.m., as Myra began teaching from Mark 4—Jesus' parable of the sower—a young white man with blond hair and a fanny pack walked into the church. The pastor, teacher, and participants eagerly welcomed him, pulling out a chair at the table and inviting him to join them.

An hour later, Myra finished teaching Jesus' parable and, with all eyes closed, the group stood for the closing prayer.

That's when the unthinkable happened, a traumatic and haunting moment that would forever be frozen in time and history, a horrific act that sent nine people to their graves and stunned an entire nation.

This story is heartbreaking, coming to you in my words and from my experience of losing my dear wife and best friend in a senseless and terrifying act of pure and calculated hate. You'll learn the true, disturbing story of the young white racist who took the lives of nine people at the Emanuel AME Church.

But this book offers much more than that. You'll also discover how I, devastated by the death of my wife, made the decision to forgive the young racist man who murdered her in cold blood as she stood praying with her fellow worshipers. Some said my public forgiveness of the young killer, as well as the forgiveness by several other victims' family members, shocked a nation and helped a bewildered, hurting community respond with unity and peace instead of the expected racially motivated riots and violence that have happened in other U.S. cities.

In this book you will gain a deeper understanding of biblical forgiveness—what it is, how it works, and why it can bring unexpected and astonishing results throughout the world, breaking down barriers of cultural, racial, and denominational differences. You will also see why biblical forgiveness is seen by society as a surprising, irrational, and illogical act.

After reading *Called to Forgive*, you will be aware that biblical forgiveness is light-years removed from the way a vindictive, vengeful society views forgiveness. And you will discover the unforeseen love, unity, and peace that forgiveness can bring into an individual's life, family, church, community, and nation.

At the end of this memoir, we include a powerful chapter-by-chapter Bible study that focuses on biblical forgiveness. It contains Scriptures to read, questions and quotations to ponder, and invitations to respond in writing to thought-provoking material. There is also space for your notes, opinions, and introspections for each chapter. The Bible study can be used as a discussion-starter for group study and dialogue, or it can be used privately for individual study and reflection.

My hope is that *Called to Forgive* will bring you an eye-opening understanding of forgiveness as viewed from God's own Word.

Anthony Thompson
Denise George
Autumn 2018

1

The Unthinkable Tragedy

The man-made catastrophe at Emanuel is among the most sorrowful and powerful stories in recent memory.

Time[1]

Bible and study notes in hand, my wife, Myra, slips through the church's side door around five o'clock, a few seconds of her smiling image captured by the security camera. As always on her way inside Emanuel African Methodist Episcopal Church, she stops and warmly hugs several other "Wednesday people," as they are called, those faithful ones who attend midweek Bible studies in addition to Sunday morning worship services. Rushing inside to the meeting room, she answers her cell phone's ring, speaking briefly with our daughter, Denise, and promising to call her back when she returns home.

The Wednesday night Bible study usually starts by 6 p.m., but on this hot and steamy June evening in historic downtown Charleston, the church has scheduled its Quarterly Conference meeting to be held before the Bible study, pushing the study time to 8 p.m.

As presiding elder for the AME Church in the Charleston District, the Rev. Dr. Norvel Goff meets with Emanuel and other local churches in his district for a Quarterly Conference at least once every three months. On this night, June 17, 2015, Dr. Goff and fifty members in attendance discuss budget issues, installation plans for the building's new elevator, and other important church business. Before the end of the extended meeting, several ministers are granted local ministry licenses, including Myra, who receives her preaching license renewal, a ministry calling she had worked hard for many years to earn. The evening proves a special and greatly anticipated event for my wife. She glows with excitement as the meeting ends and the Bible study time draws near. She will teach the Bible study for the first time at Emanuel, an outstanding honor, explaining Jesus' parable of the sower recorded in the book of Mark.

Myra's Safe Haven

Myra loves her lifelong home—Charleston, South Carolina—and especially the Emanuel AME Church. She became a newly baptized convert and church member in 1965, the tenth year of her life, becoming actively involved in the congregation's family life and numerous children's programs. After sixteen years of marriage, I have never once tried to persuade Myra to leave her church to join my denomination—the Reformed Episcopal Church. Myra is just too loyal, too devoted to Emanuel, and so in love with its people. Her commitment to God would never allow her to leave her childhood church. She considers it her safe haven from the frets and cares of this world.

A perfectionist, and very serious about her ministry and church, she feels anxious all morning about teaching her first Bible study at Emanuel. She sits at the den table working long into the afternoon until she stops and quickly dresses for church.

"I want to make sure that when I feed our people the Word, I'll be giving them the *right* Word, and that they will understand what I am saying," she tells me. "And I want to be able to answer all their questions."

"You've worked hard on it for a solid month, Myra. It's perfect," I assure her.

I plan to attend the Bible study this evening, wanting to support and encourage Myra's teaching ministry.

"I'll try to be on time for your Bible study tonight, Myra."

"You don't have to come."

"I'm coming, Myra. I want to be there. For you."

"Honey, I don't want you to come."

She doesn't want me to come? I wonder. *Why not?*

Myra and I go everywhere together, especially supporting each other at events when one of us speaks or participates. Normally she expects me to be there.

"I don't understand . . ."

"Honey, this is your church's first day of Vacation Bible School, and you know the ladies will have a lot of drama going on. You need to be at your own church."

As I think about my duties as pastor of Holy Trinity Reformed Episcopal Church, and the evening's planned events, I know she is right.

"Yes. I need to be at my church."

"Can you pick up some supper for us?" she asks.

"Sure. Captain D's? They've got a great broiled seafood platter. What about that?"

"Okay," she agrees. "Thanks. I'll see you here later tonight and we can eat together."

Myra's Departure

Sometime before five that afternoon, Myra slips into a conservative black suit and white blouse. Before she leaves for church, she calls to me from the hallway: "Honey! I'm getting ready to go. Come walk me to the door."

It is customary for Myra and me to hug and kiss good-bye upon parting—a simple, loving tradition we never fail to keep.

"You need to hurry!" she calls again as she gathers her Bible and notes from the table. "I have to be at church earlier than usual for the meeting before Bible study."

"Wait a minute! Hold on, I'm coming!" I call from the bathroom.

As I rush to finish dressing to see her off at the door, I experience a strange feeling, a sensation somewhat incomprehensible and impossible to describe. Myra seems somehow different from her usual self. This morning as we prepared for the day, even though she admitted to feeling anxious about the evening's study, I noticed Myra's face glowed with an unusual kind of happiness, her smile much more radiant than usual.

Why is she so happy? I wonder. She seems to glide across the floor as if walking on air, not wood.

I dismiss the question and puzzling feelings when details of my own church's evening program crowd my thoughts.

Before I can leave the bathroom, I hear the front door open and then close, the sound of Myra's voice greeting neighbors, her car starting and pulling out of the driveway.

Oh well, I think. *She'll understand. She knows I'm praying for her. I'll kiss and hug her later tonight.*

The Bible Study

The business meeting, led by Dr. Goff, adjourns a few minutes before 8 p.m., the crowds saying quick good-byes to each other and dispersing into the heavy, humid night. Myra and eleven of the regular Bible study participants move downstairs into the church's lower-level fellowship hall, each sitting at one of the four white cloth-covered tables.

Myra enthusiastically greets the people staying for the Bible study. She knows and loves them all. She sits down at the first table, and four others join her: the Reverend Daniel Simmons, seventy-four, a devoted father, grandfather, minister, staff member of the church, and Vietnam War veteran; Cynthia Hurd, fifty-four, a much-loved librarian for thirty-one years at the Charleston County Public Library; the Reverend Sharonda Coleman-Singleton, forty-five, a mother of three, part-time minister at Emanuel, speech pathologist, and girls' track coach at Goose Creek High School; and DePayne Middleton Doctor, forty-nine, the mother of four daughters, a choir member, promising minister, and admissions coordinator at Southern Wesleyan University's Charleston local learning center.

Polly Sheppard—seventy-two, a retired nurse—and Ethel Lance sit at the table closest to Myra's. Ethel, seventy, a widow of many years, a mother, grandmother, and great-grandmother, has worked faithfully for thirty years as the church sexton.

Felicia Sanders, fifty-eight, a hair stylist, sits at the next table with three members of her family: her eleven-year-old granddaughter; her eighty-seven-year-old aunt, Susie Jackson, a longtime Emanuel choir member; and her son Tywanza Sanders, twenty-six, a promising poet and artist who recently graduated from Allen University.

The pastor, the Reverend Clementa C. Pinckney, forty-one, wearing his customary dark business suit, makes his way to the fourth table. Pinckney holds two important positions in the state. For the past five years, he has served as pastor of the Emanuel AME Church. He is also a Democratic member of the South Carolina Senate, representing the 45th District. In order to support Myra and attend her first Bible study, he has chosen to forgo politically correct attendance—expected of him in his state role—at the Hillary Clinton presidential campaign meeting in Charleston tonight.

The pastor's wife, Jennifer, does not attend the Bible study, but instead retreats to her husband's study, located next to the fellowship hall, to catch up on some church paperwork. Her young daughter, Malana, stays with her, watching a movie while her mother works.

Preparing a Heart's Soil

When all are welcomed and settled into their seats, Myra begins to teach the carefully prepared lesson: "Studying Mark's Gospel: Preparing Our Heart's Soil." She spreads out her notes on the table, opens her Bible to Mark 4, and begins to read verses 1 through 20:

"A farmer went out to sow his seed . . . some fell along the path, and the birds came and ate it up. . . . Some fell on rocky places . . . they withered because they had no root. Other seed fell among thorns, which grew up and choked the plants. . . . Still other seed fell on good soil. It came up, grew and produced a crop. . . ."

She pauses, explaining: "The soil represents the human heart, the way we respond to the Word. The seed represents the Word of God."

Before she finishes reading the selected Scripture verses, sometime between 8:06 and 8:15, the fellowship hall door opens a bit and a young man slips inside. Myra stops reading and smiles at him. The participants look up from their Bibles and see the boyish-looking man, standing about five feet nine inches tall, a slight 120-pound frame, his tousled mop of sandy blond hair cut in a bowl shape and surrounding his pale, clean-shaven face. Dressed in a gray sweatshirt, worn blue jeans, and Timberland boots, the young white man wears a black fanny pack around his waist, the kind so many tourists in Charleston carry to hold cell phones, wallets, and cameras.

One by one, Myra and the faithful "Wednesday people" introduce themselves to him, kindly inviting Dylann Storm Roof to join the study. Pastor Pinckney pulls out the chair next to him and offers the young man a seat. Someone places a Bible in Dylann's hands. Shyly, quietly, Dylann sits down.

As part of a famous old African-American church in historic downtown Charleston, the group isn't surprised to have a visitor walk down the street, see the church lights on, and wander into Emanuel's fellowship hall. Sometimes a lonely straggler comes in for the fellowship, other times the hungry walk inside expecting to find food. Perhaps this sad-faced, wandering, lost soul wants to know more about Christ and His Word, a young seeker who hopes that within this church he'll find answers to his life's deepest and most painful questions. For whatever reason, he walks inside the church fellowship hall that evening, the Bible study members heartily accepting this young man into their small group, welcoming him warmly.

Myra resumes teaching, explaining in detail to her listeners what Jesus' parable means, lessons that Jesus' own disciples failed to understand when He told it to them two millennia ago.

"Don't you understand this parable?" a frustrated Jesus asked His closest disciples, later admonishing them: "He who has ears to hear, let him hear."

"You see," Myra begins, her eyes focusing on the group, "the disciples don't understand any of this—what Jesus tells them. . . . They don't know what He is talking about. We *must* have a desire to *hear*!"

Lifting her Bible, she continues: "Jesus explained the parable to His confused disciples in verses 13 and following. He says the farmer sows the seeds—meaning the Word. Some people's hearts are like seed sown along the path, where the Word is sown. As soon as they hear the Word, Satan comes and takes it away from them, and they produce nothing."

Seeing that everyone understands, she moves on: "Others, like seed sown on rocky places, hear the Word and at once receive it with great joy. But since they have no soil, they grow no root and last only a short time. When trouble or persecution comes, they fall away quickly."

The group asks several questions, then Myra proceeds: "Still others, like seed sown among thorns, hear the Word, but soon allow the worries, selfish human desires, and deceitfulness of life to choke the Word. They, too, fall away. Others, however, like seed sown in good soil, hear the Word, accept it, and produce a good crop."

21

Eyes to See, Ears to Hear

For much of the hour, Myra explains Jesus' powerful parable. "You see," she says, "there are people whose eyes are open but don't see a thing. Their ears are open but they don't understand a word. They avoid making an *about-face* to be forgiven."

She stops and smiles. "And as you already know, the only way we can be forgiven is to accept Jesus as our Lord and Savior. Once we accept Him, we will receive the Holy Spirit, and the Holy Spirit will give us understanding of the Word of God."

Throughout the study, Dylann seems to listen intently to Myra's words of biblical truth, all the time keeping his expression blank, his eyes staring and vacant, and saying nothing.

"Jesus said in Matthew 16:26, 'For what does it profit a man to gain the whole world and lose his soul?'" Myra continues explaining the text. "We must pray to be delivered from Satan. . . . A person's reception of God's Word is determined by the condition of his heart. Our faith and the way we live our lives will show what type of soil relates to us."

As Myra teaches Jesus' life-saving message, she must think about her pale-faced young stranger, wondering if he has eyes to see and ears to hear, and pondering the state of his heart's soil.

A Setting Sun

A few minutes after 9 p.m., Myra finishes teaching the lesson. As the sun sets on Charleston, enveloping the city in darkness, she thanks the participants for their friendship and support, and for attending her first Bible study, even though it keeps them out much later than usual. To dismiss the group, Myra and the others stand up, instinctively closing their eyes, bowing their heads in reverence, and praying: "Our Father who art in heaven, hallowed be thy—"

Suddenly, *CRACK! CRACK! CRACK!* Loud gunshots explode throughout the hall, piercing the quiet prayer time. With a Glock 45 pulled from his fanny pack, the boy-faced man opens fire on the twelve praying Bible study members. A storm of rapid gunfire rings out as he moves quickly from one table to the next, shooting the worshipers at point-blank range, shell casings hitting and bouncing one after another on the linoleum floor. In his sudden killing frenzy, Dylann Roof pauses only five times, just long enough to reload his gun with fresh clips, all the while shouting hateful racial slurs and statements.

Some victims die almost immediately, bleeding out from multiple bullet wounds that shred arteries and organs. The gunman stands over his victims, shooting them again and again as they lie moaning and dying on the floor. Others beg the shooter to stop as they grab loved ones, holding them tight, hoping to protect them from the madman and his bullets.

Some hide or play dead, miraculously escaping Roof's wrath. The pastor's wife and daughter, inside the nearby office, hear the shots, quickly lock the door, and huddle under a desk.

Roof allows Polly Sheppard to live so she can tell the story of the massacre.

"I have to do it. You rape our women, and you are taking over our country. And you have to go!" Roof shouts during the shooting.[2]

At 9:06 p.m., after firing seventy-seven bullets, Dylann Roof stops shooting, turns around, and casually walks out the door, leaving the dead, dying, and terrified behind him on the blood-stained fellowship hall floor. The church security camera catches his image as he leaves, his face expressionless, the gun still grasped in his hand.

Eight members, including the church's pastor, die on the floor from multiple gunshot wounds. One man, the Rev. Daniel Simmons, is severely injured but still alive. The faithful group of Wednesday people, so quickly and cruelly cut down by an assassin's gun, will later become known as the "Emanuel Nine."[3] Only three people in the Bible study group survive the attack: Polly Sheppard, Felicia Sanders, and her young granddaughter.

After teaching her first Bible study at Emanuel AME Church, newly licensed minister Myra Thompson lies dead on the fellowship hall floor, her body riddled with bullets, her Bible and study notes scattered, soaked in her own blood.

The Horrifying News

I learned later that evening that Dylann Storm Roof had murdered my beloved wife, Myra. The discovery body-slammed me with shock and grief. I wished with all my heart that I had gone with her to the Bible study to protect her from the killer. Late into dark future nights, I will wonder if she suffered unbearable pain after the bullets tore through her body, or if she died instantly, escaping physical agony. I will think again and again about the events of this evening, replaying the gruesome scenes in my mind.

In the long hours after I learned of Myra's death, and in the midst of my initial shock, crying, and deep sorrow, I faced personal and gut-wrenching questions pertaining to my Christian faith: "What now is my obligation to the killer? Do I choose to forgive him or avenge his diabolical deed that purposely and maliciously destroyed my wife?"

I am a self-professed Christian, a born-again believer in Jesus Christ, an ordained minister of God, and a Christ-appointed shepherd to a congregation. In these roles, I knew I would have to confront eye to eye, as never before, the unfathomable hard commands of biblical forgiveness.

Can I do it? I wondered.

Can I, in the darkest remote closets of my all-too-human heart, forgive Dylann Storm Roof for the cold-blooded murder of my beloved companion?

I also wrestled with the questions: Am I expected by God and/or by others to forgive such a *heinous* crime? I have chosen to forgive people in the past for many reasons, but does biblical forgiveness apply to this type of vicious, premeditated murder in the house of God? Does forgiveness depend upon the degree of the crime, or does it apply to all deliberate offenses we and our loved ones suffer at the hands of heartless others? Myra was an innocent woman, a child of God doing what she believed God had called her to do in His ministry. She stood in her church praying as Dylann Roof shot and killed her. Does God himself expect me to offer this young assassin my heartfelt forgiveness?

The Amish Girls

I remember how saddened and appalled I felt in early October 2006, when I heard about the bloody massacre at an Amish school in Nickel Mines, Pennsylvania. A man the young children knew, thirty-two-year-old dairy truck driver Charles C. Roberts, the father of three children, walked unannounced into a one-room Amish schoolhouse in Lancaster County. On that Monday morning, he came in heavily armed, dismissing the boys, lining up the little girls, and firing his weapon at them multiple times. Small, vulnerable, and unable to protect themselves, the terrified children wept with fear. He shot and killed four girls and wounded seven more girls. A fifth child died early Tuesday morning from her injuries. Ten Amish girls, ages six to thirteen years, became the target of this man's rage.[4]

In the screaming and chaos, the teacher somehow escaped and called for help. When police officers arrived, storming the West Nickel Mines Amish School, Charles Roberts killed himself, firing a bullet into his head from the 9mm handgun.

"Why?" everyone asked. "Why did Charles Roberts commit such a barbaric attack? Why did he kill innocent children? How could a father, with children of his own, do this?"

To this day, no one really knows. Some people believed Roberts never forgave God for the death of his first child, a baby girl who, in spite of his ardent prayers, lived only twenty minutes after her birth. They based this belief on the fact that before he shot the Amish girls, Roberts told them he was sorry for what he was about to do. "I'm angry at God and I need to punish some Christian girls to get even with him," he said. "I'm going to make you pay for my daughter."[5]

Since Myra's death, I've thought frequently about those little girls, dying on their schoolroom floor. And I have often wondered what kind of man could plan such a sadistic assault, deliberately destroying the lives of innocent, trusting children. Are we, as followers of Christ, *truly* expected to forgive such abominations? Does even God require those Amish mothers, fathers, grandparents, and friends to forgive Charles Roberts for murdering their loved ones? Shouldn't biblical forgiveness take into account the degree and nature of the cruelty of the crime and the amount of suffering it brings?

The Amish community itself answered my nagging question about biblical forgiveness. These families lived so simply among the barns, silos, and stone houses in the rolling hills and cornfields of Lancaster County, choosing to forgo electricity and other modern conveniences. They were and still are people of great faith, and in their anguish and loss they showed the world's Christians the extraordinary depth and width of genuine biblical forgiveness.

On the very day of the schoolhouse murders, as they suffered shock, pain, and sorrow, they reached out with grace, compassion, and forgiveness to the killer's family. The Amish community visited Roberts's perplexed and grieving wife and children, praying for and with them, seeking to comfort them in their own loss of a husband and father. To the widow and her now fatherless children, they took home-cooked food. As the Amish were planning funerals and burying their own children, they faithfully attended Charles Roberts's funeral, greatly outnumbering the non-Amish attendees. When money poured in from around the world to cover the Amish families' high medical bills and burial expenses, they shared it with the killer's family. They showed us a beautiful example of biblical forgiveness!

As news of the attack, deaths, and forgiveness hit television, radio, and the internet, the world was awed at the depth of forgiveness shown to the Roberts family by those people expected to most hate them. The world did not understand this kind of forgiveness that made headline news across the globe. Revenge and retaliation they could accept, as it was the way of the world. But forgiveness? And on this scale? Hardly.

A reporter, witnessing firsthand the Amish's great act of forgiveness, wrote, "The attacker preyed on the most innocent and defenseless members of a determinedly bucolic and pacifistic religious community. Within hours, the Amish announced they had forgiven him."[6]

Another sad commentary on abuse heaped upon innocent people is our nation's treatment of slaves.

A Nation's Tragic Slave History

I need only look back in our nation's tragic slave history to see the great cruelty, unfairness, and brutality that seemed unforgivable at a human level. Slavery began in America in 1619, when the Dutch brought the first captured Africans to our colonies, thus planting the seeds of a chilling, almost unstoppable slavery system that for centuries was allowed to grow into a bloodthirsty nightmare for millions of people. Generations of black people endured inhumane treatment, laboring hard under a whip, toiling long hours without consideration or compensation, receiving routine beatings as punishment, being traded like cattle by harsh, pitiless owners.

Charleston was the nation's capital of the former slave trade, the port where many kidnapped Africans first landed in the New World and came ashore. Slaves, so unfairly abused and held in bondage, built the city, and for almost two hundred years, the white population of Charleston thrived under the slave economy. Not until July 1, 1856, did Charleston outlaw the sale and auction of slaves on its city streets.[7]

How is it even remotely possible to forgive those who so selfishly bought and sold human beings, dishing out centuries of abuse upon their families and children, and profiting from their pain? Can these sins ever truly be forgiven? *Should* they ever be forgiven?

Hitler's Holocaust

More recent history also provides numerous examples of inexcusable human cruelty. I shudder when I consider the murder and maltreatment of innocent people caught up in the Nazi-inspired Holocaust whirlwind of World War II. Millions of humans endured imprisonment and slaughter due to their mental or physical disability, race, religion, lifestyle, age, or usefulness. As part of the 1941 "Final Solution" program, Germany's despicable leader, Adolf Hitler, transported Jews and others to ghettos and concentration camps, where they faced gas chambers, firing squads, medical experimentation, starvation, disease, and excruciating deaths. Only a small fraction of those imprisoned and tortured in Nazi concentration camps survived and lived to find freedom.

Dutch Christian watchmaker Corrie ten Boom miraculously survived Hitler's concentration camps. When in May 1940 the German blitzkrieg ran through the Netherlands, the ten Boom family built a secret room in their Haarlem home to hide and protect Jews in danger of arrest, imprisonment, and execution.

On February 28, 1944, Corrie and her entire family were discovered and arrested by the gestapo when a Dutch informant turned them in. Corrie and her sister, Betsie, were sent to Ravensbruck, a women's labor camp near Berlin, Germany. Betsie's health deteriorated, and to Corrie's great distress and sorrow, Betsie died before Christmas. For unknown reasons, Corrie was suddenly and unexpectedly released from Ravensbruck two weeks later. Some believe she was freed due to a Nazi official's clerical error.

After her release, Corrie wrestled with forgiveness for a long time until she finally chose to forgive the Nazi guard who brutalized her and her sister at the camp.

"For I had to do it—I knew that," she admitted. "The message that God forgives has a prior condition: that we forgive those who have injured us. 'If you do not forgive men their trespasses,' Jesus said, 'neither will your Father in heaven forgive your trespasses.'"

In her personal struggle, Corrie learned that "forgiveness is not an emotion. . . . Forgiveness is an act of the will, and the will can function regardless of the temperature of the heart."

After the war, Corrie returned to the Netherlands, setting up a rehabilitation center for fellow concentration camp survivors. Ministering to the mistreated and brokenhearted, Corrie saw first-hand that "those who were able to forgive their former enemies were able also to return to the outside world and rebuild their lives, no matter what the physical scars." She also saw that "those who nursed their bitterness remained invalids. It was as simple and as horrible as that."[8]

Corrie ten Boom suffered physically, emotionally, and mentally in the Holocaust of World War II, and she watched her loved ones die. Yet in spite of the nature and degree of Hitler's inconceivable hate, his reign of terror, and his mass murder of millions of innocents, Corrie chose to forgive. People heard her story and wondered how in the world she was able to forgive such intense cruelty. Surely the entire world watched with awe as she freely offered the gift of forgiveness to those who did not deserve it.

How Can I Forgive?

People now ask me the same question. "How could you forgive Dylann Roof for killing your wife, Myra, and eight of her friends in cold blood—such an unimaginably horrific crime—as they stood praying in Emanuel AME Church?"

My answer is always the same. I chose to forgive the racist killer because I believe and trust God's Word when He tells me that vengeance is His to repay, not mine (Deuteronomy 32:35). I need not avenge the vile deeds of Dylann Roof myself. Scripture promises me, "It is mine to avenge; I will repay."

As a Christian, a devoted follower of Jesus Christ, I choose to obey God's Word, and that means I made the decision to forgive the evil man who so wickedly and deliberately took away my lovely wife.

Scripture tells me that as I am forgiven by Christ, I am obliged to forgive others who hurt me and take from me those I dearly love. Jesus asked us to pray and practice: "Forgive us our debts, as we also have forgiven our debtors" (Matthew 6:12).

Jesus' Parable on Forgiveness

Jesus often told parables when He wanted to make a point in His teaching. When His disciple Peter questioned Jesus about forgiveness, Jesus told him a story. While some of Jesus' parables needed His explanation as to their meaning, the parable of the unmerciful servant in Matthew 18:21–35 clearly explained itself.

A servant owed a master a large sum of money that he could not begin to repay. The master ordered the usual punishment for the debtor, that his wife, children, and property be sold to repay the amount of money he owed. When sentenced, the servant fell to his knees, begging for the master's mercy and patience, asking for more time to earn the money and repay the debt. The master's heart was touched by the servant's plea. In great kindness and compassion, he canceled the debt, writing a large "paid in full" on his account and releasing him.

The "master" in this story represents God, the Father. The "servant" stands for all of humankind, the people drenched in sin, owing God a debt they can never begin to pay back in full. But God loves the humans, the wicked debtors, and on their behalf, His heart is touched with compassion. So instead of sentencing humankind to the harshest punishment, He shows surprising mercy, canceling the debt and allowing them to go free. The account is closed, paid in full.

The story is a wonderful example of God's forgiveness, His compassion, patience, and mercy. Perhaps Jesus could have ended the parable here, with the servant receiving the master's generous forgiveness, releasing him from his large delinquent debt. But Jesus continued the story, making a heart-stabbing and stunning point at its conclusion.

The servant, forgiven by the merciful master, found a fellow servant who owed him a little money. He dogged him, grabbing and choking him, demanding the money be paid back. When the fellow servant fell to his knees and begged for more time and some compassionate mercy, the forgiven servant refused and had the man thrown in prison.

When the master found out what his servant had done to the fellow servant who owed much less, the master told him in great anger, "I canceled all that debt of yours because you begged me to. Shouldn't you have had mercy on your fellow servant just as I had on you?"

The master ordered the servant thrown into jail to be tortured until he could repay the huge debt he owed. At the end of the story, Jesus further hammered the hard point of His teaching into His listeners' ears. With firm, clear words, He stated: "This is how my heavenly Father will treat each of you unless you forgive your brother from your heart" (v. 35).

Illogical Forgiveness

As I read Jesus' parable, immediately identifying with the hard-hearted servant the master so freely forgave, I asked myself, *How can I expect God to forgive me if I choose to withhold forgiveness from others, no matter how abhorrent their actions?* I read other Scriptures on forgiveness, and their points were chiseled onto my heart and mind.

"For if you forgive men when they sin against you, your heavenly Father will also forgive you" (Matthew 6:14).

And Scripture warns, in the very next verse, the one who chooses not to forgive: "But if you do not forgive men their sins, your Father will not forgive your sins" (Matthew 6:15).

As a Christian who has been forgiven by God, I must also forgive. Therefore, I forgive Dylann Roof, no matter how repulsive I find him, and no matter how savage his murderous deeds.

To the nonbeliever, as well as to many believers, the type of unconditional forgiveness the Amish community offered their children's killer, Charles Roberts, seemed illogical. It didn't make sense. The natural human response to receiving hurt from others is to hurt them back, to avenge their ghastly crimes. But that's not the biblical way to deal with barbarity. God expects unconditional forgiveness and so much more. The Amish community didn't stop with forgiving the killer. They took their forgiveness a step further, choosing to minister to his family with love and compassion. They loved the Roberts family with their food, presence, prayers, and money, thus obeying God's command: "Love your enemies, do good to those who hate you, bless those who curse you, pray for those who mistreat you. . . . Be merciful, just as your Father is merciful" (Luke 6:27–28, 36).

Mercy means compassionate love shown in tangible ways, acts of kindness like those shown to us by our heavenly Father. We do not deserve God's mercy, but He initiates it, giving it to us anyway. God desires a relationship with us, His fallen creation, but must show mercy in order to build this relationship. God's mercy comes to us through Christ. As we receive God's mercy, He expects us to also show mercy to others, loving them, forgiving them their debts.

Corrie ten Boom graciously extended God's mercy. She didn't stop with just forgiving Hitler for the horrors he and others heaped upon her and her family. She opened her own home and helped others to rehabilitate, spending the last years of her long life traveling widely, speaking publicly, and encouraging her listeners to choose biblical forgiveness over human bitterness.

Forgive Whatever Grievances

I am learning anew what I have always known, taught to me by my parents years ago, that biblical forgiveness is not optional, depending on the cold-blooded cruelty or sadistic nature or degree of the crime. Forgiveness depends on God's Word, on God's requirements for believers. The Apostle Paul wrote to the Colossians about forgiveness when he encouraged them to "bear with each other and forgive *whatever grievances* you may have against one another. Forgive as the Lord forgave you" (Colossians 3:13, emphasis added). Surely, "whatever grievances" covers all crimes, even those unspeakable horrors that forever rob us of our loved ones.

Forgiveness is ingrained in the Amish heritage, an essential part of their strong faith and character. During the weeks and months after Charles Roberts slaughtered their children, bereaved Amish parents began to view their forgiveness as "the one good thing that can come out of this tragedy."[9]

I believe God's Word calls and commands us to forgive all crimes, no matter how atrocious. God is the Judge and Jury. When we forgive, we place the unspeakable crimes in His hands and leave them there for His judgment. He has marked the debt we owe Him "paid in full." He expects us to forgive the debts owed to us by others.

The Crucifixion

Without a doubt, the most damnable crime in the world's history was the crucifixion of Jesus. After His unlawful arrest in the middle of the night, His enemies planted a sharp crown of thorns on His head, spat on Him, scourged and struck Him again and again, mocked Him, and led Him to death on a cross—the common Roman instrument of torture and punishment.

Jesus in no way deserved such a death. He spent the years of his ministry healing the blind, feeding the hungry, casting demons from the infested, raising the dead back to life, giving good health to the sick, and performing many other acts of goodness and mercy. He was guilty of no sin.

His torture began in Gethsemane when his sweat became drops of blood. Doctors now explain this rare condition as hematohidrosis, stating that it occurs under overwhelming emotional stress, and that the loss of blood produces physical weakness. Later, suffering from beatings, bruises, exhaustion, and dehydration, Jesus faced a whipping that cut through his skin, muscles, and veins, leaving His body lacerated.

Soldiers made Jesus carry His heavy wooden cross to the place of execution, and then hammered nails between the small bones of His wrists, at that time considered a part of the hand. They set the cross upright in the ground and pounded nails through the arches of both feet. He suffered hours of unutterable agony upon the cross, struggling to breathe and feeling indescribable pain. During the long process of dying, Jesus looked out over the crowd of people below Him, those who had tortured Him, and He forgave them.[10]

"Father, forgive them," Jesus said, "for they do not know what they are doing" (Luke 23:34). Then He turned His attention to one of the criminals hanging beside him, and offered him the Father's forgiveness.

"Jesus," the thief asked, "remember me when you come into your kingdom" (Luke 23:42).

Jesus answered him: "I tell you the truth, today you will be with me in paradise" (Luke 23:43).

Jesus suffered a devastating death, and yet before He passed, He forgave those who were killing Him.

As Jesus is my Lord, Savior, and my example to follow, I could do no less than to forgive the young white racist, Dylann Roof, for the heinous death of my dear wife, Myra. It was not easy, yet in this process of biblical forgiveness, I discovered that my deliberate choice to forgive allowed me a surprising sense of healing and peace, and the ability to begin to move forward in my life.

2

||||||||||||||||||||||||||||||||||||||||||

The Aftermath

The church basement had been transformed into a
slaughterhouse. And nine innocent churchgoers had
become the victims of [Dylann Roof's] racist madness.

New York Daily News[1]

In the fellowship hall of the Emanuel AME Church on Wednesday evening, dead silence marks the moments immediately following the shooting. The few people left alive in the fellowship hall are terrified, stunned. One of them, Polly Sheppard, crouching under a table, finds her cell phone. Her hands trembling, she misdials 9-1-1. The second time she dials correctly and is connected to a female dispatch operator. For five and a half minutes, the terrorized elderly woman cries into the phone, begging the operator to send help, and describing as best she can the shooter and the carnage he has left behind.

"He shot the pastor! He shot all the men in the church—please come right away," she sobs, trying to keep her voice low, believing the shooter is still in the building.

Sheppard calls out to the 9-1-1 operator with renewed panic, "He's still in here!" . . .

"He's coming! He's coming! He's coming! Please!" . . .

"He's reloading!" . . .

"God, please help me. Please help us, Lord," Sheppard prays into the cell phone. "Help us, Lord, please. . . . Please, Jesus, help us." . . .

"There's so many people dead, I think . . ."

The operator seems surprised, asking, "You said there's so many people *dead*?"

"I think they're dead, yes!" Polly exclaims as she struggles to describe the bizarre scene around her.

"Oh God, please help us." . . .

"He's still in the building, please help us. . . ."[2]

The Mayhem That Follows

Receiving the 9-1-1 operator's urgent message, Charleston police race to the church, within minutes filling the downtown streets with patrol cars, fire engines, ambulances, law enforcement officers, detectives, medical teams, and detector sniffer dogs. Inside the fellowship hall, officers find eight lifeless, bullet-mutilated bodies, each lying on the floor in a puddle of blood. The ninth victim, the Reverend Simmons, is struggling to breathe and is whisked away by ambulance.

Mayhem follows: Officers stop a possible suspect at a nearby gas station, questioning him about the shooting; an anonymous telephone call about a suspicious couple leads police to burst into the couple's townhouse, waking and interrogating them; police stop and search dark sedans (believed to be the killer's vehicle) traveling across Charleston's bridges, particularly those leaving the peninsula.

As word of the shooting quickly spreads throughout the city, confusion and chaos engulf Calhoun Street and the area around the church. Downtown Charleston becomes an entangled maze of screaming sirens, flashing lights, and panicked people wanting to know exactly what has happened. Greatly complicating matters, the city receives phone calls claiming bomb threats—the cruel and frightening tips turning out to be false.

When Medical University of South Carolina's emergency room receives the call about the shooting, they prepare for multiple casualties, remaining on standby to receive the injured. But only one shooting victim, the Reverend Simmons, comes to the emergency room alive. He dies shortly after his arrival.

Later, upon closer inspection of the nine victims' bodies, a medical examiner finds more than sixty puncture wounds, all made by Winchester hollow-point bullets. He knows the deadly power and damage of these bullets, their intentional shockwave designed to shatter bones, tear apart blood vessels, and liquefy human organs. The sales promotion for Winchester hollow-point bullets boasts that this particular bullet was "developed to provide excellent performance at an affordable price for the high volume shooter," "delivers outstanding reliability," and was designed to "ensure pinpoint accuracy and sure functioning time and time again."[3]

Dylann's cruel choice of ammunition inflicted great damage to the bodies of the Emanuel Nine. He sat in his car in the church parking lot for almost half an hour, carefully loading ammunition into his gun before he entered the fellowship hall.

The Telephone Call

The sun is just setting as I finish my Vacation Bible School duties at Holy Trinity. I consider stopping by Emanuel and catching the tail end of Myra's Bible study. Instead, for no particular reason, I decide to drive home and wait for her there. Remembering that I have forgotten to pick up the broiled seafood platter I promised Myra for dinner, I leave home, drive to Captain D's, and buy the food. When I return, I am somewhat surprised that Myra still has not come home. As I anticipate her arrival, I begin to undress, unbuttoning my shirt and untucking it from my pants.

I pause when I hear the telephone ring. A member of Emanuel demands I put Myra on the phone, claiming she *has* to talk to her. Immediately.

"She's not home yet," I tell her, somewhat mystified by the uncharacteristic tenseness and irritation in her voice. "But she will be home any minute. Can I have her call y—"

"You *need* to go to the church!" she interrupts, her voice raised and firm.

"Why?" I ask, feeling slightly perplexed. "I just *left* the church."

"Not *your* church, Reverend Thompson! You need to go to *Myra's* church—Emanuel! I hear there's some shooting going on around there."

"Shooting?!" I ask in disbelief.

"Yes!" she answers. "Shooting!!"

A thunderbolt explodes in my head. *Someone is shooting around the church?!* I imagine shots being fired outside the church building. *I sure hope Myra is safely inside the church!*

I drop the telephone and run to my car, pulling it quickly onto the street to make the short drive to Emanuel. Arriving at Calhoun Street, I stop, springing from the car and encountering a police officer stationed at a roadblock set up on the street in front of the church. I identify myself, and with great urgency tell him, "I've got to get to the church! I hear some shooting's going on. I think my wife's inside."

"No," the officer says firmly. "You can *not* pass through the roadblock."

"But my wife—"

"Don't worry about your wife," he tells me. "Everybody from Emanuel has been safely relocated at the Courtyard Marriott across the street."

"Thank God!" I shout, returning to my car. I speed to the hotel, parking illegally on Meeting Street. Without turning off the motor, I jump from the car and vault toward the hotel, carefully dodging the police dogs, people, and law enforcement officials that clog my way. When I arrive at the Marriott, I notice seven ambulances parked at the Shell gas station nearby, their sirens and flashing lights turned off, each abandoned by its driver.

That's strange, I think. *If people are shot, why are the ambulances just sitting there?*

My heart begins to beat faster. *Maybe the police officer didn't tell me the whole story.* I feel pinpricks of sweat pop out on my forehead. *Oh my God, I hope Myra is all right. Yes, yes!* I reassure myself again and again. *Myra is all right. She has to be all right! Oh God, please let her be all right!*

I run inside the Marriott, asking everybody I pass, "Where in this hotel are the Emanuel members?"

"They're all down there," a man finally tells me, pointing toward a distant room.

Oh God, thank you, Jesus! I bolt down the long hallway, feeling thankful that Myra and the others are there together and safe.

Grabbing the doorknob, I pause to take a deep breath and calm myself before stepping inside the room. When I open the door, I see Felicia Sanders embracing her sobbing granddaughter. I look to my right and see our old friend Polly Sheppard sitting in a chair with her head on a table. I look around the room, searching frantically for my wife.

Where is Myra? Where is Myra?! I can't see Myra anywhere in the room.

As if reading my thoughts, Felicia Sanders lifts her head and looks deeply into my eyes. "Anthony," she says softly, her face wet with tears, "Myra's gone."

"What?" I cry. "Oh no! She can't be gone! No! You must be wrong!"

I run from the hotel.

This is not happening! This is NOT HAPPENING!

Reeling at the thought that my wife might be "gone," I collapse onto the hotel porch beside a bed of flowers, my head hitting the concrete.

I have to find her! I have to see her!

I manage to get up, determined to go into Emanuel and see Myra for myself. I sprint across the street, past EMS workers, police officers, FBI agents, and other law enforcement officers.

I have to find Myra!

Out of breath, I leap over a tree stump by Emanuel's gate and head to the church's side door.

Just a little farther! A few more feet! You're almost there, my mind encourages the muscles in my legs. I think about Myra inside the church, terrified or hurt and needing me beside her to hold and comfort her, or to get her some help.

As I try to jerk open the church door, an FBI agent stops me, his thick arms wrapping around my resisting body, his brute strength holding me in place.

"Calm down!" he orders, tightening his grip. "Where are you going?"

"Let me go!" I shout. "My name is Anthony Thompson. My wife, Myra, is in that church. I must get to her."

The FBI agent shakes his head. "No!" he says, and then hesitates. "You—you don't want to go in there." He shakes his head, his brows knit together. "Believe me, sir, you don't want to go in there!"

"Yes, I do!" I argue. "My wife's in—"

"No, you don't," he says, his eyes softening, his body still blocking me. "You. Just. Don't."

The look on the agent's face, and the unexpected hint of compassion in his voice tear into my heart. Somehow I just know that inside the church, Myra lies dead. I feel all the strength instantly leave my body, and for the first time in my life, I completely lose control. My body goes limp, sinking to the ground. With my face against the sidewalk, I openly weep. *Surely I should be able to protect someone I love so much*, I cry silently again and again.

The Bizarre and Tragic Event

I remember only bits and pieces of that tragic night. A few days later, I read an official police report written by a Charleston detective describing my actions on that evening. His report stated that he "arrived at the incident location, 110 Calhoun Street, at about 21:40 hours . . . observed a black male running toward the church as a patrolman tried to intervene." He stated that he "tried to speak with the gentleman, who said that his wife, Myra Thompson . . . was located inside the church." The officer wrote that he "advised him that he would not be able to enter the church at this time and that the situation is very fluid."[4]

I also saw a photograph taken by a reporter on the scene at the church. In the midst of chaos and crowds, a young police officer wearing a bulletproof vest looked me squarely in the face, his right hand placed firmly on my shoulder. In the snapshot, I stood on the dark street with bright lights flashing all around me, my unbuttoned shirt hanging outside my pants, my left hand held to my face as if trying to support my head.

The bizarre and tragic events in my hometown seemed other-worldly, surreal—a strange blending and blurring of time and place. In feverish desperation and with fierce determination, I searched for my wife, wanting to make sure she was safe, and yearning to forever hold her in my arms. But my pursuit proved pointless. My wife was dead.

Almost four years have gone by, and during many long dark nights I still wrestle with her violent and untimely death. A deeply disturbing ache lingers in my heart, and as the days and nights come and go, again and again I replay Felicia Sanders' chilling, life-changing words to me:

"Anthony, Myra's gone."

My Lack of Understanding

I must admit that I do not, in any way, understand the depth of darkness that must dwell so deeply in the young mind and heart of Dylann Storm Roof. It baffles me, completely eluding my most basic human understanding, how and why Roof could plan such a deadly assault on Emanuel's members: people he didn't know, people he hated only because of their skin pigment. How could he carry out their violent murders after they so warmly welcomed him into their intimate Bible study? I cannot grasp the reason a healthy young man, his whole future ahead of him, purposely killed black church members as they prayed together in God's house. Surely I will never understand why humans hurt and kill each other, and in such intentionally cruel ways.

A Service of Horror

More than two years later, on Sunday morning, November 5, 2017, I ended my church's worship service with a blessing. The members left my church offering words of love and encouragement to each other as they headed home. *It's been a good day*, I told myself, going home to rest.

But in another city that morning, the service didn't end with blessings, and many church members were unable to go home with their families.

Twenty-six-year-old Devin Patrick Kelley, wearing black tactical gear and a ballistic vest, walked into the front door of the First Baptist Church of Sutherland Springs, Texas, and with a Ruger AR rifle, he began firing on the congregation as they sat in pews and worshiped God. In a small building with few exits, people had no place to run or hide. The twenty-six people he killed ranged in age from an unborn child to seventy-two years. One of them, Annabelle Pomeroy, was the pastor's fourteen-year-old daughter. Kelley wounded twenty other members before he finally stopped shooting and fled the building. Police later found Kelley dead in his car.

Kelley's reasons for such an atrocious act are still unknown. Some who knew him believed he was "very sick in the head." Others blamed his attack on a conflict with his mother-in-law, a member of the church.[5]

Kelley's first wife explained that her ex-husband had "a lot of demons or hatred inside of him."[6]

One church family lost nine loved ones from three generations, including an unborn child, in the church shooting. Most expected that such a huge personal loss brought this family great hostility and a hunger to avenge.

But it didn't. This family understood biblical forgiveness. While most believed they deserved a reason for the senseless murders in order to forgive the shooter, they forgave without first understanding Kelley's motive. In fact, at the funeral of their loved ones, they asked the three thousand mourners in attendance to "reject anger and instead bask in the love showed by the victims."[7]

The church pastor, Frank Pomeroy, who was away on that tragic Sunday, lost his daughter in the shooting. The next Sunday, in an emotional church service that took place in a large white tent, Pomeroy stood at the pulpit and told his congregation, "I knew everybody who gave their life that day. Some of them were my best friends. I have no doubt they're dancing with Jesus today."[8]

The pastor then preached a powerful message on forgiveness, urging the grieving church members to forgive, to choose life over darkness. "We have the freedom to proclaim Christ," he told them. "Folks, we have the freedom to choose, and rather than choose darkness as one young man did that day, I say we choose life."[9]

Must Christians Understand In Order to Forgive?

In light of the many church and school shootings of recent times, one must ask: Are Christians required by God to forgive a mass shooter who kills their loved ones when they don't understand the reasons for the murder?

Can one truly and completely forgive what one doesn't understand, what one might never understand? Does forgiveness come at different levels, depending on the crime and the rationale behind it?

One Midwestern pastor offers: "Genocides and mass shootings are in a category all to themselves . . . but those who suffered loss because of these terrible crimes can extend the lowest level of forgiveness by simply not seeking vengeance and doing their best to cope with the loss and pain that will never go away."[10]

But I must ask: Is "not seeking vengeance" and "doing their best to cope with the loss and pain" a form of genuine forgiveness? Is it enough? Is it sufficient? Can it suffice as true biblical forgiveness? Can this type of partial forgiveness bring healing to the victim's loved ones, removing the hatred and bitterness deeply rooted in the natural human heart and mind?

I don't believe so. Biblical forgiveness is a determined decision, a hard choice made with God's help and by the strength of our will. It doesn't come in levels, baby steps, or stages. It must be all-encompassing, all-forgiving, completely erasing the terrible debt owed to us by a vicious other, no matter how horrible the crime. A partial forgiveness is not forgiveness at all. It will keep us locked inside our self-made prison of resentment, hostility, and hatred. And like a weed flourishing in a flower bed, unforgiving bitterness will grow stronger with each day until it overtakes anything good that grows in the garden.

Let me give you an analogy. Forgiveness is something like salvation in Christ. When we come to Him in genuine humility and repentance, we ask for total forgiveness, a cleansing of our sinful hearts, a 180-degree turnaround, a complete change of life with new purpose, fresh insight, and a Christian worldview. We don't simply say, "God, make me a nicer person," or, "God, help me to be more generous or compassionate or patient." Instead we ask, "Lord Christ, come into my heart, forgive me of all my sins, guide my every step from this moment forward, and be my Savior and my Lord. I repent, I believe, and I trust you in all things."

This is when true change happens. Scripture tells us, "Therefore, if anyone is in Christ, he is a new creation; the old has gone, the new has come! All this is from God, who reconciled us to himself through Christ" (2 Corinthians 5:17–18).

We don't have to understand how Jesus can take our sins, suffer for us, die on a cross, rise from the grave, and offer us complete salvation and reconciliation with God. It's a mystery that on a human level we cannot ever completely comprehend. But we don't have to understand it in order to believe it, accept it, and embrace it.

When we choose to forgive someone who has hurt us deeply, we cannot grasp how God can cleanse our hearts and minds of the desire to avenge, help us to completely cancel the debt owed to us, and even one day be able to pray for and show compassionate love for the offender. But we don't have to figure out the mystery of forgiveness in order to choose to forgive. And as believers in Christ, we don't make that decision alone. Our heavenly Father is walking beside us, helping us face the pain and sorrow, showing us how to forgive, move forward, and live wholly in Him.

Frank Pomeroy, a heartbroken father and pastor, still reeling from the murder of his daughter and church members, admitted to his congregation a week after the shooting that he couldn't understand why Devin Kelley killed so many worshipers in his tiny church. But he went on to explain the forgiveness enigma: "You lean in to what you don't understand, you lean in to the Lord. I don't understand but I know my God does."[11]

The writer of Proverbs understood and agreed when he wrote, "Trust in the Lord with all your heart and lean not on your own understanding; in all your ways acknowledge him" (Proverbs 3:5–6).

Blaming the Offender

Some people believe that if they forgive the offender, they are dismissing, condoning, or excusing their crime. They fear it might appear as if they are shrugging off, overlooking, or even justifying a loved one's senseless murder at the hands of another. For some, forgiveness means they aren't honoring the beloved victim of the crime, the one whose life has been permanently marred, disabled, or taken.

But when we forgive, we don't dismiss, condone, or excuse the crime. We excuse *an accident*, because biblical forgiveness does not apply to an unintentional incident, even if the results are catastrophic. Accidents will happen and are a part of human life on earth. But Devin Kelley's and Dylann Roof's murderous actions were no accidents. They were premeditated, carefully planned. Biblical forgiveness applies to *intentional, purposeful acts*. And when we forgive the Kelleys and Roofs of our world, we are not dismissing or excusing their horrific and deadly actions. We are acknowledging that they did *indeed* hurt us and those we love. We *blame* them for what they did—the damage and death they purposely caused. But, as believers in Christ, we have the ability to *choose* to forgive them. And when we choose to forgive them completely, God produces the results, opening our prison door and allowing us to walk out free and unhindered by hate and bitterness.

I can honestly say that forgiving Dylann Roof for killing my wife lets *me* off the hook. It frees *me* from the burdens of anger, distress, and despair. And it is allowing me to move toward healing.

3

‖‖‖‖‖‖‖‖‖‖‖‖‖‖‖‖‖‖‖‖‖‖‖‖‖‖‖‖‖‖‖‖‖‖‖‖‖‖

Dylann Storm Roof

A Homegrown American Terrorist

This is an unfathomable and unspeakable act by somebody filled with hate and with a deranged mind. We're
going to put our arms around this church. . . . We're
going to find this horrible scoundrel.

Charleston Mayor Joseph P. Riley Jr.[1]

After viewing two brief videos of the white man entering and then exiting Emanuel AME Church, federal agents and local police flash the killer's grainy photograph across the nation's newscasts. The church security cameras have also filmed a black Hyundai parked beside the church door, with video images of Roof getting into it after the shooting and driving away.

Roof's father, Franklin Bennett Roof, sees the televised surveillance photos, recognizes his son, and calls authorities, confirming the shooter's name, and admitting to them that Dylann owns a .45-caliber gun, purchased with the birthday money given to him by his family.[2]

Countless law enforcement officials search for Roof throughout the long night of June 17, but with no success. The young white man has seemingly vanished.

The entire nation is stunned upon hearing news of the deadly shooting. Presidential candidate Jeb Bush cancels his Thursday morning campaign appearance in Charleston.[3]

South Carolina Governor Nikki Haley releases a statement: "While we do not yet know all of the details, we do know that we'll never understand what motivates anyone to enter one of our places of worship and take the life of another."[4]

The manhunt for Dylann Roof continues the next morning, June 18, as television news channels continue to flash his profile on the nation's screens, and police ask the public to be on the lookout for the man and the dark sedan he may be driving.

The Arrest

That morning, a North Carolina woman, Debbie Dills, who lives and works two hundred miles from Charleston, is driving to her job at a florist shop when she spots Roof's car; she recognizes the driver's appearance from the morning's televised news reports and notes that the car has South Carolina tags. She calls her friend, who is also her boss, and he calls police. Dills trails Roof's car for thirty-five miles down Highway 74 to Shelby while officers race to catch up with him. When police arrive, they stop the car, apprehend Roof, and take him into custody.[5]

The twenty-one-year-old surrenders to the authorities, fully cooperating and offering no resistance.[6]

When police search Roof's car, they discover the murder weapon, a handwritten note listing the names of several other churches, a Confederate flag, a partially burned U.S. flag, an empty box of ammunition, and a gun laser attachment used to fire weapons with better accuracy.[7]

They also find birthday cards from his mom and dad, and what appear to be suicide notes written to each of his parents. In a scribbled note to his mother, Roof apologized in advance for all the repercussions his deadly actions would cause her.

"At this moment I miss you very much," he wrote. "And as childish as it sounds, I wish I was in your arms."[8]

Authorities shackle Roof, extraditing him to Charleston and placing him in the county jail's isolation unit. The cell next to his holds Michael Slager, the white policeman charged with fatally shooting black motorist Walter Scott in North Charleston on April 4, 2015, the day after Dylann's twenty-first birthday.[9]

That afternoon in a news conference, Rae Wooten, the Charleston county coroner, confirms the shooting victims' names, releasing them to the public.

"Based on our immediate observation and the report of what happened, it is obvious these individuals suffered gunshot wounds, and as a result these individuals died," she said.

Wooten also talked about the victims' families, saying, "They are the most gracious group of grieving individuals. . . . It's a pleasure to deal with such strong, wonderful people in the face of such a tragedy."[10]

The Confession

Two FBI agents place Roof at an oval table in a small room and begin questioning him. He quickly confesses to the murders.

"I went to that church in Charleston—I did it!" he says proudly.

"Did what?" one agent asks.

"Well, I killed . . . well, I guess . . . I don't really know how many people or anything like that."

"Did you shoot them?"

"Yes."

"What kind of gun did you use?"

Roof grins and laughs: "A Glock 45. When I walked in the church, this thing was right on me, in front of me," he brags, referring to the gun. "And I was like . . . they're going to see it, you know . . .

it's big, it's heavy. It's got seven magazines, and I put eleven bullets in each magazine. They can hold thirteen, but I didn't want . . . it to like jam or anything like that."

As the agents listen, Roof continues to talk boldly, freely: "I was sitting there like just thinking about whether I should do it or not. . . . Well, I had to do it. Because somebody had to do something. Because, you know, black people are killing white people every day. . . . And they rape, they rape white women, a hundred white women a day. . . . What I did is so miniscule to what they are doing to white people every day."[11]

As Roof boasts of the murders, he remains unrepentant, explaining to the investigators that he hopes to start a race war, and he wants everyone to know what he has done. He also admits that everyone at the Bible study was so nice to him, he "almost didn't go through with it."[12]

Six weeks later from his jail cell, Dylann writes on lined paper, "I would like to make it crystal clear I do not regret what I did. I am not sorry. I have not shed a tear for the innocent people I killed. I have shed a tear of self-pity for myself. I feel pity that I had to do what I did in the first place."[13]

The FBI's Fatal Mistake

It surprised me that Roof was able to purchase the gun he used to kill my wife. I was disheartened to learn that due to errors in his federal background check, Roof was allowed to buy a weapon. FBI Director James Comey admitted that an examiner failed to see the February 2015 police report listing Roof's unlawful drug possession, a crime that would have prevented him from buying a firearm.[14]

During an FBI-arranged conference call with the victims' families, an agent apologized to us, admitting, "It's our fault. We are sorry." Before the call, we didn't know how Roof got the gun or anything about the botched background check. In some ways, this revelation quieted my spirit and gave me a new understanding into the nation's gun laws. If the system had worked in Roof's case, he would not have been able to legally buy the gun, I would still have my wife, and she would still have her pastor and church friends.

Dylann's Background

At one of the later trials, I saw Dylann's mother, Amelia Cowles, for the first time, and I wondered about Dylan's family, his background. I learned that he was a quiet child born in Columbia, South Carolina, to a white middle-class family. His parents divorced in 1991, three years before Dylann was born. As a young boy, Dylann was shuttled back and forth between his mother, who lived in Lexington, and his father, who lived in Columbia. His father remarried when Roof was five years old. Dylann struggled in school, attending at least seven different schools within nine years, flunking the ninth grade twice before finally dropping out altogether.[15]

When Dylann was a teenager, his family suffered severe financial losses. His mother was evicted from her home in 2009, and his father lost a business, falling into heavy debt. After quitting school, Dylann worked a variety of low-paying jobs. During these years, he also took an unusual and avid interest in reading white-supremacist websites, plentiful on the internet.[16]

Amelia Cowles thought her nineteen-year-old son was too introverted, and she was concerned Dylann had no job, no driver's license, and spent far too much time cooped up in his room isolated from others. Some of Roof's classmates described him as "kind of wild," a "heavy drinker," and a regular "pill popper" who constantly abused prescription drugs. A former drug charge cited Roof possessing methamphetamine, cocaine, and LSD.[17]

After the shooting, Roof's uncle, Carson Cowles, told officials the family was shocked by the killings and described his nephew as a "quiet, soft-spoken" young man. The family admitted they never saw this coming. Later, when Cowles heard South Carolina Governor Nikki Haley tell the hosts of the *Today* show that "we will absolutely want him [Roof] to have the death penalty," Carson Cowles stated publicly, "If he's found guilty, I'll be the one to push the button myself. . . . If what I am hearing is true, he needs to pay for it."[18]

Members of Dylann Roof's family offered us, the families of the victims, "their deepest sympathies and condolences," admitting that "words cannot express our shock, grief, and disbelief as to what had happened that night." They confessed to feeling "devastated and saddened," and they offered prayers for "all of those impacted by these events."

They also expressed "hope and prayer for peace and healing for the families of the victims," as well as for the Charleston community, the state of South Carolina, and the nation.[19]

A Lack of Regret

Dylann Roof's murderous actions baffled me, especially his lack of regret, remorse, or repentance after killing nine praying worshipers who welcomed him inside the fellowship hall and showed him kindness.

I chewed for a long time on Roof's hard-to-digest words: "I would like to make it crystal clear I do not regret what I did. I am not sorry. I have not shed a tear for the innocent people I killed."

He admitted the Emanuel Nine were innocent people, and boasted that he killed them. He showed pride for his actions, not a hint of regret or remorse.

I had hoped to see a true feeling of deep repentance and extreme sadness emerge from Dylann's heart. I yearned to hear him pray the prayer of the psalmist, "The sacrifices of God are a broken spirit; a broken and contrite heart, O God, you will not despise" (Psalm 51:17).

"Regret is a true feeling of remorse, deep repentance and extreme sadness over what has happened," Jennifer Davis Rash wrote.

"You will know it when you see it. The humility, the despair, the brokenness seep from the person's pores."[20]

I waited to hear of Dylann expressing genuine regret. I knew that a broken and contrite heart would give the young man a choice over the future of his soul.

"For the person walking through regret," Rash wrote, "it can provide a space for God to show us His grace in a way never experienced before. When we know more of the depth of our sin and brokenness, we can marvel even more at the unfathomable love and forgiveness offered to us through Christ."[21]

Regret. Repentance. Remorse. I saw none of these in Dylann Roof. I waited in vain. Nonetheless, I decided to forgive him.

People often ask me, "How can you forgive Roof when he has not apologized for Myra's murder and shows no pangs of conscience or contrition, lament or sorrow, guilt or shame?"

And my answer to each person is always the same: Even premeditated murder can be forgiven. I'm not saying it's easy to forgive a person who has killed your loved one, but murder is a sin just like any other sin. And according to Scripture, a sin is a sin, and we are all guilty of sin. I remind them of Romans 3:23: "For all have sinned and fall short of the glory of God."

I also direct them to 1 John 1:8, 10: "If we claim to be without sin, we deceive ourselves and the truth is not in us. . . . If we claim we have not sinned, we make him out to be a liar and his word has no place in our lives."

Fortunately, however, Scripture promises, "If we confess our sins, he is faithful and just and will forgive us our sins and purify us from all unrighteousness" (1 John 1:9).

I believe we can be so quick to pass judgment when we catch people committing sin that we act as if *we* never sinned. How can a sinner pass judgment on a sinner? It isn't our role to judge others, but God's. Our job is to forgive.

I take Jesus' words seriously when He commanded His followers not to judge and condemn others, but to forgive them their sins.

"Do not judge, and you will not be judged. Do not condemn, and you will not be condemned. Forgive, and you will be forgiven" (Luke 6:37).

Jesus plainly illustrated this command on a day when he was teaching in the temple courts. The Pharisees brought to Jesus a woman caught in adultery.

"In the Law, Moses commanded us to stone such women," they said to Him (John 8:5). Jesus replied to the rock-grasping group of men, each possessing a surplus of his own personal sins: "If any one of you is without sin, let him be the first to throw a stone at her" (v. 7).

Realizing their own guilt, Scripture tells us, "At this, those who heard began to go away one at a time, the older ones first, until only Jesus was left . . . Jesus straightened up and asked her, 'Woman, where are they? Has no one condemned you? . . . Then neither do I condemn you. Go now and leave your life of sin'" (John 8:9–11).

Another incident in Scripture also illustrates this type of forgiveness. In Acts 6 and 7, Stephen, "a man full of God's grace and power" (Acts 6:8), was seized, taken to the high priest, and then dragged out of the city and stoned to death. As Stephen fell to his knees, bleeding and dying, he did not judge or condemn his killers. He simply cried out with forgiveness, "Lord, do not hold this sin against them" (Acts 7:57–60). As he endured bone-breaking pain from hard, blunt-force blows, Stephen forgave the killers even though none expressed regret, remorse, or repentance.

I have long understood that biblical forgiveness does not rest on an offender's regret, remorse, or apology. I chose to forgive Dylann Roof with or without any response from him. I did not need an "I'm sorry" in order to forgive him.

Immaculee's Response

Perhaps the most beautiful and powerful illustration of forgiving a murderer without receiving any expression of apology, regret, remorse, or sorrow is Immaculee Ilibagiza's story of tragedy, horror, survival, and forgiveness after she lost her entire family in the 1994 Rwandan Hutu killing spree. I recently had the privilege of meeting Immaculee and heard her tell her remarkable story of forgiveness.

On Easter Sunday in 1994, Immaculee's Rwandan homeland experienced the beginning of one hundred days of one of the bloodiest genocides in human history, a well-organized plan by Hutu extremists to exterminate all Tutsis. The Hutus and the Tutsis had been friends and neighbors for years, living and working side by side, marrying each other, and caring for each other's children. A sudden spark of violence, the assassination of Rwandan President Habyarimana, began the savage Hutu killing spree, promoted and aggravated by widespread hate propaganda. The violence left Tutsi men, women, and children slaughtered in the streets. Immaculee, a twenty-four-year-old Tutsi college student and devout Catholic, lost her mother, father, and other Tutsi family members to the sudden massacre that left carnage and devastation all around her.

When the killing began, Immaculee took refuge in a sympathetic Hutu pastor's house, hiding with seven other women in a tiny bathroom, hourly fearing for her life, starving, and barely surviving the terrifying violence that surrounded her outside.[22]

One night while in hiding, Immaculee heard a woman outside screaming and a baby crying. She realized that the Hutu killers had killed a mother and left her baby on the road to die. Unable to help, Immaculee listened in agony to the crying baby all night. When morning came, the baby had stopped crying. She then heard the sounds of snarling fighting dogs. Her heart broke when she realized the baby had been eaten by wild dogs. Sickened by the disturbing sounds, Immaculee prayed for God to receive the baby into heaven. She then asked the Lord, "How can I forgive people who kill a mother and leave her baby to die?"

Before she could safely leave her hiding place, Immaculee learned that more than a million Tutsis had been murdered, including her own precious family members. With each passing day, Immaculee heard more stories of how the Hutu killers enjoyed slaughtering her Tutsi family and friends. Immaculee became angry when she learned about the horrific acts the Hutus had done to Tutsi women, children, and babies. She couldn't bear to hear another word, so horrified the government and the world had done nothing to stop the genocide of her people. She admitted that hate filled her heart, growing stronger and stronger, and she had no thoughts of forgiving anyone. She was ready to pick up a gun and kill every Hutu she saw.

"[I] wished for weapons—for guns and cannons to kill the Hutus—because I wanted vengeance so badly."[23]

The severity of her anger and rage so frightened her that Immaculee began to pray. She grasped the rosary her late father had given her and begged God for hours each day to release her from the anger and hate she felt toward the Hutus. But every time she prayed Jesus' prayer in Matthew 6:9–13, the Lord's Prayer, she trembled, stopping at the part that encouraged forgiveness, unable to continue: "Forgive us our debts, as we also have forgiven our debtors" (v. 12). She struggled with that prayer because she knew she could not forgive them.

After many days of ardent prayer, however, she felt God touch her heart, calling her to forgive the killers. Within the small, cramped bathroom, her life still in constant danger, she began to pray: "If they kill me, God, I ask You to forgive them. Their hearts have been corrupted by hatred, and they don't know why they want to hurt me."[24]

After the violence stopped, the few Tutsis left alive began to lament and bury loved ones. Deep in mourning, Immaculee asked God to "please open my heart, Lord, and show me how to forgive . . ." admitting, "I'm not strong enough to squash my hatred—they've wronged us all so much . . . my hatred is so heavy that it could crush me."[25]

When out of hiding, she mentioned to others her desire to forgive the Hutus. "You can forgive all you want to, Immaculee," they told her, "but they don't deserve your forgiveness. They deserve to be shot."[26]

Immaculee chose to forgive even the man who murdered her family. "I'd opened my heart to God's forgiveness and made my peace with the killers."[27]

Like the Emanuel Nine's family members who received no apology from Dylann Roof for their loved ones' murders, Immaculee and other Tutsi survivors received no apologies from the murderous Hutus, no expression of regret or remorse for the massacre. Yet she still chose to forgive. Not to judge, nor condemn, but forgive.

Immaculee captivated me the moment we met. I felt like I had known her for a long time. We embraced, and I felt the love of God and His grace filling my soul.

With her calm and pleasing spirit, Immaculee imparted that calm and pleasing spirit to my own soul. After she forgave the killers, she told me, she discovered the same peace I experienced when I chose to forgive Dylann Roof. It was the priceless peace Christ gave that passed all understanding.

A Heartbroken Grandfather

Even though Dylann Roof had never apologized to me or to the other victims' family members, C. Joseph Roof, his paternal grandfather, a highly respected real estate lawyer in Columbia, South Carolina, reached out to me in a personal letter written one year after the murders. He expressed sorrow and regret "from the depths of my heart . . . my sorrow and regret are endless . . . for the pain and loss you have endured."

He apologized again for his grandson, Dylann, this time publicly in April 2017 in the Charleston County Circuit Court, the first time a relative spoke on Dylann's behalf in court.

"I just want to say loudly and repeatedly and constantly we're sorry. We're just as sorry as we can be that this has happened," the brokenhearted grandfather said. "We regret it. It has ruined lives, and I cannot put those back together."

After his apology on behalf of his grandson, Joseph Roof admitted, "I will go to my grave not understanding what happened."[28]

4

The Decision

Murder may be the hardest kind of death to process, and the emotional response is much more complicated because this unfathomable grief is coupled with anger.[1]

Two days after the shooting, I suffer horribly from the jagged wound and deep aching void of indescribable loss. As I spend the sleepless nights alone in our bed, I understand with new gravity that my precious wife is dead. It is a grief as heavy as a dark woolen blanket covering me, blocking out any light, smothering any future hope.

Will I ever feel hope again? I wonder.

In shock and despair, I feel my life has no more purpose. An act of pure evil has taken my wife forever from my arms, life, and ministry, sending me on an emotional roller coaster with unexpected ups and downs and nonstop tears.

I see reminders of Myra everywhere at home: her smiling photo on the wall, the fresh flowers on the table, the loving way she made our house a warm, welcoming home.

Some say the sense of smell is a person's most powerful and memorable sense—many times stronger than the other human senses of sight, sound, touch, or taste. I believe it, and more than once I go to her clothes closet, burying my face in her blouse or robe, pretending she is still here with me. I am numb with grief, still in shock from her sudden, dreadful departure. I no longer can envision the two of us side by side, holding hands into the future. I can hardly believe she is gone.

The Bond Hearing

Dylann Roof's bond hearing is set for Friday, June 19, fewer than forty-eight hours after the gunman riddled my wife's body with bullets, causing her to die on the hard linoleum floor of Emanuel's fellowship hall.

"I'm not going to Dylann Roof's bond hearing," I tell my children, Kevin and Denise. "I want nothing *ever* to do with Roof."

Working for twenty-five years as a probation-parole agent for the South Carolina Department of Probation, Parole and Pardon Services, I had been to many bond hearings. I knew exactly what would happen.

"Roof will come out, receive a bond, and be taken back to his cell," I tell them. "I don't see any significance in going to his bond hearing. It'll be a waste of time."

But my children want to go, and they insist I go with them. After a long pause, I acquiesce, agreeing to go, but regretting my decision the moment I make it. I set some strict ground rules.

"We're going to sit down and be quiet, saying nothing to no one. As soon as it's over, we're getting up and leaving. Those are the only conditions I'll agree to go under."

The bond hearing begins at 2:00 on Friday, June 19. We find a seat in the packed courtroom, filled to overflowing with the victims' loved ones, interested onlookers, and news reporters, and we wait for the hearing to begin. Via a video link from the Charleston detention center where he is held in isolation, Dylann appears, his slight frame clad in a prison jumpsuit and bulletproof vest. He stands still, head bowed, eyes lowered, his pale face showing no expression, his hands cuffed behind his back. Two armed guards, one black and one white, wearing heavy body protection, flank him. Dylann responds only when asked to confirm his name and age, and to reveal he is unemployed.

I swallow hard. I feel my body lean sharply forward as I focus unblinking eyes on Dylann Roof.

That's him! I inwardly shout.

My muscles tense, and the taste of nausea rises from my gut and rests on my tongue. I suddenly remember something that happened weeks ago after one of the regular Wednesday Bible studies at Emanuel. When Myra came home that evening, she told me about a strange visitor who had walked into the fellowship hall, sat down, and listened to the Reverend Daniel Simmons as he taught from God's Word.

"The young man left right after we prayed the closing prayer," Myra told me.

"Did you know who he was?" I asked her.

"No," she responded. "He was a young white man with a pale face, blond hair cut in a bowl shape, and sad eyes. He was probably a homeless man. We welcomed him inside, and he stayed for the study but said nothing at all. He was so skinny, I believed he might be hungry, so before he left the church, I gave him some money from my purse."

She mentioned that this was the only time a white man had ever attended the Wednesday night Bible study at Emanuel.

"I hope he comes back," Myra said, smiling, excitement in her voice.

As I gaze at Dylann Roof via the video link, again and again my memory tells me, *That's the man! It has to be!*

I sit there stunned, realizing that twice this man heard God's Word taught from Scripture, listened to the worshipers' heartfelt prayers, accepted everyone's genuine welcome into their intimate fold, received Myra's love, concern, and cash, and then ultimately murdered them in cold blood.

I close my eyes and shake my head as if to release the memory from my mind. I feel my heart pounding as I try to both absorb and purge this powerful recollection.

I open my eyes when Chief Magistrate James Gosnell begins the hearing. The gray-haired, heavy-set judge is not popular with the Charleston community. During a previous trial, according to a judicial disciplinary order posted on the South Carolina Supreme Court's website, Gosnell used a derogatory word to an African-American defendant at a bond hearing. He received a reprimand for his language in 2005, having been charged with violating several parts of the official Code of Judicial Conduct, including that judges "shall not, in the performance of judicial duties, by words or conduct manifest bias or prejudice, including but not limited to bias or prejudice based upon race."[2]

The same reprimand recorded that Gosnell also bent the rules to get another judge out of jail after he was caught driving under the influence with an open container in his car.[3]

Judge Gosnell begins with some personal words:

"Charleston is a very strong community," he says. "We have big hearts. We are a very loving community, and we are going to reach out to everyone and we will touch them."

He then cautions his listeners against demonizing Roof's family.

"We must find it in our heart not only to help those that are victims, but also to help those in [Roof's] family as well."[4]

He continues his speech even as he receives bewildered and stern looks from faces in the courtroom.

"We have victims, nine of them," he says. "But we also have victims on the other side. There are victims on this young man's side of the family. No one would have ever thrown them into the whirlwind of events that they have been thrown into."[5]

When a Charleston attorney who represented some of the victims' families heard the judge's remarks, he was appalled, later remarking: "Understand where we were emotionally. . . . And we'd just been talking about how that boy hadn't been brought up right and his parents were partially responsible. And then the judge says, Don't be selfish, think of the other victims, his family. And I just saw red. I was like, How dare he? Does he not know what these people have lost?"[6]

The judge charges Roof with nine counts of murder and one count of weapon possession, the gun used in the brutal slayings two days before. He sets Roof's bond at one million dollars for the weapon charge, but he does not have the authority to set bond for the murder charges. He explains that Roof will be held without bail on those counts.[7]

My Public Decision

I glance at my watch and yearn to leave when Judge Gosnell suddenly surprises the courtroom with a highly irregular courtroom move. Without advance warning, the judge begins calling out the names of the victims one by one. He then asks the family members of each victim to step forward if they wish to speak. Several family members take the opportunity to address the court. During their emotional, tearful words, the gunman keeps still, quiet, his eyes unmoving and slanted downward.

I have already made up my mind not to say anything when Judge Gosnell calls on a "representative of the family of Myra Thompson."

I freeze.

I don't want to speak.

I have no idea what to say.

I glance at Dylann Roof, and that's when I hear a familiar Voice calling my name, speaking directly to my heart. I have heard it before, and I know without a doubt it is the Voice of my heavenly Father.

"*I* have something to say, Anthony," the Voice whispers.

I obey immediately and stand up. I still have no idea what will happen.

The judge looks at me and asks, "Sir, do you want to say something before this court?"

"Yes, sir," I respond.

"Please, come forward," Gosnell says, motioning me to the front of the room.

Out of the corner of my eye, I see my children's eyebrows lift and mouths drop open. The court is deathly quiet, the raw pain and tension within the room almost palpable. When I reach the podium, I stop and look intensely at Dylann Roof's face on the flat-screen monitor. I can see him, but through the detention hall's camera lens Dylann can only see Judge Gosnell. But he can clearly hear everything said to him in the courtroom.

I take a deep breath, and God puts His words into my mouth.

"I forgive you," I say to Dylann. "And my family forgives you."

I pause, unsure of what my next words will be.

"But we would like you to take this opportunity to repent. Repent. Confess. Give your life to the One who matters the most: *Jesus Christ*, so that He can change it and change your attitude. And no matter what happens to you, then you'll be okay. Do that and you'll be better off than you are right now."

While I speak, I note that Roof's eyes are fixed, unblinking, and focused on the floor. Throughout the hearing, he has not once looked up. But at the very moment I mention the name *Jesus Christ*, Dylann unexpectedly raises his eyes to the camera, and for a split second, I am allowed to peer deep into this young man's soul. I am shocked by what I see. For one unforeseen millisecond—a thousandth of a second—evil becomes careless, accidentally dropping its impenetrable guard, its mask. I am allowed to see in Dylann's eyes a small fissure in which the unanticipated, wretched look of guilt and shame slips through. The hardened racist, who killed innocent church members only because he hated the color of their skin, becomes yet another unremarkable sinner who has allowed—nay, cordially invited—evil to enter into his soul, pitch a tent, and take up residence there.

Before his eyes again glaze over with diabolical hardness, they become brief windows into the killer's pathetic soul. When I catch a sudden glimpse of Dylann's deep sense of degradation, something immediately happens within my heart and mind. I mentally drop the heavy stones of anger, despair, and hate, and I experience the unmistakable peace of Christ's love filling my entire being. At that moment, I feel free, as light as a feather. As I return to my seat, I sense God calling me to a new purpose in His kingdom, a new beginning, a new mission in Christ to spread the gospel of unconditional, biblical forgiveness.

An attending reporter observes, "Thompson's wife was not yet buried, and he [Thompson] was actually offering Roof a way to salvation."[8]

A few other family members of victims also express their forgiveness, prompting the reporter to write, "Roof kept his eyes lowered, surely hearing the dead speak along with the living. He must have felt the weakness of evil in the face of such good."[9]

The reporter then surmised: "Even atheists had to see divinity in these families built by love. God was there in that courtroom if He has ever been anywhere."[10]

The Criticisms

I spent the next few weeks in deep thought and prayer as I desperately sought to better understand what happened at Dylann's bond hearing when God so intensely stirred my heart to publicly express my forgiveness and concern for the young racist's soul. I realized that as I walked to the podium, I mentally treaded through the forgiveness process, recognizing that I, like Dylann Roof, was a sinner. In those few seconds, I examined my own life and discovered my own sin, asking God to forgive me and seeking God's help to allow me to forgive Dylann.

I still sometimes hear criticism that I forgave Dylann too quickly, having too little time to process or fully comprehend his violent crime. One critic stated that "the oversimplification of *I forgive* demonstrates a lack of understanding of the significance of the incident."[11]

I imagine this critic is wondering how I could forgive Roof just two days after the murders, when the pain of Myra's murder was so fresh and raw and I was still numb with shock and grief.

But I chose to forgive, knowing exactly the appalling significance of the incident—the heartache, the sadness, and the deep nagging loneliness of having my best friend and life companion so violently snatched away. I was not oversimplifying my difficult decision to forgive, to pardon Dylann of this horrific sin as my heavenly Father had shown His mercy to me, a sinner.

I also knew that "forgiveness alone can halt the cycle of blame and pain, breaking the chain of un-grace," and that the New Testament Greek word for "forgiveness" means, literally, "to release, to hurl away, to free yourself."[12]

Did the Apostle Paul not command the Christ-believing Colossians to release, to hurl away, to free themselves, when he wrote Colossians 3:13, "Forgive as the Lord forgave you"? I was only trying to be obedient in following his difficult teaching.

People are disturbed by this conscious decision to forgive so soon after a murder, especially one based on the deadly disease of racism. They ask, "Doesn't genuine forgiveness take longer? Isn't forgiveness a long, painful process, an agonizing journey?"

I usually respond that scriptural forgiveness is based on God's Word. Believing God's promises to be true, I made the intentional choice to fully forgive, and based upon my prayerful decision, I forgave. I knew the kind of life I would live if I chose not to forgive Dylann Roof. I would be forever locked into victimhood, a damaged slave to the evil deed of a depraved killer, destroyed and unable to escape his firm, malevolent grasp. That's what is so amazing about grace and forgiveness. They freed my soul to soar in love, in mercy, and in God's ministry to others. Yes, I chose forgiveness.

"Not to forgive imprisons me in the past and locks out all potential for change. I thus yield control to another, my enemy, and doom myself to suffer the consequences of the wrong," wrote Philip Yancey.[13]

The long journey I have embarked upon is one of emotional healing, of remembering Myra without experiencing the deep ache of how she passed or thinking about how she suffered or dwelling on the cruel unfairness of Dylann's deliberate deed. I want to reminisce about our good times together, our love for each other, and our years of marriage and ministry together. I want to be able to smile when I remember Myra, not close my eyes and shudder at the grisly way she died. That journey may take some time as I walk closely beside the Lord, depending solely on His moment-by-moment help toward restoration and healing, but I am confident I will get there.

Author Lewis B. Smedes described beautifully the forgiveness journey I am taking toward emotional healing: "Forgiving is a journey, sometimes a long one, and we may need some time before we get to the station of complete healing, but the nice thing is that we are being healed en route. When we genuinely forgive, we set a prisoner free and then discover that the prisoner we set free was us."[14]

My forgiveness came quickly, but it was genuine and complete. When I decided to forgive Dylann, my own peace began, my prison doors opened, and I began to heal. If I had refused to forgive, I knew I would live with the killing and the killer forever alive and actively stirring in my heart and mind. That's why I chose biblical forgiveness. I'm done with Dylann Roof, and he no longer has any control over me.

Forgiveness Doesn't Depend on Feelings

People still ask me if I "felt forgiving" when I forgave Dylann Roof at the bond hearing. I don't remember feeling especially *forgiving* when I decided to forgive my wife's murderer. But I knew that biblical forgiveness was not based on my personal feelings or human emotions, but on the unrelenting, unyielding fact of God's Word, a constant eternal truth not dependant on my unpredictable human feelings at any given time.

I imagine Stephen *didn't feel* very forgiving as his enemies stoned him to death. Yet he forgave and even asked God to forgive them (Acts 7:58–60).

I imagine Immaculee *didn't feel* very forgiving as the hate-driven Hutus slaughtered her Tutsi family and loved ones in the Rwandan genocide. But she forgave and eventually in her journey was able to pray without pain and struggle, "Forgive us our debts, as we also have forgiven our debtors."

I imagine Pastor Frank Pomeroy *didn't feel* very forgiving after Devin Patrick Kelley walked in the front door of the First Baptist Church of Sutherland Springs, Texas, and began firing on his faithful church members, including Pomeroy's daughter. Yet he forgave the killer shortly after the shooting, and began his own personal healing as he envisioned his loved ones in heaven, at peace and "dancing with Jesus."

I imagine the parents of the dead children in Nickel Mines, Pennsylvania, *didn't feel* very forgiving when Charles C. Roberts walked into the one-room Amish schoolhouse and killed their young, innocent children. Yet they forgave and immediately began to minister with incredible love to Roberts's hurting family.

Feelings have little to do with the firm, intentional biblical decision to forgive. As a believer in Christ, I know I will be called to forgive many hurtful others as I travel through life. Dylann Roof was just one person who caused me to have to make the difficult decision to forgive. Surely a Christian must live his entire life looking through the lens of biblical forgiveness, experiencing the inescapable cruel realities of being human and beginning the many emotional restorative journeys that must follow.

Scripture states that Peter once questioned Jesus about how many times he had to forgive people who sinned against him: "As many as seven times?" he asked.

Jesus responded: "Not seven times, but, I tell you, *seventy-seven times*" (Matthew 18:21–22 NRSV, emphasis added).[15]

In His response to Peter some two thousand years ago, Jesus spoke hauntingly and particularly to the Emanuel Church shooting —for Dylann Roof fired exactly *seventy-seven* bullets into the group of praying people.[16]

My Overwhelming Burden

During those courtroom moments after I forgave Dylann, I also remembered possessing an overwhelming burden for this young man's soul. I knew right away this burden was from God and was much bigger than I was. I hoped Dylann heard God's loving plea as the words came through my lips, calling him to repent, to confess, and to give his life to the One who matters—Jesus Christ.

A *Time* magazine reporter later interviewed me about my forgiving Dylann Roof and urging him to turn to Christ. In the article, he wrote something truly insightful, theologically loaded words that touched my very soul:

> Thompson was calling on the killer to turn himself inside out, to inventory everything wrong about his thoughts and actions—the murders, of course, but also the willful ignorance and cultivated hatred that apparently fueled him, and the vanity that would make him think he was an instrument of history, and the hardheartedness that made it possible for him to sit with his victims and know their humanity before he ever drew his gun. A true confession of his offenses would entail a wrenching calculation of the measureless grief and suffering his crimes caused in the lives of those who survived. It would comprehend the theft he committed of nine lives, and all the promise and love that lay in store for his victims. All stolen. And it would face up, as well, to the wastage of his own life and possibilities.[17]

Potential—lost and unfulfilled. Stolen lives and limitless possibilities. A wrenching calculation of the measureless grief and suffering. Yes, this reporter understood precisely the difficult route Dylann Roof must travel in order to confess, repent, and receive Christ's forgiveness and salvation. He summed up exactly what I felt when I implored Dylann to come to Christ.

In his writing, this same magazine reporter also seemed to make his own discovery about the gift of forgiveness, one that I wholeheartedly agree with: "Forgiveness is a riddle to theologians, psychologists, sociologists and philosophers. . . . For some, forgiveness speaks to the condition of the offender. . . . For others, forgiveness describes the state of mind of the forgiver: you have harmed me, but I refuse to respond in kind. Forgiveness is a kind of purifier that absorbs injury and returns love."[18]

Perhaps forgiveness is, indeed, the "purifier that absorbs injury," that purges and cleanses the forgiver's heart, making it surprisingly possible for him to return another's premeditated pain with the gift of Christ's love.

Judge Gosnell's opening words, when he encouraged those in court to consider Dylann's family as well as the victims', had upset many of his listeners, proving so disturbing and highly controversial that he was removed from office a few days later.[19]

I felt great sympathy for Dylann's mother and other family members as they were thrust into the world spotlight due to his act of premeditated murder. I don't blame them for what Dylann did on that evening, and I harbor no ill feelings against them. I blame only Dylann, and I have chosen to forgive him. I pray his family can also find it in their hearts to forgive him.

My Heart, Strangely Warmed

Not long after the initial bond hearing, I was asked to speak at Christ Church, a predominantly white, affluent congregation in Mount Pleasant, South Carolina. I talked about God and racism. At the end of the service, a mother, her young children beside her, stood up and addressed me.

"Reverend Thompson," she began, "when I heard about you and people forgiving this young man, I had to take a hard look at myself. And I have to admit that I am a racist. I see it in my family. I see it in my grandparents. I see it in my parents. My friends are racists. When I got older, I knew it was wrong, but I didn't do anything about it."

Her words astounded me. I had never heard a white person say that before, and certainly not in Charleston. I digested her unexpected words, and I asked the congregation to give glory to God for the woman's honest and intimate testimony. After that, more white people in the congregation stood up and talked about growing up in racist families, confessing their own racism and repenting of this sin. They told me they didn't want to be like that anymore.

I was elated and my heart was strangely warmed. As I traveled back home at the end of the worship service, I possessed a crisp, new feeling in my heart, one that until that moment I was not sure would ever return. I could not hold it inside. In my enthusiasm, I shouted loud and long inside my car:

"So there *is* hope after all! Believe me! There *is* hope!"

5

A Mighty Long Journey

> Our pain cuts that much deeper because it happened in a church. The church is and always has been the center of African-American life—a place to call our own in a too-often hostile world, a sanctuary from so many hardships.
>
> President Barak Obama, June 2015[1]

During the following days and weeks, Dylann Roof's life, background, and beliefs begin to surface, unfolding and reaching a public still shaking its head in horror and confusion, still unable to fathom such a shocking, racist act. I hear much more about this young man who purposely shot and killed my wife. The more I learn, the more I understand Dylann Roof to be a man who possesses pure evil in his heart and mind.

Dylann sits in jail awaiting his multiple courtroom trials, spending most of his time penning thoughts in a personal journal. Some of his entries are boyish, immature—one of them admitting that he enjoys being sad and having pity on himself because sadness is such a strong emotion.

Others depict a self-centered young man who expresses a selfish regret: "One of my only regrets is that I was never able to fall in love."[2]

But most of his recorded thoughts show his sinful soul, his inner prejudices, his ungrounded and illogical hate based solely on race. His statements send chills down my back.

"I did what I thought would make the biggest wave," he writes, as if driven by a sense of national pride, loyal brotherhood, and patriotic duty. "And now the fate of our race is in the hands of my brothers who continue to live freely."

In what is now called his "jailhouse manifesto," Roof railed against Jews, Hispanics, African-Americans, homosexuals, and Muslims. He wrote that someday his hero, Adolf Hitler, would "be inducted as a saint," and warned that unless white people "take violent action, we have no future."[3]

How interesting that Archbishop Desmond Tutu also wrote about a future, but in these incredibly different words: "Without forgiveness, there is no future."[4]

Dylann Roof's murders were labeled a "hate crime." The U.S. Justice Department announced it would investigate the killings as a possible act of domestic terrorism, since the shooting was "designed to strike fear and terror into the community."[5]

Planning the Murderous Plot

Details about Roof's activities and prejudices continued to pour forth from the media. On the morning of the shooting, after a long cocaine- and vodka-fueled night spent with his friend, twenty-two-year-old Joey Meek, Roof confided in Meek, telling him he wanted to start a race war by killing black people at a church. Roof raged on and on about how blacks were taking over the world, and how someone needed to do something about it for the sake of the white race.

Not taking his friend's threats seriously, Meek kept Roof's murderous plots to himself, having no thought of alerting police. Meek didn't know that Roof began planning the attacks against African-Americans some six months before that night. During that period, Roof spent ample time online scouting out potential targets, railing against blacks in his journal, posting photographs of himself on social media with a Confederate flag, and wearing flags of defunct white-supremacist regimes in South Africa and Rhodesia. He posted on his internet website (called "The Last Rhodesian") a manifesto of white supremacy, and bought a Glock 45 handgun and hundreds of rounds of ammunition. Roof yearned for revenge for his perceived offenses by the black race against the white race.[6]

Some of his internet images showed him holding a gun while standing outside South Carolina's Museum and Library of Confederate History, and posing in front of a sign that reads, "Sacred burial site. Our African ancestors." He also posted a photograph of himself standing on and burning an American flag.[7]

In his online personal manifesto, written before the shooting, Roof admitted he had not been raised in a racist home, but became "racially-awakened" by the 2012 Trayvon Martin shooting, the black Florida teen killed by George Zimmerman—who was acquitted of the murder.

"At this moment," Roof wrote, "I realized that something was very wrong. How could the news be blowing up the Trayvon Martin case while hundreds of these black on white murders got ignored?"

He mentioned that he "had no choice," and chose Charleston because it was the most historic city in his state, at one time having the highest ratio of blacks to whites in the country.

"We have no skinheads, no real KKK, no one doing anything but talking on the internet," he wrote. "Well someone has to have the bravery to take it to the real world, and I guess that has to be me."[8]

He also broadcasted online his views on African-Americans and segregation.

"Segregation was not a bad thing," he wrote. "It existed to protect us from [African-Americans]. . . . Not only did it protect us from having to interact with them and from being physically harmed by them, but it protected us from being brought down to their level. Integration has done nothing but bring whites down to [the] level of brute animals."[9]

Roof continued, commenting negatively about Jews, Hispanics (whom he called "our enemies"), and patriotism.

"I hate the sight of the American flag," he wrote. "Modern American patriotism is an absolute joke. People pretending like they have something to be proud [of] while White people are being murdered daily in the streets."[10]

After reading Roof's online manifesto, Assistant U.S. Attorney Nathan Williams concluded, "You can see what kind of hatred he had: a vast hatred that was cold and calculated."[11]

"The evidence, along with his manifesto, hundreds of photos, and a confession to the FBI," according to a news report, "draws a portrait of a young white man consumed by racial hatred who carefully planned the killings, picking out meek, innocent black people who likely wouldn't fight back."[12]

Others believed that Dylann's taped confession "was that of a confused, wannabe warrior who soaked up hate on the internet and waged a mission of no clear purpose against people who had done him no wrong." They described how the jury in Roof's federal hate crime trial "listened intently as Roof regurgitated venomous online hate for blacks by way of explaining his bloody shooting rampage through Emanuel AME Church."[13]

Dylann was just one of the many proponents of the rising white supremacist violence in the United States. In 2017, white supremacists committed the largest share of domestic-extremist-related killings, claiming eighteen lives, and highlighting the danger of racist rhetoric and hateful ideas. Dylann Roof's writings showed that he bought into the "modern white-supremacist ideology . . . the belief that white people are on the verge of extinction, thanks to a 'rising tide' of non-white populations (supposedly controlled by a Jewish conspiracy)." Some white supremacists and other racists, like Dylann, "justify their actions as attempts to 'save' their race," saying the white race is being threatened with genocide or extinction, making it easier for them "to justify or rationalize violence in the name of preserving the race."[14]

Dylann was shown to be obsessed with white supremacists' claims, thinking himself to be one of their devoted soldiers, called to the mission of eliminating those he felt threatened his race. It took only a short time of internet study on hate-based websites for Dylann to buy into their white supremacist beliefs and carry out its lethal consequences.

Propelled by white supremacist teachings, Roof had made six recent trips to Charleston from his home in Columbia, South Carolina. Authorities believed Roof made these drives to case the church and plan the shootings at Emanuel.[15]

After his arrest, Roof told FBI officials that he was "worn out" by the Emanuel shooting and didn't plan to commit more killings that night after he fled Charleston. But based on further examination of the GPS in Roof's car, a newly unsealed court document two years later revealed that after the Emanuel shooting, he drove twenty miles to another African-American church—Branch AME Church in Summerville, South Carolina. Like Emanuel, Branch AME Church also held a Wednesday evening Bible study. The new information gave officials reason to wonder if Dylann had been planning another massacre on that same night. Evidence showed that he slowed his car and stopped at the Summerville church for two to three minutes and then drove away.[16]

Dylann Chooses Charleston

Dylann Roof carefully researched the racial history of South Carolina, Charleston, and the Emanuel AME Church before he chose his shooting location. His premeditated plan to kill people as they worshiped at Mother Emanuel in Charleston, South Carolina, was not a random choice, but a well-thought-out and deliberate decision. His internet research made him highly aware that the African-American church was more than just a place for members to meet, greet, and worship. Throughout its many years, Emanuel had been known as a spiritual refuge and "a beacon and as a bearer of the culture."[17]

In a sermon at Emanuel in 2013, Pastor Clementa Pinckney stated from the pulpit, "What the church is all about is the freedom to be fully what God intends us to be and have equality in the sight of God."

And then, as if prophetic, Pinckney added, "And sometimes you got to make noise to do that. Sometimes you may have to die like Denmark Vesey to do that."[18]

Two years after making his Denmark Vesey statement, the pastor himself lay bleeding and dying on the floor of Emanuel's fellowship hall.

Race-Related Tension

The pastor's killer, Dylann Roof, grew up in Columbia, South Carolina, where a large Confederate flag waved proudly above the city's State House Capitol Building, the same tendentious flag Roof displayed on the license plate of his car. Perhaps he saw the flag as other white supremacists did, "a reminder that the hatred behind the proclaimed right to own another human being has never left our shores."[19]

Dylann knew about the long history of race-related tension that lurked beneath the old cobblestone streets of Charleston's historic downtown district, a deep-seated hostility threatening to erupt at any moment with volcanic violence. He frequently visited the 345-year-old city that, on its surface, was steeped in Southern gentility, graced by moss-covered oak trees and blooming azaleas, and boasted of beautifully preserved plantations like Magnolia Plantation, Boone Hall Plantation, and Drayton Hall, all built and sustained by the whipped, scarred backs of slaves.

Dylann also knew the pain suffered by African-Americans at Charleston's busy harbor, where eighteenth-century ship captains unloaded their weary human cargo after a lengthy, deadly trek across the Atlantic's Middle Passage. The port, only a five-minute walk from the Emanuel AME Church, saw more than 40 percent of North America's enslaved Africans disembark from the filthy hulls of ships. After a long, terrifying voyage, the chained Africans experienced an almost unbearable time of quarantine at Sullivan's Island Pest Houses, so as to become "fit" to be sold in Charleston's popular slave auctions.

During the Atlantic slave trade, the city processed nearly half of all incoming slaves from the African West Coast.[20]

"Charleston's racial history runs deep," one reporter wrote. "The 'Holy City' was once home to one of the state's primary slave ports, where beaten and bruised black bodies were auctioned off to white owners. Yet while the days of slavery are long gone, racism still persists throughout the town."[21]

Knowing Charleston's history of slavery and hoping to ignite the city's and nation's past and present racial unrest, Dylann purposely chose Charleston, sometimes called "the cradle of racism," as the city for his hate crime.

During his taped two-hour confession, Dylann responded to FBI agents, laughing repeatedly and making exaggerated gun motions, stating that he "targeted Charleston and Mother Emanuel because they were historic and would resonate with people as he tried to avenge perceived black injustices against whites."

"I didn't want to go to another church," he admitted, "because there could have been white people there. . . . I just knew [Emanuel] would be a place where there would be . . . black people."[22]

He admitted he wanted to leave at least one person alive to tell about the shooting, and complained that his victims "complicated things" when they hid under tables during the massacre.

He also told agents that he chose the church because he wanted to slaughter those who were more likely to be meek and wouldn't shoot back, explaining that the Wednesday night Bible study provided an easy target.

Leaving bullets in a magazine of the gun, Roof admitted he planned to kill himself after murdering Emanuel members, but changed his mind when he saw no police and could simply walk out the door.[23]

The Rebuilding of Mother Emanuel

Two years earlier, when Pastor Pinckney mentioned the name Denmark Vesey in his sermon, he knew Vesey still held great significance in Charleston. Emanuel AME Church, a "revered symbol of black resistance to slavery and racism," founded in 1816–1818 by black pastor Morris Brown, became the spiritual refuge for Vesey, the freed slave and Methodist carpenter. In 1822, Vesey planned a slave rebellion in Charleston, but the revolt failed. Receiving a death sentence, Vesey and thirty-five of his black supporters were hanged, and Mother Emanuel was dismantled. The congregation met underground in secret until the Civil War ended, and they rebuilt the church. But the church was again demolished in 1886 when Charleston experienced the largest recorded earthquake in the history of the southeastern United States. Mother Emanuel rebuilt, refusing to be buried and forgotten.

For the young white supremacist hoping to start a race war, the choice of the Emanuel AME Church, the city of Charleston, and the state of South Carolina proved the perfect place to inflame racial violence and fuel more bloodshed. In his jailhouse diary, he claimed he wanted to make a huge impact by taking an action that "would make the biggest wave," and kill blacks "at a significant church."[24]

The Sixteenth Street Baptist Church, Birmingham, Alabama

Charleston isn't the only city in the nation that has had its past marred by violent and rampant racism. Recently I visited and spoke in another Southern city with a race-related past as dark and ugly as Charleston's. For years, Birmingham, Alabama's, strict Jim Crow laws meant the state's black residents couldn't ride in the front seats of city buses, vote without first passing unfair exams under the threat of violence, eat in restaurants, use certain toilets, drink from water fountains, shop at some department stores, live in "white" neighborhoods, work in higher-paying leadership jobs, swim in public pools, etc. The city's leaders and active Ku Klux Klan made sure these segregation laws were harshly enforced.

Birmingham's Sixteenth Street Baptist Church and Charleston's Emanuel AME Church have much in common, both being long-time "revered symbols of black resistance to slavery and racism." Founded about a half century later than Emanuel, Sixteenth Street Baptist Church served as a gathering place for most African-American social events, as well as a concert hall, a public auditorium, and a lending library when blacks weren't allowed to use the city's public library.

Like Emanuel, Sixteenth Street was the first black church in Birmingham, organized in 1873. During the early 1960s, the church became the meeting place of the civil rights movement, supporting marches and demonstrations for black equality, led by Rev. Dr. Martin Luther King Jr., Rev. Fred L. Shuttlesworth, James Bevel, and significant others.[25]

In 1963, Sixteenth Street experienced a racially motivated hate crime: a deadly assault upon its church members at the hands of white supremacists. Four Ku Klux Klan members planted sticks of dynamite outside the basement of the church building, timing them to go off during the morning worship service on September 15.

That morning, Pastor John Cross planned to preach his sermon at 11:00, "A Love That Forgives." But at 10:22, just as members began to pour from their basement Sunday school classes into the sanctuary, the dynamite exploded, crumbling a thick brick wall, breaking windows, injuring twenty-two church members, sending terrified churchgoers racing to exit doors, and killing four young girls in the basement restroom.

Dr. King called the heartbreaking massacre one of the "most vicious and tragic crimes ever perpetrated against humanity."[26]

President John F. Kennedy stated, "If these cruel and tragic events can only awaken that city and state—if they can only awaken this entire nation to a realization of the folly of racial injustice and hatred and violence, then it is not too late for all concerned to unite in steps toward peaceful progress before more lives are lost."[27]

The bombing and the girls' deaths proved to be the "shot heard 'round the world," beginning the city's and nation's deep soul-search about civil rights and leading to legislation such as the Civil Rights Act of 1964 and the Voting Rights of 1965.[28]

A fifth little girl survived the blast in the restroom that killed the four other children. When the dynamite exploded, Sarah Collins Rudolph, Addie's sister, was hit with a storm of flying glass and debris, resulting in a lost eye and a three-month hospital stay. A half century later, Sarah recalled her experience after the bombing: "When I would go to bed at night, I would just cry all night long, just why did they kill those girls?"

Sarah decided to forgive the white supremacists.

"Being bitter won't bring the girls back, won't bring my sight back," Sarah said fifty years later. "So I had to forgive because it was what God wanted me to do."[29]

Forgiveness Complicated by Racism

As Sarah Collins Rudolph forgave, I, too, chose to forgive Dylann Roof. When Dylann opened fire on Emanuel's church members, he told them, "I'm here to kill black people." He stated no other reason for the massacre except for the fact that he hated black people.

Since I publicly voiced my forgiveness for Dylann at his bond hearing two days after the shooting, sincere Christians and others have repeatedly asked me this question: "Does biblical forgiveness require 'forgiving the debt' when the vicious crime is complicated by centuries of deep racial hate, violence, and cruel injustices? Does our heavenly Father really expect us to forgive such horrifying hate crimes?"

I consider it a reasonable and justifiable question due to the nature of the crime. My answer is always immediate. "Yes. He does."

During my lifetime, I have met many people who refuse to forgive hate crimes—those deeply disturbing acts of violence based on a person's skin color or race or lifestyle choices. They happen so frequently these days that new laws are being passed, such as the 2009 Matthew Shepard and James Byrd Jr. Hate Crimes Prevention Act.[30]

As incredible as it sounds, in 2016 more than half (almost 59 percent) of the nation's crimes were "motivated by hostility based on race/ethnicity."[31]

Hate crimes, and whether or not they are forgivable, have become popular radio and television talk show topics as people everywhere are voicing opinions on forgiving and/or *not forgiving* those who commit hate crimes. In a recent CBS *60 Minutes* story, an invited guest asked the interviewer, "How can someone possibly forgive somebody who would kill or maim in the name of white supremacy?" He then added: "Those are the people who are *irredeemable*."[32]

Recently I heard a black Catholic author admit, "Forgiveness does not come easily to me. I am fine with this failing." Referencing the Emanuel Church shooting, she added, "I deeply respect the families of the nine slain who are able to forgive this terrorist and his murderous racism. I cannot fathom how they are capable of such eloquent mercy, such grace under such duress."[33]

I am discovering more and more that hate crimes can be huge obstacles to forgiveness. People tell me that crimes based solely on hate "generally hurt more than general crimes." They suggest that "hate crimes inflict greater harms on their victims."[34]

I can understand why this is true. According to the American Psychological Association, hate crimes are not only an "attack on one's physical self, but . . . also an attack on one's very identity . . . [producing] psychological and emotional damage, intense feelings of fear, vulnerability, anger, depression, physical ailments . . . and difficult interpersonal relations—all symptoms of post-traumatic stress disorder."[35]

Outrage and anger seem to be expected and common responses to hate crimes, arising "from a deep sense of personal hurt and betrayal . . . [producing] feelings of powerlessness, isolation, sadness and suspicion . . . [and violating] the equality principle, striking at the core of the victim's self."

A hate crime tells the victim, "You're not fit to live in this society with me. I don't believe that you have the same rights as I do. I believe that you are second to me. I am superior to you."[36]

Such was the underlying message of slave purchasing and human ownership that, over long, dark centuries of continuing victim abuse, layer upon heavy layer of deepening anger, frustration, and exasperation were added, thus complicating one's choice to forgive ongoing hate crimes.

Anger is not an emotion I feel, or have felt, about Dylann's act of murder. Some criticize me, saying, "Anthony, it's not *human* not to feel anger, one of the most natural and understandable stages of the grief cycle, especially when racism is involved."

They theorize about the possible negative health impact on me and other African-Americans of "forgiving acts of white racism"—"post-traumatic slave syndrome," they call it—implying that our forgiveness means "repressing justifiable feelings of anger and outrage" that are "transmitted from generation to generation." Internalized anger, they say, "driven deep into the unconscious, contaminated by unresolved pain . . . becomes problematic."[37]

They see the African-American's forgiveness of white racist crime as some sort of shortcut around anger, believing the black church teaches its members that it is un-Christian and unspiritual to be angry about racial injustices. Some may wonder if forgiveness is simply a way to eliminate anger from the black Christian's heart.[38]

While it might seem understandable that black people feel angered by a white racist's cruelties, I must again admit that I have never felt anger toward Dylann—shock, numbness, and deep despair at my wife's sudden and brutal death at his hands, yes—but not anger. I know if I allowed myself to feel intense anger, the fiery rage inside me would complicate my decision to forgive Dylann, making me want to do something drastic about the murder, to seek revenge. If I focus on anger, the fury in my heart and mind will cloud my judgment about biblical forgiveness. If I ever feel anger at Dylann, even for one second, I instinctively and immediately let go of it, refusing to allow uncontrolled wrath to consume me, giving Dylann Roof yet another victim of his hate crime.

The Enormous Cost of Forgiveness

I am also hearing some critics of forgiveness say that black people forgive a white person's intentional hateful acts because, like past slaves who fear further violence at the hands of white masters, forgiveness proves a way to protect themselves.

If that theory is true, doesn't that make forgiveness *cultural* rather than *biblical*, a kind of ethnic ritual in America that "functions to atone for the past racism . . . or in an attempt to provide African-Americans a way to move forward and acknowledge historic and recent racial pain"?[39]

One African-American writer strongly believes that cultural, ritual forgiveness and forgetfulness allow "racism or white silence in the face of racism [to] continue to thrive."

She writes, "We [black Americans] have had to forgive slavery, segregation, Jim Crow laws, lynching, inequity in every realm, mass incarceration, voter disenfranchisement, inadequate representation in popular culture, micro-aggressions and more. We forgive and forgive and forgive and those who trespass against us continue to trespass against us."[40]

85

Many believe that "in a culture of ritual forgiveness and forget-fulness, no one is called to account for historic deeds done against others," a way that seems to "absolve America of its violent history of racism."[41]

Some argue that this type of cultural forgiveness is based on weakness, not strength, and that "by forgiving racist crime so quickly and easily, black people cheapen their forgiveness."[42]

I don't agree. The forgiveness I expressed to Dylann Roof at the bond hearing just two days after the shooting was not based on anger, weakness, cheap forgiveness, or fear of future violence toward me. My forgiveness came quickly, but certainly not easily. Forgive-ness was not an easy fix, nor was it easily offered or easily lived. And I did not forgive Dylann because society and the church expected me to pardon him. It cost me something to forgive Dylann Roof.

I agree with a black pastor in Phoenix, Arizona, who wrote, "When someone chooses to forgive, we are watching someone pay an enormously heavy and personal cost, . . . It requires daily 'working out'—a daily willingness to look at the scars of injus-tice and choose to *press deeper into grace* instead of turning back toward anger and revenge."[43]

What is grace? It is the free and unmerited favor of God, as manifested in the salvation/redemption of sinners, the forgiveness of sins, and the bestowal of unearned and undeserved blessings.

Let me stop here and clarify the word *anger*. Anger isn't always a negative emotion. *Constructive* anger, used in the right way, can bring justice to felons and can motivate people to help stop hate crimes. It can also call for a nation to seriously rethink the FBI's too-brief three-day gun-waiting period, a commonsense move that will lengthen the gun-waiting deadline, allowing the FBI a more workable timetable and possibly keep dangerous weapons out of potential killers' hands.

Anger is like fire. It can warm your home or destroy it. It all depends on how it is used.

I am reminded that Jesus himself used constructive (righteous) anger—and a handmade cord whip—to empty and cleanse God's temple of money mongers who were intent on scamming the praying populace and making a quick buck.

"Get these out of here!" He shouted, referring to their cattle, sheep, doves, and coins, while overturning money exchange tables and scattering profits. "How dare you turn my Father's house into a market!" (See John 2:12–16.)

Surely it was constructive anger that motivated prosecutor Doug Jones to reopen the Sixteenth Street Baptist Church massacre case that killed four Sunday school girls. After the 1963 bombing, FBI Director J. Edgar Hoover, "not exactly a proponent of the civil rights movement," sealed the files, ensuring that a court couldn't use the documented material as evidence to prosecute the attackers. But Jones successfully convicted two Klansmen, Thomas Blanton Jr. and Bobby Frank Cherry, in 2001 and 2002 respectively, almost four decades after the hate crime.[44]

Apartheid in South Africa

The racial violence and hate crimes in Birmingham and Charleston remind me of how black South Africans suffered between 1948 and the early 1990s during apartheid ("separateness"). When I read the biography of Nelson Mandela, I felt great admiration for his God-enabled ability to forgive South Africa's past hate crimes. During Mandela's lifetime, South Africa had its own rigid Jim Crow laws segregating black Africans from white society and denying them the right to vote or live in certain areas. In 1948, the National Party won control of the government and codified the nation's long-present segregation and inequality into the official, rigid policy of apartheid.[45]

Objecting publicly to the nation's dark time of apartheid, Mandela was tortured and imprisoned for twenty-seven years. His release came in 1990, a time when South Africa embarked on its journey to full democracy.

Many of his angry black devotees felt betrayed when Mandela called for black Africans to forgive and reconcile with their white enemies instead of seeking revenge for the decades of unjust violence and pain they experienced at the evil hands of apartheid.[46]

I also admire Desmond Tutu, a contemporary of Mandela and former archbishop of Cape Town, South Africa, who suffered horribly during apartheid. He, like Mandela, called for equality, the end of apartheid, and forgiveness.

Desmond Tutu considered forgiveness a gift to the forgiver as well as to the perpetrator, stating, "It would be grossly unfair to the victim to be dependent on the whim of the perpetrator. It would make him or her a victim twice over. The gift has been given. It is up to the intended recipient to appropriate it."[47]

Tutu also gave a specific formula for forgiving hate crimes, asking South Africans to, first and second, tell the story and name the hurt, saying that in order to forgive one must "admit the wrong and acknowledge the harm." For the third and fourth steps, he encouraged the victims to grant forgiveness and then either renew or release the relationship.[48]

"Offering forgiveness prevents us from being destroyed by a corrosive resentment," he stated. "It helps us grow in being magnanimous."[49]

Called to Forgive

I forgave Dylann because I was called to forgive. I believe forgiveness "recognizes that the love of God is more powerful than white racist hatred."[50]

When I made the conscious decision and commitment to forgive Dylann Roof, my forgiveness meant that Dylann would not be allowed to control my life forever. My decision came from God's strength, not from my human weakness.

A reporter for the *Washington Post*, writing about forgiveness in light of racial hate crimes, commented, "The extraordinary act of forgiveness might remind us that the nation's most historically oppressed group does a better job of doing what we all say we want most: being decent and human, even when it seems impossible."[51]

No doubt, again and again I will be asked the question, "Does biblical forgiveness require 'forgiving the debt' when the vicious crime is complicated by centuries of deep racial hate, violence, and cruel injustices? Does our heavenly Father *really* expect us to forgive such horrifying hate crimes?"

Again, my answer is an unequivocal "*Yes*, God does."

My forgiveness of Dylann Roof, even though complicated by layer upon layer of racial cruelties over past centuries of slavery, came not as a historically required or oppressed/oppressor-expected offering.[52] And it was certainly more than my trying to be "decent and human." My forgiveness stemmed directly from the teachings of Jesus Christ, and came as a merciful gift from a fellow sinner who had been forgiven by God's grace and mercy. I offered my forgiveness unselfishly and generously to an unrepentant young racist, whom I hoped with all my heart would also ask God for His mercy, grace, and forgiveness.

Scripture tells us that God can forgive those people who repent, putting their faith and trust in Christ for their salvation—even a murderer! After all, He forgave the Apostle Paul, a first-century domestic terrorist who murdered Christians just because they believed in Christ. Surely Paul's evil acts and hate crimes were designed to strike fear and terror into the Christian community. Paul stood on the sidelines when Stephen was stoned to death, proudly giving his approval (Acts 22:20). When Paul gave his sinful life to Christ, however, God forgave him, redeemed him, and then used him mightily in His kingdom work.

"None of us deserves God's forgiveness . . . we all have sinned. . . . But the good news is this: God loves us, and Christ came into the world to save us. When we repent of our sins and receive Him into our hearts, God has promised to forgive us—completely and fully."[53]

Surely no one, not even Dylann Roof, is irredeemable.

6

||||||||||||||||||||||||||||||||||||||||||||||||||

Missing Myra

Myra Thompson taught our state and country how to
love. . . . [Anthony,] you and your family taught our
state and our country how to forgive.

South Carolina Governor Nikki R. Haley,
at Myra Thompson's funeral[1]

On Monday, June 29, 2015, I prepare myself mentally and
emotionally to bury Myra. Our daughter, Denise, chooses
her mother's burial outfit, an ivory St. John dress and jacket.
Just after ten thirty, we return Myra to her childhood sanctuary,
her beloved Emanuel AME Church, the place of prayer and worship where her vibrant life ended twelve days ago. Myra prayed her
last words to God here within these old sacred walls, a spiritual
refuge for her as well as for generations of African-Americans
before her. As a newly licensed minister, Myra taught her first and
final Bible study here while looking into her killer's eyes, her heart
touched by the young man's sad expression and skinny frame,
her mind wondering about his personal relationship with God.

The crowds lining Calhoun Street grow respectfully quiet when the hearse pulls up, stopping in front of the historic church. As pallbearers lift and carry Myra's mahogany coffin, hundreds of sympathetic onlookers, having arrived four hours before, hold up handwritten signs that declare: "Love Wins. Every. Single. Time."

I sit still and quiet during the memorial service, feeling numb, isolated, hardly seeing anybody. My eyes are dry but my heart cries great tears for the wife I miss so much. I focus my gaze on my children and grandchildren, all the while reminiscing about Myra, remembering her smiling face, our first meeting, our joint ministries, and how her life ended so abruptly, so cruelly.

As I look around the church, I see Myra's fingerprint on every wall, on every pew, on every surface. Myra was a devout woman with a clear sense of purpose, the perfect choice to lead the church's property committee. She and Pastor Pinckney shared a passion and a vision for restoring and preserving Emanuel's building. They worked hard together, one brick and board at a time, spending long hours on the projects. With three main projects finished, they had turned their attention to the restoration of the church sanctuary.

South Carolina Governor Nikki R. Haley stands at the podium, looking out over the wall-to-wall crowds, and addresses the mourners: "Myra Thompson and those eight angels," she says, "brought someone into a Bible study that did not look like them, that did not sound like them, and did not act like them, in the name of trying to love."

I think about the other eight victims, praying together, dying together, and I feel great empathy for their family members. Four victims have already been buried; four more still need to be.

Haley pauses, touched by emotion: "[Myra] is a woman who I want to strive to be. She wanted every person she came in touch with to make them better."

The governor breaks down emotionally, almost crying when she apologizes for the church shooting, the attack that "happened on my watch."

Our son, Kevin, tells the crowd of mourners about his mother: "As a child," he says, "I used to pray that I'd pass before my mom. Because I couldn't handle the pain."

Our daughter, Denise, mentions her mother's love of conversation and the many phone calls they shared. "A quick phone call is never a quick phone call," she says, smiling.

She looks at the casket covered with red roses and white orchids. Then she speaks directly to her mother entombed within it: "I have finally accepted that your job here on earth is done. It's not a *good-bye*. It's a *see you later*."

Charleston's mayor, Joseph P. Riley Jr., tells the mourners that Mrs. Thompson "went from studying the Lord's word downstairs, in a blink of an eye, to meeting him upstairs," adding, "We all know he said, 'Myra, I know you.'"[2]

After her "going-home celebration" service, surrounded by vast arrangements of the flowers she most loved, I watch mourners assemble along the portable iron barricades on Calhoun Street, singing "Amazing Grace," the famous hymn written by former slave trader John Newton.

In 1747, when Newton gave his life to Christ during a terrific storm at sea, he made a complete life transformation, spending the rest of his days working to end the international slave trade.[3] I think about the sinful slave trader as I hear the words to his hymn. Surely, if God could forgive John Newton and so drastically change his heart and life, I know He can do the same for Dylann Roof.

As I stand beside Myra's grave, I say a silent good-bye, placing my wife in the beautifully manicured Carolina Memorial Gardens, her final resting place.

Grieving Myra's Passing

During the following days and weeks, the house I once shared with Myra is deathly quiet. I feel so depressed and in such despair that

I cannot function, unable to perform even simple everyday tasks. During the first three days after her death, as I lay in our bed, I feel her gentle touch on my arm and neck, and I sense her presence. I can't explain it; I just feel it. It lasts a whole month, happening at the same time each night.

For weeks I mourn. I don't want to get out of bed in the mornings, and when I do, I stay in my pajamas all day, refusing to answer the ringing telephone or doorbell. I miss Myra sleeping next to me, and I often roll onto her side of the bed, hoping to feel closer to her. I can't sleep. I can't eat. I don't care if I brush my teeth or wash my face. On Fridays I somehow pull myself out of bed to work on Sunday's sermon. During the church worship service, I go through the expected motions, pretending to be positive in attitude and pasting a smile on my face. But my heart hurts, and underneath the forced optimism I feel sad, drained of energy, not caring much about anything.

Psychiatrists say that grief is the inevitable process we experience as the result of a loss, claiming the universal five stages of grief are denial and isolation; anger; bargaining; depression; and finally acceptance and peace.

I passed through the stage of *denial* when I learned on the evening of June 17 that Myra was gone. I never experienced *anger*, but I *bargained* for two days, thinking *if only, if only, if only*. If only I had been with Myra at the Bible study, maybe I could have protected her.

My grief was complicated because of the way Myra died—the killer sentencing and executing her because her skin tones were darker than his. I *accepted* my wife's passing at the bond hearing two days later when I chose to forgive the killer, although I felt the lingering presence of *isolation*. But now as I lay her to rest, remembering her and celebrating her life, I seem to be stuck in the *depression* stage of grief—the type of grief that refuses to let her go, to tell her good-bye. It is painful, but I know I must let her go. But I'll need God's help to do it.

Reminiscing

Before Myra is finally laid to rest, I think back to how she and I first met, nearly forty years ago. We were both students at Benedict College in Columbia. One day, Myra missed her bus ride home so I offered her a ride. From there, we each went our own way in life, marrying other people, working different careers, and rearing children. We lived in the same town, and occasionally we passed each other on the street and said a brief hello.

A decade later, Myra and I both were divorced. One day out of the blue, Myra called me and we talked. Soon a relationship began. We dated, fell in love, and married, settling down together with our children in a modest brick home near The Citadel's baseball field.

We loved each other and enjoyed a strong marriage built on the foundation of Christ and Scripture, each of us wholeheartedly supporting the other's call to God's ministry.

Even though Myra and I were both born and reared in Charleston, we came from very different backgrounds. Myra's childhood home was one of dysfunction, with an absentee father and an ill mother. Myra and her three young brothers and sister were split up and placed among various relatives. Myra was fortunate, growing up with relatives and Christian neighbors Isaiah and Sarah Coakley, who introduced her to Mother Emanuel, encouraging a lifelong relationship with the Lord and the church.

A faithful and hard-working single mother, Myra had worked her way through college and a host of later graduate degrees. She loved teaching, especially disadvantaged students, and for many years taught eighth grade in Charleston. She possessed a myriad of spiritual gifts—giving, helping, teaching, and counseling—and used them unselfishly to help others. A friend described her as "a very energized, serving-God type of person."

When she was later in life, a door of ministry opened for Myra, and she was anxious to use her impressive gifts in an even greater way.[4]

Charleston's Mayor Riley said of her, "Myra will always be here in the memory of this church. She was a martyr in the continuing fight to human dignity."[5]

My loving mother and father created an organized and stable home for me. My father, Albert R. L. Thompson, served faithfully in the US Navy. His father was a deacon and co-founder of Charleston's Gethsemane Baptist Church. My grandfather taught all his children to love and respect others, my father being the prime example of his father's virtuous qualities.

My father enlisted in the US Navy at a time when black men could rank only as stewards or cooks. He became both, undisturbed when facing the challenges of racism and discrimination, elevating himself to the highest rank he was allowed to hold—with integrity and great dignity.

A smart and capable man, he took an exam, hoping to rise to the rank of chief in the Navy. Three times he passed the test, but each time the rank of chief was given to a white man. As a child, I overheard my parents talking about this incident many times, as they decided not to allow it to put a wall between them and the white people they knew. I'm sure they sometimes felt angry about the unfair lack of promotion, but I never heard a derogatory word from them about the white men who, time and again, were granted the position.

South Carolina's Black Code

The state of South Carolina passed "Black Codes" immediately after African-Americans were granted new freedoms by the Constitution of 1865. They later became known as Jim Crow laws. Slavery was absent, but segregation proved an effective means of enforcing social inequality in South Carolina. Laws kept blacks and whites from interacting together within society, forcing them to use separate toilet facilities, water fountains, and restaurant and waiting room entrances, and making blacks sit in the backs of buses and other vehicles of public transportation. Black children couldn't go to white schools, couldn't swim in Charleston's public swimming pools, and couldn't enjoy the beaches at the Isle of Palms, Sullivan's Island, or Folly Beach. Every minor social law that sought to separate black and white society was enforced by sheer terror. During those years, white supremacy and racism were unleashed and allowed to grow mightily.

In 1951, the year before I was born, the South Carolina General Assembly established the Gressette Committee, an official legislative committee created to fight all new efforts at desegregation and to block any and all equal rights for blacks.[6]

Most of the rest of the Southern United States followed suit, holding on tightly to unfair laws that restricted the freedoms of African-Americans.

I was ten years old in 1962 when Dr. Martin Luther King Jr. visited Charleston, preaching at Mother Emanuel, urging church members to register to vote. The next year, 1963, I remember watching the television news showing Birmingham police attacking and arresting young black demonstrators with German shepherds and fire hoses as the children and youth marched nonviolently protesting unfair segregation laws.

"Mom," I asked, "why don't black people fight back?"

"You don't try to hurt people back when they hurt you," she told me.

Dr. King came back to Charleston on July 30, 1967, three years after the Civil Rights Act passed. He spoke at Charleston County Hall on King Street. My mother took me, then a fifteen-year-old, to that rally that brought three thousand people out on a sweltering summer day to meet and hear the civil rights leader.

An aura of fear and tension mingled in the air in anticipation of his visit, rumors starting and growing that Dr. King was coming to Charleston to stir up trouble. Dr. King told us that he didn't come to Charleston to start a riot or to kill anybody, like white men were announcing. He said he was just tired of white supremacy.

I soaked up his words like a sponge, when during his sermon, Dr. King taught me about nonviolence. He answered the question

I had asked my mother four years before, and brought me a wider understanding of racism's evil. I hung on to his every word, words of such wisdom I will never forget them.

"We live in America," I remember Dr. King saying. "We have to face the fact that, honestly, racial discrimination is present. So don't get complacent. We made some strides. We made some progress here and there, and it hasn't been enough. It hasn't been fast enough."

I well remember how Dr. King closed his speech: "We have a long way to go," he stated. "The plant of freedom has brought only a bud, not a flower. Long way to go."

Tragically, on April 4, 1968, only eight months after I attended his speech in Charleston, Dr. King was shot to death in Memphis. My teenage heart was broken, but Dr. King's murder didn't surprise me. Even at such a tender age I understood all too well the results of white supremacist hatred and violence.[7]

Just as my mother and father always looked for a better way to deal with the US Navy's racism, my mother showed me, through the wise words of Dr. King, that violence and hatred were no way to live.

In 1969, a year after her husband's murder, Coretta Scott King visited Charleston, starting a nonviolent march on the steps of Mother Emanuel in support of disenfranchised hospital workers. My mother joined Mrs. King, even as the South Carolina National Guard threatened them with bayonets, arresting about nine hundred demonstrators, including my mother and the church's pastor. I was afraid for my mother but very proud of her. When she returned home from jail that night, she told me, "I'm alright. I didn't get hurt, and we didn't fight them back. I went to jail instead."[8]

A Rebel with a Cause

As an adult having to deal with racial injustice, discrimination, and unfairness, I became something of a rebel. In 1996 I worked as a probation-parole agent for the South Carolina Department of Probation, Parole and Pardon Services. I argued and fussed about racism, yelling at the top of my voice as I pointed out the "black-white problem" in that office, demanding immediate changes. Every time a white man pushed my wrong button, I'd get after him. But it never worked out for me; I was always in trouble, never knowing peace.

One year God taught me a lesson I never forgot. A new Agent in Charge took over our office, his primary mission to get rid of me. Initially I fought him with everything I had: my mouth, the office manual of rules and regulations, and a prominent black attorney. I was fed up and angry with the white man, the unfair system of government, and whoever else threatened my life and my family's welfare. I gave the agent more than enough grounds to remove me from my supervisory position. And he did, demoting me and placing me where I had no authority over any white person. This proved to be the proverbial straw that broke the camel's back, enraging me, and tempting me to do something stupid.

Fortunately, before my stupidity took over and I reacted in a way I would regret, God shouted in my ear, "Stop, Anthony! Stop right now! Change your ways. *I* will fight your battles."

I listened to His voice, took His advice to heart, and began to change in little ways every day. Workers still provoked me, but I didn't respond to them as I once did. After hearing God's voice, I forgave them for their ill treatment and I experienced a new peace, knowing for sure that God was in control and had my back.

After a while those employees who had been treating me so unfairly began to leave the agency—some resigning, others terminated. When I retired after twenty-five years, the agency called me back to work for another two years.

On June 17, 2015, when a young white supremacist killed my wife, God again reminded me what I must do to find my peace, telling me to be nonviolent, to find better ways to deal with this tragedy. I looked to God, His Word, and the church, and I found peace. God enabled me to tell Dylann Roof, "I forgive you, and my family forgives you."[9]

Myra's Call to Ministry

Sometimes, even though I try hard to control it, my mind wanders to Emanuel's fellowship hall on the night of June 17, 2015. I imagine the last minutes of Myra's life as she taught God's Word and prayed. I cringe when I think about Myra's thoughts and fears when Dylann began to pelt her body with bullets. I wonder if she experienced long moments of excruciating pain or if she died immediately. I pray she didn't suffer. I wonder if she saw the gunman shoot the dear friends who sat around her, those dedicated Christians praying with her.

I know she was frightened when the gunfire began, for Myra scared easily. Even little things like spiders unnerved her. I remember Myra calling me in a panic one Sunday morning from our home. My cell phone rang just as I stepped into the pulpit to preach in the worship service at my church.

"Anthony, come home!" she squealed into the phone. "There's a lizard in the bedroom, and you've got to come home *right now* and take care of it."

During the past few years, I watched Myra change and grow into ministry. When she received a calling from God, she envisioned herself teaching the Gospel.

"I think God's calling me into ministry," she told me. "I want to get my ministry license."

"You're in for a lot of hard work."

"Anthony, if I don't do anything else in my life, this is what I want to do."

I think often about Myra's future ministry that was snatched from her—the Bible studies she would have taught, the people she would have met, and the lives and hearts she would have touched for Christ. She doesn't have those opportunities now, with her ministry cut so short.

I often ask God why He called her into His ministry, grew her heart and mind to pursue it, allowed her to work for years to earn a ministry license, and then, the very first time she "officially" taught a Bible study, she was killed.

I cannot understand why He allowed her to both begin and end her official ministry all in one evening.

But I don't have to understand God's reasons. I am called to believe Him and to trust that God knows what He's doing. That's enough.

My New Calling

My parents taught me the value of biblical forgiveness as a child. I have preached a lifetime on the topic of biblical forgiveness. After Myra's murder, I knew my family, congregation, friends, and others would be watching me closely to see if I could truly practice what I preached. Surely it was the ultimate test of my beliefs and teachings.

At the bond hearing, not only did I hear God calling me to forgive Dylann, but He also called me to a new ministry—that of teaching and preaching biblical forgiveness. I prayed, asking God why He called me into a new ministry, gave me a new mission, only two days after my wife's passing. "Why do you want me to undertake a new ministry, teaching and preaching biblical forgiveness, especially at a time like this? How can I? It is impossible right now. I am deeply grieving my wife's passing. I need time to mourn my loss, attend to my personal healing, and learn how to live life without her," I prayed.

But I obeyed God's call and discovered anew that relying on Him and His Word brought me strength and changed my attitude and heart. In trying to be who God wants me to be and do what He wants me to do, He has soothed my spirit. I now understand that He began to prepare me for this new calling a long time ago. And God is already sending me out to share my story of loss and forgiveness.

In My Journey to Healing

I am making numerous discoveries about people and all the things that keep them from forgiving someone who has hurt them or their loved ones.

I am meeting people who think they can forgo forgiveness if the criminal fails to restore what he stole from them. The biblical Zacchaeus, the dishonest tax collector Jesus met while passing through Jericho (Luke 19:1–9), is a good example of a repentant sinner making things right with the people he hurt.

In first-century Israel, Roman rulers made a man pay income taxes, as well as import and export taxes, crop taxes, sales taxes, property taxes, emergency taxes, and on and on. Tax collectors, usually Jewish, were dishonest men who openly deceived their own people, skimming money off the top for themselves and working in greedy collaboration with Roman occupiers, the Jews' enemy.

The Jewish people hated tax collectors, especially Zacchaeus, who had become wealthy by extorting large sums of money from them, lining his own pockets with their hard-earned coins. They ostracized him from Jewish society, not wanting to be seen with him, declining his dinner invitations, and not inviting him to their homes.[10]

One day, as Jesus passed through his city, Zacchaeus climbed a tree in order to see Him in the crowd. When Jesus came to that particular sycamore-fig tree, He stopped, looked up, and focused his eyes on Zacchaeus.

"Zacchaeus," Jesus called, "come down immediately. I must stay at your house today."

Luke tells us that a stunned Zacchaeus "came down at once and welcomed him gladly" (Luke 19:6). Yearning for salvation and owning up to his many sins, Zacchaeus told Jesus, "Look, Lord! Here and now I give half of my possessions to the poor, and if I have cheated anybody out of anything, I will pay back four times the amount" (v. 8).

Zacchaeus's unexpected words came from a sinful heart that yearned to be forgiven. He came to Jesus hoping the restitution of funds and selfless compensation to his victims would make things right, allowing him to receive Jesus' forgiveness.

Jesus looked deep into the tax collector's heart and saw Zacchaeus's honest desire to compensate people for the money he had stolen from them, to put things right. Jesus forgave him, announcing: "Today salvation has come to this house" (Luke 19:9).

But unlike Zacchaeus, who could return the unfairly taxed money he had stolen, Dylann Roof has caused a loss he can never repay. He cannot return Myra to me.

"Does anyone really move on from such a tragedy?" a civil trial lawyer wrote in a commentary for the *Orlando Sentinel*. "The short answer is no. . . . Even if the gunman is punished for his crimes, that will not bring back their loves ones."[11]

Lack of reparation for a crime like murder can keep Christians and others from forgiving a perpetrator. While money and stolen items can be reimbursed, lost lives cannot.

Fortunately, my forgiveness of Dylann doesn't rest on his desire or ability to bring back my wife. I forgave him fully knowing the damage he had caused could never be undone. Surely it is a myth to think forgiveness must depend on compensation and restoration. Myra is gone. She's not coming back.

Commonplace Killings

In this day and age, deadly shootings in public places are becoming commonplace—a sad commentary on our populace and nation. The number of deaths overwhelms me as I look back over the past eleven or twelve years. Hundreds of people have been killed and wounded in schools, malls, churches, workplaces, salons, navy yards, military locations, clinics, conference halls, nightclubs, airports, and other public places. For each person who dies at the hand of a gunman, hundreds of loved ones experience shock, anger, frustration, fear, depression, sadness, and many other debilitating emotions.

I am discovering that many people think they will find closure and peace only after their loved one's murderer is executed, with the killer getting what's coming to him—his just deserts. But that is not necessarily so.

"While it's easy to understand why people would seek the harshest punishment possible after a terrible crime, studies cast doubt on whether harsh punishment in general, and capital punishment in particular, actually brings the relief and peace of mind the victims deserve," according to *Greater Good Magazine*.[12]

Dylann's execution might somewhat satisfy a human desire for "an eye for an eye," punishing the murderer and legally avenging the crime. But it will not bring the victims' loved ones closure and the peace of mind and heart they might expect.

Peace and closure come only from God through biblical forgiveness.

While I still walk the long, painful road to complete healing, I have already found closure and inner peace. It came the moment I forgave Dylann Roof.

Perhaps some people want Dylann to be executed, but I don't. I want him to be alive, using the long days of a life sentence to ponder what he has done, to contemplate the words I said to him at the bond hearing. I want to see Dylann give his life to Christ, to receive God's forgiveness and salvation, and to live for Him during the time he has left on earth. I pray that will happen.

7

A Community and Nation React

> [Dylann Roof] was hoping to divide this state and this
> country. But what he doesn't know is what he did is
> going to bring us a whole lot closer.
>
> South Carolina Governor Nikki Haley[1]

Stunned and confused, the city of Charleston, as well as the entire nation, holds its breath after Dylann Roof's massacre Wednesday evening at Mother Emanuel, leaving nine African-American worshipers dead. Fearing how the city will react, and with good reason, many predict raw violence exploding in the streets. After all, that has been the recent pattern with white-on-black crime. They base their expectations on hard fact, painfully remembering the racially charged incidents that sparked violence over the past few years in Ferguson, Baltimore, Berkeley, and other cities across the nation. The media repeatedly broadcasted the frightening scenes that resulted in bloodshed, destruction of property, arrests, injuries, and looting. Some of the crimes were so violent and out of control they required emergency help from the National Guard.

Ferguson, Missouri, Riots

Consider Ferguson, Missouri, and the events that happened in 2014. A relatively stable, working- and middle-class community of 21,000 people, Ferguson witnessed weeks of barbarity in its streets after a white police officer shot and killed an unarmed black teenager, Michael Brown. Street violence increased when a jury refused to bring charges against the officer. Moving along Ferguson's West Florissant Avenue, protesters tore apart the predominantly black community, throwing objects at officers in riot gear, breaking police cruiser windows, and setting fire to buildings. In the chaos of gunfire, tear gas, and smoke, Governor Jay Nixon deployed the Missouri National Guard. Four years later, a stretch of West Florissant Avenue still remains a path of painful memories.[2]

Street Violence in Baltimore, Maryland

Less than a year after the Ferguson unrest, a racial incident in Baltimore, Maryland, caused similar street savagery. On April 12, 2015, six police officers (three black and three white) arrested Freddie Gray, a twenty-five-year-old black man. In the van on the way to the police station, something sinister happened to Gray, as he arrived at the Western District police station in "serious medical distress." A medic unit examined Gray, determining he was "in cardiac arrest . . . critically and severely injured." After undergoing emergency double surgery on his spine, Gray died a week later. Charges of homicide were brought against the six officers, but later all charges were dropped.[3]

After Gray's death, anger-fueled riots broke out in Baltimore with days of fierce fighting between demonstrators and police. Protesters set fire to cars and buildings. Looters stole powerful opioids from a third of the city's pharmacies, their uncontrolled use adding more violence to the mayhem. The civil unrest and rioting caused injuries to police officers, led to numerous arrests, and damaged the city's businesses. The mayor declared a city curfew, condemning the "thugs" intent on "destroying our city." The Maryland Army National Guard was summoned to help provide security.[4]

Staten Island Death Sparks National Protests

The year before the Emanuel shooting, New York City police officers in Staten Island arrested an unarmed black man—Eric Garner, forty-three years old and the father of six children. White officer Daniel Pantaleo pressed Garner to the sidewalk, holding him down, ignoring the man's repeated "I can't breathe" pleas. Garner died that afternoon, the coroner's report listing his death a homicide.[5]

After the grand jury decided not to indict Officer Pantaleo, protests broke out in cities around the country, including New York City; Philadelphia; Chicago; Miami; Las Vegas; Seattle; Washington, DC; and others. As far away as Berkeley, California, protesters looted and damaged buildings, caused injuries and arrests, and threw rocks, bricks, bottles, and pipes at officers. Police responded with smoke and tear gas.[6]

A City Erupts in Grace

Understanding the typical violence associated with race-related crimes in the United States, Dylann Roof envisioned and hoped his murderous actions would trigger a massive and hostile nationwide response intensifying into a long-overdue race war. He chose the racial powder keg, Charleston, the heart of the old Confederacy, as the point of origin, hoping bloodshed and battle would spread like wildfire across the country. He must have figured, *What better place in the United States to start a race war than in Charleston?*

In many ways, Roof was "not an anomaly but, in fact, a product of American history, a history shaped by a legacy of white supremacist thought dating back to the founding of the country.

The 'heritage' of the Confederate States of America was of unabashed commitment to white supremacy and the perpetuation of chattel slavery."[7]

But after the murders—and to everyone's shock—Charleston witnessed no rioting, no assaults, no violent protesting, no arrests, and no bloodshed. Instead, the stunned and hurting city of Charleston erupted in *grace*, in surprising and courteous goodwill one to another, black and white, Christian and Jew. The whole world watched as some of the victims' loved ones reacted to the murders by passing the expected violence and responding with love, kindness, and forgiveness. Like buckets of cool water poured onto a smoking fire, the love and forgiveness shown to Dylann Roof extinguished all potential flames long before they flared up. These selfless, forgiving actions, flowing out from deeply hurting hearts, took a firm hold on the riot-ready nation and summoned peace, tranquility, and compassion. The city became a shining example of brotherly love, uniting hearts, races, and faiths, and quelling potential pandemonium. Expected disruption and disarray became endearment and devotion. Expected bedlam became benevolence; lawlessness became acts of loving-kindness. Potential havoc became hands that reached out to grasp the hands of others across the city's age-old cultural divisions and crusty layers of civil unrest.

The city's unusual and gentle response baffled the hordes of news reporters filling Charleston's streets with media trucks, microphones, and cameras. They anticipated the predictable pattern of violence that swallowed up civilians and cities and made dramatic media and print coverage. They stood on tiptoe waiting to record yet another racially inspired explosion, more fighting, more injuries, and more fires.

But when on Charleston's old historic streets love and forgiveness happened instead, overcoming and extinguishing the expected violence, they were visibly confused. As they watched biblical forgiveness in action, witnessing its peaceful results on the city and nation, they scratched their heads in confusion. Perplexed, they readjusted their camera lenses to record accounts of compassion, of people coming together as one, all the while asking deep theological questions about this strange and potent power of forgiveness. They arrived in Charleston aiming to film bloodshed and riots, to capture sensational shots of revenge and violent confrontation. Instead, they returned home with portraits of people showing biblical forgiveness in vivid, compassionate color, blacks and whites embracing, each offering love, support, and comfort to one another.

When Charleston's Mayor Riley witnessed firsthand the results of biblical forgiveness in his city, he stated, "A hateful person came to this community with some crazy idea he'd be able to divide, but all he did was unite us and make us love each other even more."[8]

A Nation Awed

Immediately, the almost unbelievable stories of demonstrated peace, brotherhood, and harmony filled online and print media.

The *Washington Post* published the article "'I Forgive You.' Relatives of Charleston Church Shooting Victims Address Dylann Roof." The *Post*'s reporter wrote, "One by one, those who chose to speak at a bond hearing did not turn to anger. Instead, while [Roof] remained impassive, they offered him forgiveness and said they were praying for his soul, even as they described the pain of their losses."[9]

Another article headline read, "Racism Can't Destroy This Charleston Church," acknowledging, "It has rebuilt before. It will rebuild again."[10]

Huffpost carried the online news story, "Thousands Walk Hand In Hand Across Ravenel Bridge to Show Support for Mother Emanuel Church," reporting, "On Sunday evening, hours after Emanuel AME Church opened its doors for the first service following the killing of nine of its congregants Wednesday, thousands in Charleston took to the streets in a show of support and solidarity."[11]

After the initial news headlines broke, television commentators, newspaper editors, radio talk-show hosts, and legions of others began to debate and ask questions about this unusual forgiveness phenomenon:

"What exactly is forgiveness?"

"How long does it take to forgive?"

"Does Dylann Roof deserve forgiveness?"

"Is it too soon for forgiveness in Charleston?"

"Is forgiveness really best for the community?"

"How can an African-American forgive a white racist murderer?"

"After the shooting, why did a city erupt in love and compassion instead of chaotic destruction?"

News reporters knew how to write tantalizing copy about violence. They did it all the time. But love? Compassion? Forgiveness? Not so much. When they wrote their articles about the Charleston shooting, they focused on virtue instead of violence, asking questions they themselves could not answer. Some made a stab at reporting the meaning of biblical forgiveness, but unless they were Christ-followers and Bible believers, they fell short, confusing their already bewildered secular readership.

One reporter from the *Christian Examiner* got it right, however, when he wrote that Dylann Roof hoped to start a race war but his action "has had the opposite effect, allowing the grieving families to put the Gospel's power on full display for not only Roof but for a watching television audience."[12]

The Gospel's Power

Yes, the Gospel's power went on full display in Charleston and awed the entire country. During the days after the shooting, quiet and somber crowds gathered around Mother Emanuel, most people struggling to hold back tears. The makeshift memorials of flowers grew in front of the church, many people crawling under the long length of yellow police tape to place bouquets. Compassionate donors pledged thousands of dollars to the Mother Emanuel Hope fund set up by Mayor Riley to help the victims' families pay for funerals, counseling, and other needs.[13]

Thousands of people gathered in downtown Charleston at the College of Charleston's arena to attend an evening vigil and prayer service. The whole city was mourning the deaths while at the same time openly rejecting the young white racist's hatred. The visible acts of love set off a godly chain of events as blacks and whites embraced and comforted each other, crying together in Charleston's streets.

Churches in the Holy City were crowded with mourners attending vigils, praying together, and showing a united front of support. More than fifteen thousand people of all colors and faiths joined hands, creating a human chain of love that stretched for two miles and crossed the bridge that connects Charleston to Mount Pleasant.[14]

As I watched people come together, hand in hand, standing on the Arthur Ravenel Jr. Bridge, I was struck by the deep symbolism it presented. After many years of broken bonds between Charleston's black and white residents, the bridge of flesh and blood became an unmistakable statement to all with eyes to see, an incredible human connection bridging a gap between two diverse, and often warring, cultures. The strong human chain extended far beyond the visible length of the suspension bridge crossing the Cooper River and overlooking Charleston Harbor and the Atlantic Ocean. It reached deep within that harbor, across past generations of abuse, a cruel and unjust history of slavery. Linked together in the unity chain, each person bowed a head, honoring the fallen Emanuel Nine with five full minutes of silence. Their physical eyes may have been closed during the quiet time of deep contemplation, but the eyes of their hearts were wide open, basking in the divine hope that came as a result of visible love and forgiveness openly shown one to another.

The Confederate Flag

The symbolism of unity grew deeper when after decades of failed bills and protests, the Confederate flag was ceremoniously removed from the South Carolina State House grounds. The state legislature donated the flag to the nearby Confederate Relic Room and Museum. I was glad to see this event take place, as the flag was an outdated relic, a longtime symbol of the Confederacy and the institution of slavery it once fought hard to preserve.

Dylann Roof grew up in its shadow, the large Confederate flag flying proudly in his birthplace city of Columbia since 1961, the symbolic banner that many believe helped fuel his hatred for African-Americans. He displayed the flag on his car's license plate, posed with it in internet postings, and embraced its contentious ideology.

"Some will assert that the Confederate flag is merely a symbol of years gone by, a symbol of heritage, not hate," NAACP President Cornell Brooks stated. "But when we see that symbol lifted up as an emblem of hate . . . as an inspiration of violence, that symbol has to come down."[15]

And down it came, its controversial thirteen stars never again to wave in Columbia's changing winds, making a profound statement to all, and newly freshening the air in South Carolina—and beyond.

Acts of Loving-Kindness

When Bishop England High School alumni from the class of 1970 heard that Myra was one of the shooting victims, they, along with many friends and admirers of Myra, asked permission to memorialize Myra by restoring the garden behind my church in Charleston, Holy Trinity Reformed Episcopal Church. Donations poured in and devoted friends worked hard and long in the blazing Saturday sun to re-create the garden.

"It is truly a special day with profound meaning to all of us," one of the donors said. "This tragedy impacts us all."

"With determination, we turned inspiration into perspiration for beautification," someone commented, and Myra's Garden will bloom into the future, becoming a loving legacy and an inspiration to all who seek a moment of silence and beauty.

In Charleston and around the country, numerous activities, programs, tributes, services, and memorials honored the slain Emanuel Nine. The nation's Jews joined in the solidarity events, peacefully protesting the senseless attack, identifying with the victims, saying that they, too, knew firsthand about persecution.

"The Jewish and African-American communities have a warm and long heritage together. Unfortunately, the anti-Semitism of the shooter also creates a bond," Rabbi Yossi Refson stated.[16]

President Obama traveled to Charleston to speak at the funeral of the Reverend Clementa Pinckney, Emanuel's murdered pastor. When Obama suddenly burst into a touching solo of "Amazing Grace," mourners rose to their feet, joining him in song.

The president commented that the killer likely assumed he "would deepen divisions that trace back to our nation's original sin." But then he added, "The alleged killer could have never anticipated the way the families of the fallen would respond when they saw him in court in the midst of unspeakable grief, with words of forgiveness."

He admitted that the country had responded to the church shooting "with a thoughtful introspection and self-examination that we so rarely see in public life."[17]

The Indestructible Word of God

The Bible, God's Holy Word, brings out both the best and the worst in people. Biblical forgiveness, visibly practiced in Charleston, prompted spontaneous praise from some, hard questions from others, and cruel criticism from many. But this reaction wasn't anything new. Throughout history, unbelievers have tried to destroy the Scriptures, not realizing that God's Word is indestructible.

According to Isaiah 40:8, "The grass withers and the flowers fall, but the word of our God stands forever."

Jesus himself said, "Heaven and earth will pass away, but my words will never pass away" (Matthew 24:35).

Myra based her Bible study at Emanuel on the *seed* (from Luke 8:11), a symbol representing the enduring Word of God.

Throughout human history, the enemies of Christianity have sought to destroy God's Word, attacking it, burning it, and criticizing its accuracy. But as promised by Scripture itself, God's Word has miraculously survived. It continues to teach us about Christ's forgiveness, holding us accountable to practice it openly and sincerely.

Devoted Christ-believers understand the power of biblical forgiveness, smiling and nodding to each other when they see its Spirit illuminating and empowering human souls. Christ's followers know its lasting value, for they are part of the Shepherd's fold, the sinful yet redeemed sheep that delight when they see secular society pause, express awe, and ask searching questions about faith and Scripture. The sheep are not at all surprised when biblical concepts, deeply believed and visibly practiced, bring profound, handholding changes in hearts and minds, and spawn peaceful results like those witnessed by the world in Charleston.

Surely, "the kind of love that Jesus commands is possible only in the measure that we have the divine life in us, that we have received a gift that enables us to love as God loves."[18]

Charleston's Apology

I sincerely believe that biblical forgiveness, genuinely and publicly voiced to Dylann Roof by some of the victims' grieving family members, changed our city. It proved the instrument of peace that quelled potential rioting and violence in Charleston, the city avoiding what was experienced in most U.S. cities after dramatic racial incidents and deaths. It transformed people's hearts, minds, and attitudes, and made them think more deeply about life, love, forgiveness, and the lasting value of God's Word.

In June 2018, three years after the Emanuel Church shooting, another miracle happened, one that ensured the continued racial healing of Charleston from its shameful and abusive past.

On June 19, the 153rd anniversary of the ending of slavery in the United States, the city of Charleston officially apologized for its role in regulating, supporting, and fostering slavery and the resulting atrocities inflicted by the institution of slavery. The Resolution to Recognize, Denounce and Apologize for the City's Involvement with Slavery also stated that the prosperity and robust economy of this city began with a dependency upon the free labor, technical expertise, and craftsmanship of those peoples who were enslaved.[19]

Some believed, as Councilman James Lewis did, that a "resolution does nothing. It apologizes for something that happened before our time."

But others, like Councilmen Robert Mitchell and Dudley Gregorie, saw it differently.

"We have to start somewhere and get to a point where we can move forward," Mitchell stated. "So, as a city, we are starting now."[20]

It's about time.

In our city, overshadowed by a history of racism, injustice, and fear, people are listening, opening their eyes, ears, and hearts, and waiting to experience healing and unity on a new and deeper level. I urge them to pay close attention, for God is surely at work in Charleston.

8

Honoring Myra's Wishes

Dylann is not a part of my life or the life of my children. That's why we forgave him so that we can move on. We're through with him.

Anthony Thompson, 2016

Before Dylann's trial begins in early December 2016, eighteen months after the shooting, the court appoints renowned capital defense attorney David I. Bruck to represent Roof. Attorney Bruck is known for taking the nation's hard cases, defending those whom society labels as *monsters*, those people who commit crimes the public considers inexcusable and unpardonable. Aware of a client's unquestionable guilt, Bruck tries to convince juries to give life sentences instead of death sentences.

Two years before, Bruck represented the Boston marathon bomber, twenty-one-year-old Dzhokhar Tsarnaev, who planted two pressure-cooker bombs on Boston's Boylston Street. They exploded at the marathon's finish line, killing three spectators and injuring more than 260 others. But in spite of Bruck's carefully prepared arguments, Tsarnaev received the death sentence, "the final chapter to a brutal, emotionally exhausting trial that brought forth indelible images of an unspeakable crime."[1]

Bruck also defended Susan Smith, the South Carolina mother who, in 1994, drowned her two young sons. This case did indeed end in a prison sentence; she was spared from death by execution.

Attorney Bruck claimed Dylann Roof was not mentally capable to stand trial, and asked that Roof undergo a psychiatric examination. Eight doctors questioned the young man, revealing that Roof "did not suffer from any mental disease or defect," that he was "alert, focused, and confident," "cogent and articulate," and had "an extremely high IQ."[2] In light of these findings, Judge Richard Gergel moved to trial.

On December 7, Roof enters the somber courtroom, his hair freshly trimmed in its usual bowl shape. He wears an oversized gray-and-black-striped prison jumpsuit, and prison-issue sneakers sporting his hand-drawn Celtic crosses—hate symbols embraced by white supremacists. Surrounding him are the victims' family members, their friends, clergy, Roof's mother, his paternal grandparents, and others.

Lead prosecutor Jay Richardson delivers his opening statement, telling of Dylann's carefully planned murders, the hate letters, and the disturbing details of his crime. Hearing these discoveries about her son for the first time, Mrs. Cowles slumps down into her seat. The grisly details of his cold and calculated killings are too much for her to handle. As she grabs her chest and collapses to the floor, she cries out, "I'm sorry! I'm sorry! I'm sorry!" The courtroom scene becomes an emotional one, touching the hearts of spectators and court personnel who cry with her. Some in the courtroom watch Dylann's reaction, claiming he never glances back as his mother suffers a heart attack and is rushed to the hospital. She survives it, but never returns to the trial.

At one point, after hearing the heartfelt words of family members, people in the courtroom openly weep, unable to hold back tears, making it necessary for the judge to call a short recess.

On another day during the trial, people view the graphic photographs of the crime scene—the victims lying in pools of blood around the circular tables where they stood and prayed, the shell casings, cartridge magazines, Bibles, and purses scattered all around them. The photographs again leave the courtroom in tears.[3]

I refuse to attend the trial on that particular day, not wanting to see photographs of the bloodbath in the church fellowship hall, nor of Myra's bleeding body having been mutilated by Dylann's eight bullets. I didn't want to see my wife like that, those images in my head for the rest of my life.

My absence on that Thursday, however, means that I miss viewing the church security camera's video of my wife's final moments of life. The court shows a six-second clip of Myra as she strode purposefully, joyfully in the church side door at 5 p.m., and slipped out an hour later to go to the fellowship hall.

The federal victim witness coordinator later gave me that particular section of the tape to watch. *That was the Myra I love, know, and want to remember.*

Throughout the days of the trial, Dylann sits still, emotionless, zombie-like. The witnesses shed tears; their voices shake when they speak, but none of them gives a personal opinion on whether Roof should receive the death penalty or life in prison. They leave that decision up to the men and women of the jury, consisting of ten women and two men, nine of the jurors white and three of them black.[4]

During the trial, Roof often argues with Mr. Bruck, the attorney who wants to save him from execution by presenting the young man as mentally ill. But on December 15, the court finds Roof guilty of the crimes, convicting him of thirty-three charges.

Before the next trial begins in early January—the penalty phase of the trial—Dylann pens a three-page motion from jail stating that he no longer wants to work with Mr. Bruck because the attorney is "too Jewish," and is his "political and biological enemy."

"His ethnicity was a constant source of conflict even with my constant efforts to look past it," Roof writes. "Trust is a vital component in an attorney-client relationship, and is important to the effectiveness of the defense."[5]

In order to make sure everyone understands that he is mentally sound and well aware of the crime he committed, Dylann decides to represent himself during the sentencing trial. When attorney Bruck visits Roof in jail before the trial begins, Dylann threatens to "come to Mr. Bruck's house and kill him."[6]

On the first day of his trial, Roof becomes his own defense attorney, assuring jurors he is psychologically healthy and demanding that they ignore everything they hear and have heard to the contrary from the former defense attorney. During the long trial days, Dylann calls no witnesses and offers no evidence.

Lead prosecutor Jay Richardson calls twenty-three witnesses. I am one of them, and when my turn comes, I cry as I talk about Myra, our marriage, and the strength of our loving bond. As I hold our wedding photograph in my hands, looking at it often, I tell the court, "She is the one I prayed for." When I share with the jury what would have been our future plans, I break down emotionally, lamenting that she's no longer alive to share in those dreams.

I sit in the courtroom listening to the heartbreaking words of the other witnesses. As I think about Myra, I pray for Dylann. I yearn to hear him speak in his closing statement, and I wonder what he will say. I hope that for an instant he will let down his façade, exposing a sorrowing soul. I hope to see a tiny crack of light illuminating from the young man's hardened heart, believing that somehow in the past two long years of incarceration, he has surely thought back over his life, pondered his actions, realized the many people he has hurt, and perhaps asked God to forgive him.

But I am disappointed. On the last day of the trial, January 10, after the prosecution rests, Dylann addresses the court, offering his closing statement. I lean forward to better hear what he will say. The frail young man stands and speaks arrogantly: "I felt like I had to do it. I *still* feel like I had to do it."[7]

He offers no apology for the murders, shows no regret, no remorse. His words indicate that if a future opportunity presents another chance to kill African-Americans, he will do it again. He acts as if he deserves no forgiveness, only punishment.

"God have mercy on his soul," I whisper instinctively, shaking my head in awe, realizing that Dylann has learned nothing during the long days of his imprisonment. He has simply wasted the time, giving his heart's growing weeds of hate and hostility time to put down deeper roots, strangling and choking out any last possible seedling of guilt, sorrow, repentance, remorse, or regret. His words will echo in my mind for weeks: *"I felt like I had to do it. I still feel like I had to do it."*

I look around the courtroom at the others who hear Dylann's hard, unrepentant words, noticing the downcast and disbelieving expressions on their faces. No doubt they, too, are awed and sickened by the killer's continued brashness, arrogance, and senseless hate.

In his five-minute closing statement, Dylann also tells the court, "I have the right to ask you to give me a life sentence, but I'm not sure what good it would do anyway." He pauses and then says abruptly, "That's all."[8]

Judge Gergel sentences Roof to death eighteen times, handing down an additional fifteen life sentences for the hate crimes and other charges.

"This trial has produced no winners, only losers," the judge states. "This proceeding cannot give the families what they truly want, the return of loved ones."[9]

As I exit the courtroom, my heart is heavy. I relive the memory of the tragedy that took Myra away from me. The trial digs her up—all the pain and horrors stabbing my heart, only to bury her again by Dylann's desire—"I *still* feel like I had to do it."

A *New York Times* reporter approaches me, putting a voice recorder up to my mouth.

"Mr. Thompson," he asks, "after hearing Roof's testimony today, do you want to take back your gift of forgiveness to him?"

I feel the question is an honest one, asked by a fellow human being who accepts society's definition of forgiveness but fails to understand or comprehend the concept of *biblical* forgiveness.

"No," I tell the reporter. "I forgave him and I'm not going to take that back ever. Dylann is not a part of my life anymore. Forgiveness has freed me of that and of him completely. I'm not going to make him a lifetime partner."

During the months after the trial, I prayed daily for Dylann's soul. I knew God could work a miracle in Dylann's life, and that *only* God could reach deep into the young man's heart of stone and stir it. My role in life was to move forward, every day remembering Myra, thanking God for the gift of our time together, and praying for her murderer.

Our Nation's Terrifying Trend

Three years later, on February 14, 2018, I watched the television news with renewed sadness. A gunman, Nikolas Cruz, fired an AR-15 semi-automatic rifle outside and inside Marjory Stoneman Douglas High School in Parkland, Florida, just north of Fort Lauderdale.

As I saw medics rush the stretcher-bound bleeding bodies into rows of waiting ambulances, I remembered June 17, 2015, painfully reliving the horrors I experienced that night and knowing that many more loved ones would experience similar pain.

The shooter was a mere teenager, nineteen, two years younger than Dylann Roof was at the time of the Emanuel shooting. The two massacres were somewhat similar. Investigators discovered that before the shooting, Cruz made graphic cell phone videos revealing his cryptic plans, alerting the world that he planned to become the "next school shooter of 2018," and threatening to kill "at least twenty people" at that particular high school.

"When you see me on the news, you'll know who I am," Cruz said and smiled. "You're all going to die . . . Yeah," he added, "can't wait."[10]

On that Valentine's Day, Cruz shot thirty-four people, killing seventeen and wounding another seventeen. He then escaped the building by mixing in with the students fleeing outside to safety.

Within hours in nearby Coral Springs, police found and arrested Cruz.

"You come to the conclusion this is just absolutely pure evil," Florida Governor Rick Scott remarked after learning of the massacre.

I fear that shooting deaths and injuries are becoming a terrifying trend in our nation and world—copycat killings. In just the first four months of 2018, shooters targeted and carried out killing sprees in more than a dozen elementary, middle, and high schools in Texas, Louisiana, Kentucky, California, Alabama, Virginia, and other states, murdering thirty people and injuring another forty.[11]

After each shooting, I mourn with the parents, grandparents, and friends who must bury someone they love, a person purposely slaughtered by a hate-filled terrorist bearing a gun. I feel empathy for them as I can now mentally step inside their shoes, seeing and experiencing the world from their perspective. I've been there, and I understand all too well the pain each one experiences, the long, depressing hours of sadness and loneliness, the overwhelming, weeping grief that threatens to consume each day.

Grief and Tears

Since Myra's death, I often think deeply about grief. The dictionary defines *grief* as deep sorrow, especially sorrow caused by someone's death. I am personally acquainted with all the synonyms associated with the word *grief*: misery, sadness, anguish, pain, distress, heartache, agony, torment, affliction, suffering, woe, desolation, despair, and many more, too deeply painful to put into words.

I find healing for my grief in God's Word, my anchor in the storm that keeps me securely fastened and focused on Christ. I fear that, like Peter seeking to walk on water, I will sink into the darkness if I take my eyes off Jesus. I often wonder how nonbelievers cope with life's unexpected hardships, with the deaths of loved ones, with the agonizing grief that lingers, its long, icy fingers stretching deep into the future before finally beginning to fade.

I think I could drown in the sheer volume of tears I've cried over the past three years. I wept for Myra, for the other eight victims' families, for all those who grieved a loved one's shooting death, and for Dylann Roof. My tears came as a natural human response to the sorrow, suffering, and sadness I saw around me. Tears are a universal phenomenon, revealing human grief, a broken heart. They connect our souls, human to human, as together we share in the mutual grief caused by a fallen world. And with each tear that falls, I feel an extraordinary connection, a close brotherhood, with the living Christ, who, in His life of flesh and blood, also wept, showing us His tears, His own broken heart.

Whether we cry over our own pain, or the pain of someone else, tears are a gift of grace from God. They provide a release from tension and sadness. They cleanse our soul. Tears are a necessary and instinctive human response to suffering that we have owned from the moment of our birth. They touch our heart at its most inward places, possessing the power to melt the masks we wear, uncovering the mystery of our deepest selves, the true and honest side of us seen only by God. Tears reveal that which makes us vulnerable, a response to the hardships of life, opening up to light the infected secret places within us that threaten to fester and decay. They bring focus to the intolerable, the inexcusable—clearer vision of those things in life that are senseless and tragic. Tears signal a voluntary letting go of control, an admission of powerlessness, an urgent summons for God, and a step toward healing.

"Tears are one of the many ways we release our sadness, one of our many wondrous built-in healing mechanisms," Elisabeth Kübler-Ross wrote.[12]

When my denominational leaders in the Anglican Church in North America received news about Myra's murder, the bishops in South Carolina immediately responded, acknowledging her loss with a universal truth about grief and tears: "It is right that you feel sickened and angry. It is right that you struggle to know what to do. We all do. Scripture tells us that in the diminishment or suffering of one the whole church suffers. We are enjoined to weep with those who weep and to mourn with those who mourn. Today, we mourn and we weep with our brothers and sisters at Emanuel Church and all of Charleston."[13]

"Jesus wept." The Scripture writers recorded a river of tears running throughout the Bible, never shying away from what they represented and why they flowed. I have thought many times since Myra's death about the tears Jesus openly shed when His friend Lazarus died (John 11). When He experienced the deep heartbreaking sorrow of loss, He cried. His tears show me His human side, the part of Him I can identify with, and the great distress of His heavily burdened heart. He knew He would restore Lazarus's life, bringing him up from the grave, but even so He cried at his friend's death (v. 35).

In His tears, I believe Jesus showed us the heart of the Father, a Father who suffers with us when tragedy moves into our lives, overwhelming our fragile hearts, consuming our minds with grief, despair, and bereavement.

Jesus cried for Lazarus, but perhaps He also cried for himself as He prepared to face His own death on the cross, the high cost of humankind's redemption; the weight of the world's sins would soon be placed on His shoulders, providing the gift of undeserved grace, of eternal life, to Lazarus, to me, and to those around the world who will believe in Him. *Thank you, Jesus.*

Perhaps in that moment of grief, Jesus also cried for His mother, who would stand beneath the cross with swollen eyes and tearstained cheeks, watching her son suffer the agony of torture and death.

Maybe Jesus cried as He peered into the future, envisioning Dylann's boyish face and blood-stained hands, perhaps counting all the Dylanns in the past and future who had chosen, and who will choose, wrong paths, making irreversible decisions that result in lost lives, forfeited potentials, and hardened hearts. Perhaps He wept as He saw all those who allowed the weeds of hate to fill their hearts, growing deep, sturdy roots that would eventually destroy themselves and others.

Surely as He stood by Lazarus's grave, Jesus cried for all those reasons, despising the enemy death, which comes to us at such unexpected times and violently snuffs out life, joy, fellowship, and dreams. Maybe His tears came from the anger and outrage He felt as He saw evil triumphing on earth, causing so much pain and loss. Jesus knew God would have the last Word, but in the meantime, perhaps He wept over a sinful and suffering world.

I don't know all the reasons why Jesus cried in John 11, but I thank God for divinely guiding John to record Jesus' strong emotions with two profoundly powerful but simple words: "Jesus wept." Jesus' tears give me permission to weep, to cry for the things that bring pain to God's heart, and to my own heart as well.

I pray that Dylann Roof will one day cry a flood of tears as he looks back over the tragedy that is his life, as he contemplates the eternal existence of his soul, as he considers the depth of his wrongdoings. I pray for the inner pain in his soul to crack wide open his seemingly impenetrable heart. For how else will the Lord Jesus be invited to enter in unless the heart of the young racist breaks in sorrow and repentance?

Jesus Still Weeps

"Jesus wept." The oft-quoted words of Scripture continue to bring healing to me and to others who identify with Christ, believers who strive to be obedient, to follow God, and to live according to His Word.

Almost twenty-five years ago, another incident in our nation brought heartache and shared tears. White supremacist Timothy McVeigh and his co-conspirator, Terry Nichols, two young men filled with anger and hate, took the lives of 168 people inside the Alfred P. Murrah building in Oklahoma City, Oklahoma. McVeigh parked a rented truck outside the Murrah building. Filled with fuel and ammonium nitrate, one of the most common fertilizers in the U.S., the homemade truck bomb exploded at 9:02 on the morning of April 19, 1995, destroying buildings, property, and lives.

McVeigh carefully considered other federal buildings in different states before he finally chose Oklahoma City. He later explained that the location of the Murrah federal building provided excellent camera angles for media coverage after the explosion so as to better spread his anti-government message. Like Dylann, McVeigh had little regard for the lives he took of people he had never met.

Of those killed, nineteen were young children playing in the building's day care center. McVeigh coldly referred to their deaths as "collateral damage."[14]

Terry Nichols, who received a life sentence, asked survivors and families of the victims for forgiveness, admitting, "Words cannot adequately express the sorrow I have had over the years for the grief that so many have endured and continue to suffer. I am truly sorry for what occurred."

He also said he had asked God for forgiveness and found "a real and personal relationship with God through . . . Jesus Christ."[15]

But Timothy McVeigh, like Dylann Roof, proudly confessed to the killings, offering no apology, showing no remorse. McVeigh's execution came by lethal injection at 7:14 a.m. on June 11, 2001. Before his death, he spent his final days of life at the Terre Haute prison, the dreaded maximum-security facility in Indiana.

Like Dylann, McVeigh also showed no regret over the lives he took and the people he hurt, admitting, "I understand what they felt in Oklahoma City. I have no sympathy for them."[16]

McVeigh's defiance and hard heart remained intact right up to his execution, as revealed in the words he chose to hear at the end of his life. Before he died, he asked a prison warden to read aloud the poem *Invictus*, penned by William Ernest Henley in 1875. The poem's title means "unconquerable" and proudly, arrogantly boasts the most foolish, laughable claim in the universe: "I am the master of my fate: I am the captain of my soul."[17]

Sadly, it proved a fitting poem for the young man with a godless heart, a hate-filled mind, and a grandiose sense of self.

After the Oklahoma City bombing, Mayor Ron Norick appointed a 350-member Memorial Task Force to create a memorial to remember those killed in the Alfred P. Murrah building. The design and development of the memorial was based on a strong mission statement: "We come here to remember those who were killed, those who survived and those changed forever. May all who leave here know the impact of violence. May this memorial offer comfort, strength, peace, hope and serenity."[18]

Included within the memorial was a large statue of a standing Jesus. Carved in white stone, Jesus' head was lowered as if in disbelief and sorrow, His right hand lifted and covering His tearstained face. His left hand, clenched in a fist, rested on His heart. The statue's simple inscription read, "And Jesus Wept."

The powerful image and profound words from Scripture needed no explanation to the many hearts aching with loss, as they communicated deeply and clearly the only path to comfort, strength, peace, hope, and serenity: Jesus.[19]

Forgiving the Unforgivable, the Inexcusable

In our society today, we often see deliberate acts of violence that we label *inexcusable*. Some crimes continue to send chills down our spines decades after they happen. One example happens in 1994, only six months before Timothy McVeigh's bomb explodes in Oklahoma City.

Susan Smith, twenty-three, the South Carolina mother of two young sons—Michael, three, and Alex, fourteen months—strapped her children into her 1990 Mazda, released the car's brake, put the gear in drive, and jumped out as the car rolled into John D. Long Lake. She stood on the bank watching for six long minutes as her car with her children sleeping in the back seat slowly sank into the lake. Both boys drowned, buried in the grave of dark water.

Trying to conceal her involvement, Smith made up an incredible story about a black man forcing her out of the car at gunpoint and driving off with her children in the back seat. Nine days later, however, her lies caught up with her. She confessed to killing the children, causing the nation to shake its head in horrifying disbelief and shock. Divers found the car turned upside down in the lake, the children dangling from their car seats, a small hand pressed against the window.

Inexcusable. I can think of no other word that better fits the depravity of this deliberate crime.

Defended by David Bruck, the same attorney appointed to plead Dylann Roof's murder case, Smith was charged with two counts of murder, the court rejecting the death sentence and sending Smith to prison for life.[20]

From prison more than two decades later, Smith explained her gruesome and senseless crime, still offering no motive: "I am not the monster society thinks I am. I am far from it. Something went very wrong that night. I was not myself. I was a good mother and I loved my boys. . . . There was no motive as it was not even a planned event. I was not in my right mind."[21]

Susan Smith carried the burden of her deadly actions with her as she journeyed throughout life. Her ex-husband—the boys' father, David Smith—also carried a heavy burden when for many years he refused to forgive his wife for the murders.

David Smith described his heartache and grief after the murder of his two sons by his ex-wife. "I didn't know how to put one foot in front of the other. Didn't know what I was going to do," he said. "My whole world literally—like everything I had left, they were gone. Just like that. . . . My whole world just stopped. I had to remind myself to breathe."[22]

Years passed as David Smith wrestled with his anger toward Susan, reliving the suffocating pain of her inexcusable crime, unable to find answers, striving to take small steps toward living with the overwhelming grief.

In 2000, after years of struggle and countless sessions with therapists, Smith began to understand the true concept of forgiveness.

One day as he sat on his couch, he took a deep breath and stated, "Okay, I forgive her."

He admitted that the act of forgiving Susan came as a big relief, one that "lifted that burden off my soul."[23]

David Smith later told Larry King in a television interview about his forgiveness toward his ex-wife: "I had to, because *that* [unforgiveness] was only going to eat me up and . . . subdue my life for the rest of my life. So I had to come to grips with that, forgive Susan for what she'd done."[24]

David's forgiveness enabled him to move forward, remarry, and begin a new life. But he admitted he never fully recovered from the grief of losing his two children.

"There's always this nagging and gnawing heartache," he said. "It's there every day, even if I'm not always conscious of it."[25]

Perhaps the nation will always consider Susan Smith a murdering monster, claiming her crime unforgivable, inexcusable. Few people could understand how David Smith could forgive his ex-wife for killing his sons in such a frightening, horrible way.

Dylann Roof's crime can also be viewed as unforgivable, inexcusable. And few people can understand how I, and others, can forgive him. When I chose to forgive Dylann, I made a willful decision that forever canceled the debt he owed me and my family—the inexcusable, unpardonable debt.

I forgave him because I truly believe that "to be a Christian means to forgive the inexcusable, because God has forgiven the inexcusable" in me, and that to refuse to offer forgiveness "is to refuse God's mercy for ourselves."[26]

I forgave Dylann Roof, and I will never take it back. Ever.

Must the Offender Respond?

Society leads people to believe that forgiveness cannot be one-sided, and that in order for the forgiveness transaction to be genuine and complete, the offender must respond positively to the victim's offered gift of forgiveness.

But that's not true, and it keeps many people from experiencing the peace that comes from forgiveness because they see their one-sided forgiveness as incomplete. If the offender had to respond, accepting the offered forgiveness, then he would dictate and control the victim's choice to forgive. Forgiveness would then depend on the offender's response, not the victim's decision to forgive.

I forgave Dylann Roof. I expected no response from him, and he has never acknowledged nor accepted my forgiveness. Even though one-sided, my forgiveness was genuine and complete. If my forgiveness depended on Dylann's acceptance, then my act of forgiveness would be impossible. If I needed his approval, acknowledgment, or acceptance, and he refused to give it, I would be eternally locked in the prison of unforgiveness, unable to know the peace that passes all human understanding, unable to put him behind me and move on with my life and ministry.

Receiving no response of remorse from Timothy McVeigh, the majority of the Oklahoma City bombing survivors and victims' family members refused to forgive the murderer for robbing them of their children, spouses, and loved ones. A woman who lost her two young grandsons in the building's day care center perhaps spoke on behalf of the majority when she stated, "I was glad when [McVeigh] died. I will never forgive Timothy McVeigh."[27]

On a strictly human level, her lack of forgiveness is understandable. The natural human response to deep hurt is hatred, retaliation, and revenge. Not forgiveness.

Some, however, did choose to forgive the heartless bomber.

At the hour of the bombing, Paul Heath, a psychologist, worked at his desk in the Alfred P. Murrah Federal Building. He struggled for three months to forgive McVeigh, the man who killed so many of his co-workers and friends.[28]

Another survivor, Randy Ledger, still bears the bombing scars on his face and neck. The blast severed his carotid artery, almost ending his life. Before the killer's execution, Ledger struggled to write a letter to McVeigh, offering his forgiveness. "It's just something that I have to do to let this go," Ledger explained, adding that the letter "also will contain prayers for him because he still seems to be unrepentant, unremorseful." He added, "That's what hurts the most is that he's going to die and it just seems that there's no reason for him to do this."[29]

Timothy McVeigh went to his execution, dying with his eyes open, after receiving a lethal cocktail of injections. McVeigh's lawyer, Robert Nigh, apologized to the relatives of his 168 victims, expressing his own sorrow that his client had never showed remorse, had never apologized for the people he purposely killed.

If McVeigh ever knew that some of the victims forgave him, he never acknowledged or accepted their forgiveness. Fortunately, his response wasn't needed.[30]

Does Forgiveness Require Reconciliation?

Society places a dangerous expectation on the one who forgives, demanding that forgiveness must bring reconciliation and/or reunion with the offender. This misguided and frightening myth keeps Christian wives returning to tyrannical husbands who hurt, threaten, and abuse them and their children. These women often choose not to forgive the abuser for fear they'll be required to reconcile and reunite with him. As statistics show, an abused wife's reluctant return to a savage husband can sometimes mean a death sentence for her and her children.

This myth also keeps people from forgiving past sexual abuses. Even if, for their own sake, they want to reach out in forgiveness to an abuser, they don't, as they fear their forgiveness will mean reconciliation and/or reunion, adding further degradation and possibly allowing more sexual abuses in their lives. Instead, they forfeit the peace that accompanies biblical forgiveness, not willing to make themselves vulnerable and available to the future whims of the sexual predator.

Reconciliation—the restoration of a relationship—should happen *only* when the abuser has received necessary treatment and healing and no longer abuses his victim. Reconciliation, however, may not be possible in some cases, for it depends on the choices of two people, not just one. It takes two people to restore a healthy relationship. The decision to forgive in no way rests or depends on relational reconciliation or reunion taking place. If it did, victims of rape would be forced to reconcile with rapists, and abused wives would be forced to live with violent husbands.

"There are people who have wounded us to such a degree that it is not healthy for us to be in relationship with them . . . we need to establish boundaries that create a safe buffer between our world and theirs. Yet, for the sake of our own spiritual and emotional health, it is critical that we forgive these people—even when relational reconciliation is not our goal."[31]

Giving forgiveness does not automatically mean *trusting* the pain-causing individual. One can forgive an offender without putting her trust in the person who brutally violated that trust. Biblical forgiveness demands that we forgive, not that we become a doormat, a continual victim.

When student Daniela Menescal forgave Nikolas Cruz for shooting bullets into her back and leg on Valentine's Day during the Parkland, Florida, high school massacre, forgiveness did not require Daniela to have a relationship with him. She didn't have a relationship with him before he tried to kill her; why on earth would she want one now? A Christian, she forgave Cruz for her own peace and well-being, stating, "It's a miracle that I'm alive. . . . Even for all he caused . . . I forgive him."[32]

Society's Illogical Forgiveness

Preconceived and false notions dreamed up by a Hatfield-McCoy society can cause otherwise forgiving Christian people to spend entire lifetimes holding on to unforgiveness, destructive anger, and bitter, health-destroying grudges. To the unbeliever, forgiveness is illogical. It defies reason. It doesn't make sense to our sinful human self. We prefer to choose revenge, causing the offender as much pain as possible for his hurtful actions. Our human nature wants to keep alive the red-hot embers of bitterness, rejecting the peace of forgiveness, forever stoking the glowing coals that burn in our hearts, and embracing a new identity: victimhood.

I am convinced that society will never fully understand biblical forgiveness.

"In the wake of these terrible events, the pardon offered to Roof on the part of families of some of the victims was, depending on one's perspective, edifying, puzzling, or unnerving," wrote Robert Barron, an auxiliary bishop of the Archdiocese of Los Angeles.

"As many of the negative and puzzled reactions prove, what the relatives of the Charleston victims did is, on the merely human level, inexplicable. To offer pardon to a wicked man, who in no sense gave indication of regret or repentance, is just so strange that something else, we are convinced, must be going on," observes Barron.[33]

When I forgave Dylann Roof, Christ was at work in my heart.

"Real forgiveness, the kind that Jesus speaks of, is an act of love, and love is an act of the will. When we forgive, we lift the burden of responsibility from the shoulders of the offender. We give a very specific gift: the exoneration of the obligation to right the wrong done. Forgiveness is the writing off of a debt."[34]

Our forgiveness, when based on Scripture instead of society, transcends logic and reason. Writing off a deserved debt sends shockwaves across the internet, television, and news programs, and believing that forgiveness somehow absolves the killer from his crime, society may criticize a victim's forgiveness. But in no way did my forgiving Dylann Roof exonerate him from his murderous act. He alone is to blame, and I blamed him. But I can forgive Dylann and still expect him to receive justice, the punishment he deserves as determined by a judge and jury. Dylann planned and carried out an inexcusable crime, and he'll pay the consequences given him by a court of law. But I can, and do, forgive him.

Do I want a future relationship with Dylann Roof? Of course not! I had no relationship with him before the shooting, and I certainly want no relationship with him now. Dylann is facing execution. His life will be cut short, affording not much time for a relationship with anyone. And as I expressed earlier: Dylann is not a part of my life or the lives of my children. That's why we forgave him, so that we can move on. We're through with him.

Surely complete reconciliation and restoration will take place one day in heaven when God "will wipe every tear from their eyes. There will be no more death or mourning or crying or pain, for the old order of things has passed away" (Revelation 21:4).

I am leaving it in God's hands, trusting Him completely to deal with it. I will continue to pray for Dylann, hoping that before he dies, he'll beg God for forgiveness. But I am done with Dylann. I am laying down my heavy burden, never again to pick it up. I'm moving on, walking forward, just as I know Myra would wish me to do.

9

||||||||||||||||||||||||||||||||||||||||||||

The Deadly Dis-ease
of Unforgiveness

Now is the time to focus on God.

Anthony Thompson

Hate and unforgiveness prove such powerful emotions, becoming states of mind and heart that destroy everything they touch. One of the saddest, most disturbing stories of hate and unforgiveness happened decades ago and still brings tears to my eyes whenever I recall it.

Simon Wiesenthal, an Austrian Jew born in the Ukraine in 1908, and his wife, Cyla, suffered greatly during the Hitler years when, in 1942, the Nazi hierarchy put into operation the "Final Solution," the systematic annihilation of Jews. Within months, eighty-nine of their family members perished. Imprisoned in concentration camps, Simon and Cyla were skin and bones and barely alive when an American armored unit liberated them on May 5, 1945.

In his book *The Sunflower*, Wiesenthal told of an incident that occurred while he was a concentration camp inmate. He was sent with a prison workforce to clean a hospital filled with wounded German soldiers. As he scrubbed floors, a nurse interrupted him, asking if he was a Jew. When he told her yes, she took him to the bed of an old, dying Nazi soldier named Karl.

Karl admitted to Wiesenthal that he was unable to find any peace for his tortured soul until he confessed to a Jew the crime that had burdened him for years. He then told Wiesenthal a story that sent chills down the Jewish prisoner's spine.

Karl described how he and his comrades, sent to fight in Russia, killed more than two hundred Jews—men, women, and children— by cramming them into a house packed with cans of flammable petrol, throwing hand grenades at them through open windows, burning babies and entire families alive, and shooting with machine guns anybody who tried to escape. The gruesome scene and agonizing guilt burdened Karl, and before he died, he yearned to find freedom from it.

Lying in a hospital bed in constant pain and waiting to die, Karl confessed his sins to Wiesenthal, wanting to finally come clean and be forgiven before he passed.

"I have waited many long and dark nights to find a Jew to serve as a representative of the Jewish people, that I might beg his forgiveness," he told Wiesenthal. "Without forgiveness, I cannot die in peace. And I know my time is running out."

Wiesenthal listened quietly to Karl's confession and the dying man's urgent pleas for forgiveness. But even with Karl's deathbed apology, Wiesenthal could not bring himself to forgive the German soldier. He simply turned his back to Karl and left the repentant man's room without saying a word. The next day, the nurse told Wiesenthal that Karl had died.

Wiesenthal's decision *not* to forgive the dying Nazi burdened him for the rest of his life, bringing to his mind again and again over long years the haunting question: "Ought I to have forgiven him?"

After the war, Wiesenthal dedicated his entire life to aggressively hunting down Nazi war criminals, all the while believing that "God must have been on leave during the Holocaust."[1]

Bringing guilty Germans to justice, he made dead sure they answered for their participation in Hitler's Holocaust. He never rested from his ongoing pursuit to hunt down and punish those who committed inexcusable crimes against the world's Jews. He claimed to have brought more than 1,100 criminals to justice.

Some might say that Wiesenthal's anger was constructive, that he used the powerful emotions of hate and unforgiveness for a good and just purpose. Surely the guilty Nazi war criminals deserved to be punished for their World War II atrocities to the Jewish people. Many people around the world greatly admired Simon Wiesenthal for making it his life's work to hunt down and exact revenge on Nazis who had fled punishment. But I wonder what happens to a lone man's mind, heart, body, and soul when he is so driven, so consumed, so burdened for an entire lifetime by unforgiveness, anger, hatred, and resentment. Surely Wiesenthal paid a high personal price in health and relationships when he alone took on this government-sized task.

Harboring hate and unforgiveness "is like carrying a heavy burden—a burden that victims bring with them when they navigate the physical world."[2]

On September 20, 2005, Wiesenthal, a tired old man of ninety-six years, died of kidney disease in Vienna, Austria, the anguished face of the dying German, Karl, still on his mind and the unanswered question still on his lips: "Ought I to have forgiven him?"[3]

The Medical Consequences of Unforgiveness

Science is beginning to take a hard look at the consequences of unforgiveness, noting the infirmity it can bring to minds, emotions, and bodies. Medical books now classify unforgiveness "as a disease" . . . [suggesting that] "refusing to forgive makes people sick, and keeps them that way."

"Harboring these negative emotions, this anger and hatred," Dr. Michael Barry states, "creates a state of chronic anxiety." He explains how chronic anxiety produces excess adrenaline and cortisol, thus depleting "the production of natural killer cells, the body's foot soldier in the fight against cancer."[4]

Recent studies show that people who hold grudges report higher rates of heart disease and cardiac arrest, elevated blood pressure, stomach ulcers, arthritis, back problems, headaches, and chronic pain than those who don't hold grudges. Those who practice forgiveness report greater personal well-being, including lower levels of depression, fewer physical health complaints, and higher levels of life satisfaction. Scientists also discover that those who require the offender's contrition—his apology—in order to extend forgiveness report lower levels of well-being.

"By requiring the offender's contrition, we're letting a person who harmed us decide if or when we can benefit from forgiveness. That's giving the wrongdoer a lot of control over our lives."[5]

Fifty Years of Unforgiveness

The late Eric Lomax knew how living with hate for half a century could lock a man into a personal prison. One of thousands of British soldiers the Japanese held captive in 1942, Lomax was forced to help build the 418-mile Siam-Burma Railway. He and the other POWs suffered from malnutrition, overwork, and disease. At the hands of Japanese prison guards, he endured relentless torture and beatings, brutality that broke his arms, hips, and ribs. He remembered one abuser in particular, Takashi Nagase, a Japanese interpreter who was especially cruel to him.

A broken young man and overwhelmed with hate, Lomax survived the war and returned to Scotland, the country of his birth. He was damaged mentally, emotionally, and physically, weighing only 105 pounds. He discovered that during his forty-two-month imprisonment, his mother had died and his father had remarried. He had no home to return to in Scotland.

"In 1945," Lomax wrote, "I returned to Edinburgh to a life of uncertainty, following three and half years of fear, interrogation and torture as a POW in the Far East. . . . Inside I was falling apart."

For the next five decades, Lomax nurtured his hate and anger, fantasizing about painful ways to torture and kill the Japanese abusers, especially Takashi Nagase. His long years of loathing Nagase destroyed his relationship with his father, broke apart his marriage, and separated him forever from his two daughters. For years, he experienced violent mood swings, memory flashbacks, and painful mental trauma.

Eric Lomax was one of the many people who refused to forgive the inexcusable and ended up paying the inescapable price of unforgiveness.[6]

But fortunately, Eric Lomax's story didn't end in unforgiveness. A half century after his brutal beatings and imprisonment by the Japanese, Lomax and his abuser, Takashi Nagase, scheduled a face-to-face meeting in Kanburi, Thailand. Nagase greeted Lomax with a formal bow. Taking Lomax's hand in his, the old, bent-over Japanese man apologized to him again and again for his past cruelty.

"I am so sorry, so very sorry," Nagase sobbed.

Emotionally touched by Nagase's sincere expression of regret, Lomax forgave him. The two men became friends, keeping in touch, and visiting each other until their deaths. Lomax later wrote a book about his World War II ordeal, admitting, "Some time the hating has to stop."

Eric Lomax lived in a state of dis-ease for fifty years before he finally forgave Nagase. Unforgiveness crippled his mind and emotions and destroyed his closest relationships. His forgiveness was based on Nagase's repentance and face-to-face apology, and while this type of societal forgiveness—*conditional* forgiveness—can bring some healing, it is far different from biblical forgiveness.

Scientific studies show that participants who believe God has forgiven them for their own sins and wrongdoings are more likely to offer others *unconditional*, unrestricted, and unqualified forgiveness.[7]

Unlike society's forgiveness that is packed with myths, biblical forgiveness has no strings attached to it. It is forgiveness without conditions, needing no apology, no compensation for the loss, no face-to-face meeting, and no response from the offender. It is simply a victim's unquestioning forgiveness given as a gift of grace to the offender. Even if one-sided, it is complete and absolute, proving far more powerful than a societal forgiveness based on a series of conditions. With biblical forgiveness, victims choose to forgive another person because they, themselves, have been completely forgiven by God. Their own sinful debt has been paid in full with no conditions—an undeserved grace gift from their heavenly Father.

I have forgiven Dylann Roof completely because God has forgiven me completely. To society, this type of no-strings-attached forgiveness seems illogical. But to Christ-believers who have experienced God's loving and complete forgiveness, biblical forgiveness makes perfect sense.

Consumed by Hate

As of this writing, Dylann has now had three long years to think about his murderous crime. He goes from court to prison still embracing hate, having issued the powerful emotion *carte blanche* to dictate his life, his actions, and his future. He holds on tightly to his hostility and warped beliefs like a baby clings to a favorite blanket, wrapping himself in its pseudo security, giving it permission to seep into every word he speaks and everything he does.

I know that God can change Dylann's heart and attitude, making him become who He wants him to be, doing what He wants him to do. And I pray that it will happen in this young man's life.

But hatred seems to give Dylann a purpose in life, giving the drifting loner a sense of belonging to a large nationwide group of white supremacist brothers, and of fighting for a cause he imagines is greater than himself. His journal scribbles indicate that he believed an army of supporters cheered him onward in the battle for white supremacy.

"I would rather live in prison knowing I took action for my race than live with the torture of sitting idle," Dylann wrote in his "jailhouse manifesto."[8]

His statement reminded me of Satan's words spoken in John Milton's *Paradise Lost*: "Better to reign in hell, than serve in heav'n."[9]

I marvel that someone with Dylann's high IQ could be lured into such idiocy, so compelled to fight for such foolish beliefs, so eager and willing to give his life for an insane, dead-end ideology. He is a pitiful young man who feeds his hatred, allowing it to ruin his own life and bring crushing pain and destruction into the lives of many others. To the slaughtered victims' family members and loved ones who chose *not* to forgive the young killer, Dylann has become the guard who now controls their lives, who holds the keys to their own personal prison cells, and who opens the door wide to allow hate, resentment, and bitterness to enter and take root in their hearts and minds. Only biblical forgiveness can take away Dylann's control and keys, and open locked prison doors.

After Dylann's April 2017 trial and federal death sentence, the unrepentant young white supremacist was transferred to a high-security U.S. federal prison in Terre Haute, Indiana, which houses male inmates awaiting execution. He is the first person in United States history to be convicted of a federal hate crime and sentenced to the death penalty.

Day after day he sits on death row, likely living in solitary confinement in a closet-sized cell, his meals pushed through a narrow slot in a door, his recreation nonexistent. He is given a bed, sink, and toilet, and is allowed to leave his cell only three brief times each week when he is placed inside an inescapable cage. He waits alone and isolated, day after day awaiting his scheduled death, which might take many years to happen. I pray that Dylann's years of solitude and isolation will give him time to think, to reason, granting him some deeper understanding into his own mind and heart, perhaps forcing him to his knees in repentance, and begging God for forgiveness.

But without God's direct divine intervention, I don't expect Dylann to experience a positive change of heart and mind while inside the Terre Haute prison. According to new studies conducted on inmates sequestered in solitary confinement, isolated prisoners suffer heavy mental tolls, with about a third becoming "actively psychotic and/or acutely suicidal." One board-certified psychiatrist stated that prison solitude "can cause a specific psychiatric syndrome, characterized by hallucinations; panic attacks; overt paranoia; diminished impulse control; hypersensitivity to external stimuli; and difficulties with thinking, concentration and memory," and that some "inmates lose the ability to maintain a state of alertness, while others develop crippling obsessions."[10]

Some researchers found that solitary confinement beyond fifteen days led directly to severe and irreversible psychological harm. Without any human company and/or conversation, and "without anything to do, the brain atrophies . . . vision fades. Isolation and loss of control breeds anger, anxiety, and hopelessness."[11]

I worry that Dylann's racist hate will be nurtured in prison, not diminished, his tortured mind no longer able to make clear decisions—the choices that can change his eternal destination.

I often think about Dylann when I contemplate Psalm 139: "For you created my inmost being; you knit me together in my mother's womb. I praise you because I am fearfully and wonderfully made" (vv. 13–14). God created a human being, and gave him the breath of life.

How can a person choose to distance himself from his loving Creator?

Does everything within him not cry out for God? Begging Him to "search me, O God, and know my heart; test me and know my anxious thoughts. See if there is any offensive way in me, and lead me in the way everlasting" (vv. 23–24).

Does he not suffer from the deep vacuum in his wicked heart, the empty cavernous chamber St. Augustine claims must be filled by God and God alone? "Thou hast made us for Thyself, O Lord, and our hearts are restless until they rest in Thee."[12]

Has he so suppressed God's gentle whisper to his heart that he no longer hears it?

When Dylann dies from execution, he will leave behind him a path lined with grieving loved ones, an existence littered with death, destruction, and the endless tears of his many victims.

God gave Dylann life and breath, stamping His own image onto him, and Dylann has wasted God's gift, leaving a terrifying legacy, and dooming himself to the demons of hatred and hostility, debauchery and evil.[13]

I pray that God will help him before it is too late.

10

The Path to Healing and Peace

> When God speaks, *nothing* is transformed into *something*. And that's what the Word of God can do for our lives.
>
> Anthony Thompson

On Saturday, October 30, 2010, Robert and Wanda Smith's son, Tony, thirty-four years old, drove to his regular job at a restaurant in Cincinnati, Ohio. At 11:30 p.m. an armed, Halloween-masked, seventeen-year-old high school student came into the restaurant waving his gun. The teen struggled to open the cash register, and in the process jammed it shut. He then demanded that Tony open the register. Tony tried but couldn't release the jammed cash drawer. In frustration and rage, the robber fired his gun, shooting and killing Tony.

Recently I met the Rev. Dr. Robert Smith in Birmingham, Alabama, when a group of friends invited me to a dinner party. We had an opportunity to talk, each of us having lost a loved one to a shooter.

The longtime African-American pastor and seminary professor recently wrote a book, *The Oasis of God: From Mourning to*

Morning, about the night he and his wife received the telephone call every parent fears and dreads. The call came at 11 p.m. after Dr. Smith had preached his closing sermon at a three-day conference in Louisiana. He and his wife ate dinner and returned to their hotel room to sleep and pack for a flight home the next morning. Wanda answered the phone when it rang, uttering not a word. After a minute or two, she quietly hung up.

"Baby, what's wrong?" Robert asked her.

"It's Tony."

"What do you mean?"

"He's been shot," she whispered, not knowing if Tony was alive or dead.

Robert headed for the restroom, shut the door, and turned off the light. He prayed to God that his youngest son would survive the gunshot.

An hour later, at 11:56, the Smiths received another phone call telling them Tony was dead. The Smiths grieved their son's loss and the wreckage his murder would cause their families.

In his book, Robert wrote, "There are some moments that are frozen in time: December 7, 1941—the attack upon Pearl Harbor by the Japanese; April 4, 1968—the assassination of Dr. Martin L. King, Jr.; September 15, 1963—the bombing of the Sixteenth Street Baptist Church, Birmingham, AL, where four young black girls lost their lives. . . . For me, time was frozen on October 30, 2010, 11:56 p.m., the time when our son was pronounced dead. . . . Although we continue to live, that moment is frozen in time."[1]

I also, like the Smiths, have a moment that is frozen in time: June 17, 2015—the day I lost my precious wife to Dylann Roof's violence and hatred. The Smiths and I both experienced the same numbness and pain, prolonged and intensified by trials, long hours when we had to sit in a courtroom and hear the horrifying details of the tragedy again and again, reliving the nightmare while we stared at our loved one's killer.

Why? Why? Why? It is such a senseless and cruel death.

During the trial, the Smiths met the teenage robber for the first time. They watched his mother and some of his family members weep in juvenile court as the judge read the verdict: aggravated murder in the death of Antonio Smith, and aggravated robbery. He sentenced the teenager to many years in prison.

Robert chose to forgive his son's murderer just as I made the decision to forgive Dylann.

"I forgive him," Robert stated, "and 'I love him in Christ—even though the wound to my heart is still open.'"

"I love him in Christ." Surely it is the only way a Christ-follower can love the murderers of our society, those killers who cause wounds so deep they never truly heal.

In September of 2012, Robert wrote a letter to the young man, addressing it to the penitentiary where he was serving his time. He prayed the young man would be receptive to it. Smith told him that he had caused much pain to him and his family, and that "Jesus loves and forgives you and so do I." He asked friends and colleagues to pray that he would respond, accepting his forgiveness, and understanding God's love for him.

Nine months later, in May 2013, the man replied to the letter, expressing how sorry he was for the family's loss. Smith wrote him again in June, and received a second reply, one that sincerely asked why Dr. Smith wanted to stay in contact with him after he had killed his son and hurt his family so much.

"Because God loves you," Smith answered. "And He is loving you through me. I want you to see that God is able to recycle, reclaim, and restore your broken life. God redeems pain. I cannot let *you* go because God will not let *me* go."

Biblical forgiveness and Christ's love go hand in hand. Believers not only *forgive* in Christ, they also *love* in Christ. They understand the depth of hatred, sin, and evil, as well as the pain they cause. And they know that God in Christ can redeem the lost soul that harbors all. We have all sinned, every one of us, and without Christ, we are all doomed. But God has made a way for us, for with God nothing is impossible.

This is the reason why a Christ-believer forgives a murderer, a wicked and selfish person who robs him of a loved one. Because he, too, has been forgiven by God through Jesus Christ. He hopes that each lost soul, like himself, will turn to Christ in repentance, be forgiven and accepted into God's family, forever experiencing Christ's redemption. This was why Robert Smith could tell his son's murderer: "I only want you to know Tony's God and to serve Tony's Christ. My greatest hope is that one day you and Tony will bow side by side at the feet of our Lord in glory and worship the One who has redeemed you both by His blood!"

I pray that young man receives Robert Smith's forgiveness, and that he repents, seeking God's forgiveness, just as I pray that Dylann Roof receives my forgiveness.

Indifferent to Christ's Forgiveness

As mentioned earlier, when Jesus was crucified, hanging on a cross, struggling for every breath, He freely forgave the soldiers, onlookers, and rulers who gazed up at Him with blood on their hands. No doubt, they heard Jesus' words to the Father on their behalf when He shouted them from the cross: "Father, forgive them, for they do not know what they are doing" (Luke 23:34).

Scripture indicates that Jesus' forgiveness seemed to have no life-changing effects upon the people who crucified Him. In fact, Luke wrote that they responded to Jesus' words of forgiveness with sneers and mocking: "He saved others; let him save himself if he is the Christ of God, the Chosen One" (Luke 23:35). "If you are the king of the Jews, save yourself" (Luke 23:37).

Matthew wrote that those "who passed by hurled insults at him, shaking their heads and saying, 'You who are going to destroy the temple and build it in three days, save yourself! Come down from the cross, if you are the Son of God'" (Matthew 27:39–40). Even as He approached the Father, addressing their sins and need of forgiveness, He received unrelenting ridicule from the chief priests, the teachers of the law, and the elders (Matthew 27:41).

They even took His clothes (Luke 23:34).

Did anyone standing at the base of the cross acknowledge, accept, or even respond to Jesus' forgiveness? No, it seemed that nobody did. Jesus forgave them, the very ones who watched, sneered, mocked, and hurled insults, yet they were not affected for ill or good. They were simply unresponsive to Jesus' forgiveness, stopping up their ears, rejecting His offer. If Jesus had withheld His forgiveness and cursed them instead, would it have made any difference to them? Probably not. They just didn't seem to care.

The same thing can happen when believers offer forgiveness to those who have deeply hurt them. The offender shows indifference, rejecting the gift of forgiveness, continuing to sneer, mock, and hurl insults at the one who tries to show him God's love and plan of redemption.

To this day, more than three years after I forgave Dylann, he remains indifferent, seemingly callous and uncaring about the state of his eternal soul.

A magazine reporter summed up a number of people's negative opinions about my choice to forgive Dylann when he wrote, "I do not know if I could have had the compassion of Anthony Thompson, who exhorted Roof to 'repent, confess, give your life to the One who matters the most, Christ . . . so you'll be okay.'"

So "Roof will be okay?" the writer queries, then responds: "Why should his future be hopeful when he snuffed out nine precious lives?"[2]

The Lack of a Response

Some people still argue that the forgiveness I expressed to Dylann on June 19, 2015, is not complete because I have received no response from him and he has not acknowledged and accepted my forgiveness. They believe that a "one-sided forgiveness" is invalid, and that in order for forgiveness to be valid and complete, the offender must accept it.

But that's not true of biblical forgiveness.

"If forgiving depended on the culprit owning up, then the victim would always be at the mercy of the perpetrator. The victim would be bound in the shackles of victimhood," Archbishop Desmond Tutu said.[3]

My forgiveness was and is genuine, valid, and complete even though Dylann has not responded in any way.

"As the victim you offer the gift of your forgiving to the perpetrator who may or may not appropriate the gift but it has been offered and thereby it liberates the victim," Tutu said.[4]

As far as I know, Dylann simply ignored the gift I laid at his feet, refusing to pick it up, unwrap, open, and accept it. He just didn't seem to care, and that is his privilege.

I can do nothing now but continue to pray for him.

Others criticize me for forgiving Dylann because they believe I should have allowed him to suffer for his crime.

"You should have refused to forgive him, Anthony," they told me. "He needs to suffer, to feel pain for what he did."

But no amount of my unforgiveness will make Dylann Roof suffer or feel pain. My actions, my feelings, and my words have no control over him—none whatsoever. Whether he does or does not suffer the guilt of his crime is not in my hands.

If I had decided *not* to forgive Dylann, *I* would be the one suffering, lingering in sorrow, living in despair each moment for the rest of my life. *I* would have no inner peace or productive future ministry. *I* would one day become a bitter old man, still living in hatred, yearning for revenge, and locking myself into a self-made prison. And *I* would live there in misery forever. My forgiveness, as I expressed it to the young racist, brings *me* God's peace, not necessarily Dylann. He must fall to his knees, repent, and deal with His heavenly Father himself.

Nonbelievers are confused by this type of biblical forgiveness—a victim's free offer of mercy and grace to someone who has hurt them deeply. Some people tell me that my forgiving Dylann, striving to move beyond the tragedy, and trying to resume an active ministry, negates my love for Myra. They say that if I really loved her, I could not have forgiven her killer and moved onward with my life.

That, of course, is absurd. Forgiveness does not diminish my love for Myra. I move forward into life and ministry because I *do* love Myra. If I could speak with her right now, she would tell me to forgive her killer, wash my face, comb my hair, and jump with both feet back into the business of God's work. I am sure of that. She would want me to continue to carry out God's call upon my life, work we both loved, work we shared. The last thing Myra would want is for me to live an entire lifetime caught in the relentless grip of unforgiveness, forfeiting years of good health and relinquishing a lifetime of God-given potential ministry. Had I been the one murdered instead of Myra, I would want her to forgive my killer and move forward.

I'll always love Myra, forever thanking God for giving us such wonderful years together as husband and wife. I know that one day I will greet Myra in person, giving her the long-overdue kiss I meant to give her on June 17, 2015, before she left our home to teach the Bible study at Emanuel AME Church.

Because Believers Sin

I also chose to forgive Dylann because I, a believer devoted to Christ, still need God's continual forgiveness.

Even those of us redeemed by Christ and adopted into God's family have within our hearts the capacity to hate, sin, betray, and even murder. But the good news is that without exception, "righteousness from God comes through faith in Jesus Christ to all who believe" and that believers "are justified freely by his grace through the redemption that came by Christ Jesus" (Romans 3:22–24).

And all of us, even the most faithful believers, fall into sin—our spirits eager to obey God's Word, but our human flesh weak—striving to live in a corrupt and wicked world, temptations always surrounding us. For believers who stumble, God forgives again and again.

Jesus told the story of a prodigal son who requested his inheritance while his father was still alive, a dastardly demand in ancient Jewish culture. The loving father gave his son his wish and provisions, allowing him to leave the family home and wander to the "far country." The boy squandered his wealth in wild living. When he ran out of money, he found employment feeding pigs, the foulest, most unclean bottom-of-the-barrel job for a Jewish man. He was so hungry, he longed to fill his stomach with the pods that the pigs were eating, but no one would give him anything to eat.

The story ends with the starving man "coming to his senses" and traveling back home to his father in embarrassment and repentance. He prepared to tell his father that he was no longer worthy to be called his son.

But he was his father's son, a permanent member of his father's family. His sins in the far country didn't cast him out of the father's family, only out of close and constant communion with his father. No doubt, the father waited day after day, watching at the window and hoping his son would come home.

While the son "was still a long way off, his father saw him and was filled with compassion for him; he ran to his son, threw his arms around him and kissed him" (Luke 15:20). The running father, his long robes flapping in the wind behind him, surely proved a disgraceful sight to his proper and reserved Jewish neighbors, who knew and loathed the actions of the wayward son.

The father welcomed his son home with a robe, ring, sandals, and feast, exclaiming, "For this son of mine was dead and is alive again; he was lost and is found" (Luke 15:24)!

While we refer to this story as the parable of the lost or prodigal son, it is really all about the loving, forgiving Father who waits, watches, and runs to meet him, to celebrate His humbled and repentant son's return to the close communion of the family fold.

Surely we believers are called to forgive others—even the most vile person—because we ourselves are in constant need of God's forgiveness, the undeserved gift of mercy and grace that reaches out to us, God's children, again and again, and welcomes us home.

The late J. Oswald Sanders understood this concept when he wrote, "A study of Bible characters reveals that most of those who made history were men who failed at some point, and some of them drastically, but who refused to continue lying in the dust. Their very failure and repentance secured to them a more ample conception of the grace of God. They learned to know Him as the God of the second chance to His children who had failed Him—and the third chance, too."[5]

The Apostle Paul also understood how Christians battled wrong-doing every hour of every day. He admitted, "I do not understand what I do. For what I want to do I do not do, but what I hate I do. . . . I know that nothing good lives in me, that is, in my sinful nature. For I have the desire to do what is good, but I cannot carry it out" (Romans 7:15, 18).

Simon Peter certainly knew that the loving Father was the God of the second and third chance. In Scripture, Jesus predicted that His faithful follower, Simon Peter, would betray Him, and said directly to His devoted disciple, "Today—yes, tonight—before the rooster crows twice you yourself will disown me three times" (Mark 14:30).

Peter responded, insisting, "Even if I have to die with you, I will never disown you" (Mark 14:31).

After Jesus' arrest and before His crucifixion, Peter, fearing for his own life, sat by a fire in the courtyard of the high priest.

A girl asked Peter, "You are not one of His disciples, are you?" Peter answered, "I am not" (John 18:17).

Two others asked Peter the same question, and twice, with salty fisherman's oaths, the disciple denied even knowing Jesus.

When the rooster crowed, just as Jesus predicted, Peter remembered the Lord's words. He broke down and wept (Mark 14:72).

After His death and resurrection, Jesus appeared to Peter and several disciples early in the morning on the shores of Lake Galilee. The disciples, who had been fishing all night, recognized Him. Jesus cooked some of the fish they caught and invited them to breakfast with Him.

After they finished eating, Jesus focused His eyes on Simon Peter, asking him, "Simon son of John, do you truly love me more than these?"

"Yes, Lord," Peter responded. "You know that I love you."

Jesus told him, "Feed my lambs."

Again Jesus asked Peter, "Simon son of John, do you truly love me?"

And once again Peter answered, "Yes, Lord, you know that I love you."

"Take care of my sheep," Jesus said.

The third time Jesus asked Peter the same question, Peter felt frustrated, hurt. He responded, "Lord, you know all things; you know that I love you!"

"Feed my sheep, Peter," He said a third time. (See John 21:15–17.)

Jesus' forgiveness, thrice given to Peter for each time he betrayed Him, was redemptive, healing. Peter accepted Jesus' gift of forgiveness, allowing it to mend his broken and guilty heart.

Forgiveness had a profound effect upon Peter's life. It transformed him. Peter spent the rest of his days in active ministry, feeding Christ's sheep, going out enthusiastically into an evil world with the Good News of Jesus Christ, His love, His resurrection, and His redemption.

Does Forgiving Mean Forgetting?

Society believes another common myth about forgiveness. They read and misinterpret those Scriptures that seem to indicate that God is forgetful, that He develops a kind of Alzheimer's disease after He forgives. They believe the words *forgive* and *forget* are written in the Bible. They aren't. Without deep thought or spiritual guidance, they quote the Lord's words in Isaiah: "I, even I, am he who blots out your transgressions . . . and *remembers your sins no more*" (Isaiah 43:25, my emphasis).

The word *forget* means "to fail to remember," to "lose facts from the mind." From my years of biblical study, I know that He is incapable of failure, of *failing to remember*, of losing facts from His mind. We cannot place our anthropomorphic characteristics on God, believing that His mind is in any way like our human mind. God forgives, and He chooses *to remember our sins no more*. He decides that when He forgives us, He will no longer hold our wrongdoings against us—will no longer punish us for what He has pardoned. He has purposely, deliberately chosen to remove our transgressions from us "as far as the east is from the west" (Psalm 103:12), and to hurl "all our iniquities into the depths of the sea" (Micah 7:19).

I don't think it is humanly possible for me to forget that Dylann Roof murdered my wife. And neither do I want to forget it. I chose to forgive him. I chose to refuse to hold his actions against him. I chose to put behind me my desire to violently, eye for an eye and tooth for a tooth, avenge her murder. I chose not to dwell on that, replaying every grim detail over and over in my mind. I chose not to hate Dylann for hating the color of my skin, the only reason he destroyed nine beautiful lives and caused deep pain in the lives of hundreds, if not thousands.

But I certainly cannot forget what he has done, living the rest of my life pretending that the tragedy never happened by his hand.

God gives us the gift of memory for a good reason, a practical purpose. Memory makes us who we are, allowing us to live and function from day to day without having to relearn everything we do. Memory allows us to hold important information in our minds, to understand and avoid fearful encounters or situations, to build lasting relationships with others, and to learn important lessons that keep us alive and grow us in Christian maturity. Memory records our experiences, the things we have learned throughout long lives. It helps us to recognize with joy the face of a friend, and it helps us to recognize with warning the face of a foe. Memory of a past failure keeps us from repeating that failure again and again, and from falling prey to an offender's repeated pain and torture. Memory keeps us from trusting those we need to distrust, thus safeguarding our own lives and the lives of our loved ones.

We dare not forget what we suffer, for it is in our pain that we learn the great lessons we will never learn in frivolity and prosperity. Personal adversity gives us understanding and compassion for others who suffer pain and loss. We can empathize with them in their heartbreak because our hearts have also been broken in similar ways. When Robert Smith told me of his son's death by gunfire eight years ago, he became to me one who knew firsthand the trauma I experienced three years ago. He ministered to me as a wounded healer who could empathize with the depth of my own pain. We shared an insight into the sudden loss of a loved one, an understanding of the grief associated with a murder, and the hardships imposed upon a victim's family during long court trials when we had to hear repeated details of the death. I felt an immediate affinity with Dr. Robert Smith because we were joined together by suffering, we remembered the lessons we had learned, and we had experienced the grace of God when we both faced the unforgettable but spiritually illuminating teachings of sorrow.

We not only must remember our past pain individually, but collectively. In our own century, the world must never forget the rise to power of one man, Adolf Hitler, and the fifty million people who died because of him. Nor must we forget the Holocaust when specific persons—Jews, gypsies, the physically and mentally infirm, and many others—were put to death as part of a nation's racist agenda.

Holocaust survivor Simon Wiesenthal wrote, "There is no denying that Hitler and Stalin are alive today. . . . They are waiting for us to forget, because this is what makes possible the resurrection of these two monsters. Even before I had had time to really think things through, I realized we must not forget. If all of us forgot, the same thing might happen again, in 20 or 50 or 100 years."[6]

We must never forget how black South Africans suffered cruel injustices during the government-sponsored apartheid, when more than 3.5 million people were removed from their homes and plunged into poverty and hopelessness after the unjust separation of blacks and whites enforced by harsh laws.[7]

A survivor who personally suffered during South Africa's apartheid, and a Christian who later led the nation to forgive and heal,

Desmond Tutu wrote, "Forgiving is not forgetting. It's actually remembering—remembering and not using your right to hit back. It's a second chance for a new beginning. And the remembering part is particularly important. Especially if you don't want to repeat what happened."[8]

Tutu also believed that "without memory, there is no healing."[9]

Observing Remembrances

It is important that we, as human beings, observe together the anniversaries of tragedies and painful happenings that bring sorrow to the world's people. In great distress and sadness, Jesus and His disciples took their last supper together, eating bread and drinking wine in preparation for Jesus' upcoming death and resurrection.

"Do this in remembrance of me," He told them. (See Luke 22:7–30.)

Two thousand years later, believers in Christ, like the disciples who ate the last supper with Jesus, take the bread and drink the wine that represents His body and His blood, in remembrance of Him and the price our redemption cost Him.

The city of Charleston also holds special annual remembrances, commemorating the tragedy on the night of June 17, 2015, when a white supremacist gunned down African-American Christians praying together in the fellowship hall of the Emanuel AME Church. Each year we come together as a city to honor the beautiful lives snuffed out: Myra Thompson, Cynthia Hurd, Susie Jackson, Ethel Lance, DePayne Middleton Doctor, Tywanza Sanders, Sharonda Coleman-Singleton, Daniel Simmons, and Clementa Pinckney.

In June 2016, one year after the shooting, people traveled across the country to join Charleston as the city held a twelve-day observance, hosting a series of services, memorials, and remembrances of the victims, the survivors, members of the church, and people in the community. Hundreds attended the remembrance functions. As part of the observance, people were encouraged to perform acts of kindness—*Acts of Amazing Grace Day*—in an effort to counter the evil act committed by Dylann Roof.

"With thousands of acts of grace being performed around the world, we will surely make the world a better place," the church website proclaimed.

They remembered with sorrow the tragedy on that dark night, and at the same time they remembered it as an opportunity to respond to hate and violence with unexpected love and affection. The church was nominated for a Nobel Peace Prize. The city chiseled the names of the dead on schools and libraries. Artists honored the victims in portraits and murals. All the city churches tolled their bells nine times, once for each victim, and encouraged their members to "let all that you do be done in love."

I was asked to lead the Wednesday evening Bible study at Emanuel in June 2016. I taught from Mark 4, the parable of the sower, using Myra's own blood-splattered notes she labored so diligently to write when she taught it the year before. More than two hundred people attended, meeting in the church sanctuary instead of the basement fellowship hall where the shooting happened. No cameras were allowed inside the sanctuary. In prayer, the congregation lifted up Dylann Roof's name, calling upon God's mercy for him as he awaited two death penalty trials in the coming months. We also prayed for his family members.

In June 2017, on the second anniversary of the shooting, Charleston and other cities around the world held commemorative programs and events. The remembrance, given the name The Light of Hope, gave people of all ages the opportunity to engage in meaningful dialogue about unity among the races; participate in the Hate Won't Win Unity Walk; hold ecumenical worship services; provide free books for children, a gift from the Cynthia Graham Hurd Foundation; distribute school supplies for students in grades K–12, sponsored by the Myra Thompson School Supply Distribution; hold events for middle school students with opportunities to participate in workshops and forums on topics such as diversity, tolerance, respect, and inclusion; arrange a Senior Citizens

Luncheon; give concerts; and host exhibits, all in honor of the slain Emanuel Nine and the five survivors. I was again asked to lead Emanuel's Wednesday evening Bible study, this time co-teaching with Emanuel's new pastor, the Reverend Eric S. C. Manning.

"We just wish and hope that we can continue to have forums concerning racism and hate, continue to reach over different denominations and different races to know each other before we come to a conclusion of who we are and who we are not," I told my listeners. "We just hope and pray this will continue—not just now, but forever."

How essential remembrances are to human beings, to cities, to countries, and to the world! Remembering honors the victims and survivors; it brings people together in prayer and dialogue, and leads to positive change. Charleston Mayor John Tecklenburg closed the second anniversary remembrance with these words: "It is the remembrance. It is the prayers. It is the celebration, in a way, of love, but it's also a commitment to positive change in our community in their honor and in the reflection of that key [tenet] that love will conquer hate."[10]

The third anniversary remembrance, in the summer of 2018, coincided with the two-hundredth anniversary of the Emanuel AME Church. Especially remembered were the church's "tumultuous beginning—and the many intervening years with their triumphs and traumas."[11]

"We could not help but celebrate this bicentennial of the founding of this church with glory and praise," Rev. Manning stated. "We have persisted in the face of racial hostility, survived the [dismantling] of the church . . . in 1822; its destruction in an earthquake in 1886; and the horrific murders of nine members of the congregation on June 17, 2015."[12]

The program for this third year's remembrance included partnering with other city churches to provide opportunities for citizens to engage in meaningful dialogue about unity among all races.

"We want to be the place where others may engage in dialogue about achieving racial reconciliation once and for all," Manning stated. He called the Emanuel Nine "faithful martyrs who fell victim to racism and hatred, who are now living in eternal victory."[13]

At a special morning service, plans for the building of the Emanuel Nine Memorial were unveiled. The memorial will be dedicated to reversing the spread of hate with a message of unyielding love and forgiveness. The architects who designed New York's 9/11 Memorial, Michael Arad and Peter Walker, have been chosen to create the Emanuel Nine Memorial, a white stone structure with two long, smooth, high-backed benches that "arc up and around, like sheltering wings . . ." providing a "sense of enclosure, and like a pair of arms, [cradling] visitors inside this space."[14]

The memorial will also feature a gentle fountain inscribed with the names of the victims, and a garden space open to everyone and "dedicated to life and resiliency."[15]

"The design reminds me of so many different things," William Dudley Gregorie, a member of the Charleston City Council and Mother Emanuel, stated. "It reminds me sometimes of a ship for enslaved people who were going to freedom. Sometimes it reminds me of the wings of angels. Sometimes it reminds me just of the arms of God."[16]

Surely, with each passing year, as the Emanuel Nine Memorial welcomes visitors from around the world and we pause together for our annual remembrance, our church and our city will take one more step forward on the path to healing and peace. I am hopeful, not thinking so much about the tragedy anymore, but about where we are going from here.

I pray with many others that we will continue to remember together what happened at Emanuel AME Church on June 17, 2015, allowing each anniversary of the tragedy to shine a bright light in Charleston and throughout the nation, never forgetting what the Word of God can do in our lives and in our city, forever changing our attitudes and changing our hearts, helping us to become who God wants us to be, and helping us to do what God wants us to do.

Epilogue

My Letter to Dylann

To: *Dylann Storm Roof*
c/o The United States Penitentiary, Terre Haute
Terre Haute, Indiana
September 2018

Dear Dylann,
　More than three years have passed since you killed my beautiful
wife, Myra Thompson. As I am now emotionally ready to write
you a personal letter, I pray you will read each word, seriously
pondering their life-giving message.
　On Wednesday evening, June 17, 2015, at the Emanuel AME
Church in Charleston, you shot eight bullets into my wife's body.
She died in a pool of her own blood on the fellowship hall floor.
You destroyed Myra and eight of her friends as they prayed together. They were all strangers to you. You killed them simply
because you hated African-Americans. You've indicated no other
reason for the cold-blooded murders except that you despised the
color of their skin.
　I wish you had been able to see past their skin pigment and deep
into their tender hearts. Each one loved the Lord, served Him with

his or her whole life and, in individual and unique ways, reached out to actively minister in Christ's name to hurting people. By orchestrating their untimely deaths, you robbed the world's needy sheep of nine loving shepherds.

But I have forgiven you, Dylann. I have painfully missed Myra every hour of every day for the past three years. She was my best friend, my life companion, and my fellow minister. I loved her beyond words. You deliberately took her away from me, away from her family and friends, and away from those who so desperately needed her future Christ-centered ministry.

Do you remember, Dylann, when I expressed my forgiveness to you at the Bond Hearing only two days after my wife's death? Her blood still fresh on the fellowship hall floor, I sat in the courtroom that day deeply grieving her loss, feeling completely numb inside, my mind still struggling to absorb the crushing shock of her murder.

I didn't want to go to the Bond Hearing on that Friday. But God had different plans, leading me to stand up in court and publicly forgive you. Those were God's words I spoke to you that day, the message He whispered to my heart.

Do you remember what I told you? "I forgive you. And my family forgives you. But we would like you to take this opportunity to repent. Repent. Confess. Give your life to the One who matters the most: Jesus Christ, so that He can change it and change your attitude. And no matter what happens to you, then you'll be okay. Do that and you'll be better off than you are right now."

I said those words, and I meant them as I watched you on the video monitor, noting especially your downcast eyes, fixed and focused on the floor. Yet, at the moment I mentioned the Lord's name, Jesus Christ, you raised your eyes to the camera for a split second, just long enough for me to peer deep into your soul. It startled me to detect the mammoth amount of guilt and shame in such young eyes. I saw pure hate, hate for yourself and hate for others, the type of diabolical enmity that comes into a person's life by invitation only. Dylann, you've invited Evil to enter into

your soul, allowing it to take up permanent residence there, giving it permission to control your thoughts, dictate your actions,
and determine your future. In doing so, you have destroyed your
own life as well as the lives of many others. How I wish you had
opened up your life instead to God's abundant love for you, begging his forgiveness, rejoicing in His redemption and, in His name,
ministering to others, not murdering them. The deep passion with
which you hated could have instead been the passion with which
you deeply loved.

In my work in South Carolina's Probation-Parole, I've met
other young men like you. They too were lost, consumed by self-
contempt, loathing all those who were different from them. Some
woke up to God's Word, God's love, and made a life worth living.
Others gave Malice and Evil free reign, allowing the nefarious
twins to seduce their minds with vile ideology, and maneuvering
them to live wicked, wasted lives.

Dylann, as you look back over your life, the way you've lived it,
and as you envision your ill-fated future, condemned to execution,
are you pleased with what you see, the legacy you will leave? Where
are your white supremacist brothers now? They aren't cheering
you on. They have forgotten you, moving on to spread their doc-
trine of hate. And now, you sit in prison, reaping what you have
sown—seeds of death and destruction.

Some of us have forgiven you, wiped clean the scribbled slate
of your horrific sins, purposely extinguishing our burning human
desire for revenge. Others, however, have not. They hold in their
hearts a heavy burden, one that might forever weigh them down,
coloring every word they say and influencing every action they
take. Without divine intervention, hate and violence always breed
more hate and violence, and the cycle continues until it becomes
a way of life and death.

My wife studied long and hard for the Bible Study she taught
you on that Wednesday night at Mother Emanuel. She wanted to
make sure her listeners understood clearly the meaning of Jesus'
parable of the sower. You sat quietly in the chair beside Pastor

Pinckney as Myra so carefully, thoroughly described God's Word to you, comparing it to healthy seeds ready to plant, sprout, grow, and thrive. Seeds that would one day produce a bountiful harvest that would feed and nourish a starving world. She explained to you the type of good soil needed to produce a generous, healthy harvest, and she warned you about scattering good seed on hard, stony, or thorny ground. Were you listening? Did you have ears to hear God's Word and God's warning as He spoke through Myra's heart and lips?

The hard, stony, and thorny ground represents the state of your heart, Dylann, a heart shut tight, impenetrable, refusing to hear God's Word, spurning God's offered gift of love and redemption. The clock is ticking, and before it is too late will you please listen to God's plea, accepting the invitation Jesus so generously extends to you? Will you consider making an about face to be forgiven? Otherwise, I'm afraid you'll spend all eternity regretting it.

You should know, Dylann, you have deeply hurt my family and me. You made the deadly decision to kill, you loaded the gun, and you fired the seventy-seven shots. How could you murder the Bible Study members after they had so warmly welcomed you into their intimate fold, handing you a Bible, the Parable of the Sower passage marked for you? What were your thoughts as you held God's living Word in your hands, the same hands that only minutes later brought bloodshed and death?

I blame you, Dylann, and only you for killing my wife in such a heinous, despicable way. My forgiveness in no way dismisses your premeditated actions. Nor does it excuse or condone your deliberate crime. I blame you therefore I can choose to forgive you.

I must admit that when I forgave you, I didn't feel very forgiving. I felt numb, my grief raw, and my body and soul racked with pain and sorrow. But fortunately the way I felt had nothing to do with my decision to pardon you. I based my forgiveness on God's unchanging Word, not on my ever-changing human emotions. Forgiving you proved a choice my will made quickly, as I sought to obey God's Word. But do not believe that the decision *came simply or easily. I deeply loved my wife, and I miss her still. I chose to forgive you, Dylann, but I dare not ever forget the tragedy you planned and carried out. Surely, without memory, there is no healing.*

You might have tried to make it easier for me to forgive you had you shown a sense of regret and remorse for killing Myra. I yearned to hear an apology from your lips, and to see a pang of conscience, lament, or sorrow for what you did. But I did not hear or see even a hint of contrition. Instead, you stated arrogantly and with venom: "I would like to make it crystal clear I do not regret what I did. I am not sorry. I have not shed a tear for the innocent people I killed." Your later closing court statement on January 10, 2017, echoed the same sentiment: "I felt like I had to do it. I still feel like I had to do it."

Surely, your lack of remorse and your eagerness to kill black people again if given the opportunity, made it difficult for me to understand you, but not difficult to forgive you. My heart hurt when you said those tragic words. But my forgiveness was complete, requiring no apology from you, no words of remorse, no explanation, and no acceptance. Even with no response from you, my forgiveness was finalized, even though one-sided. My choice to write off the great debt you owed me, to lift the burden of responsibility for Myra's death from your shoulders, has been accomplished. I will never take it back. My forgiveness is complete, done, and finished.

Dylann, as you spend your final days of life isolated in prison, I doubt that you've heard what resulted from your massacre. You admitted to killing the "Emanuel Nine" because you wanted to start a war between our nation's black and white races. You chose the city of Charleston, South Carolina, the "cradle of slavery," and the Emanuel AME Church, where black people worship God, because you thought the murders in those places might have had the greatest impact, causing racial riots, arrests, deaths, and eventually escalating to war. But how ironic it is that the monstrous actions you brought about in order to advance hatred and evil have instead brought unexpected and unusual acts of love, kindness, and compassion. Stories of peace, brotherhood, and harmony have been highlighted in national and international newspapers, in social media, and on the Internet. Magazine editors and television producers have proclaimed the Gospel's power loud and clear to a watching world. The topic of Biblical forgiveness is still on the tip of the nation's tongue, as more and more people seek to understand the kind of forgiveness that can pardon a killer who preys on praying church people.

Others changes have happened too, Dylann, in Charleston, in South Carolina, and in the nation.

The Confederate flag no longer flies above Columbia, South Carolina, your birthplace. The outdated relic of slavery and hate that you have long admired, now gathers dust in a museum.

The hearts of our nation were strangely warmed when thousands of black and white hands joined together across Charleston's Ravenel Bridge, making a strong public statement against the evils of white supremacy and racism.

A bevy of sweet-smelling flowers and acts of loving compassion have overwhelmed our city, expelling forever the caustic stench of racial hate.

The entire city has erupted in grace, money pouring in from around the world to cover the victims' funeral expenses, thousands gathering each year to remember the slain believers and to perform acts of kindness in their honor.

Monuments and memory gardens have been planned and created, a United States president publicly sang the hymn Amazing Grace *in Charleston, and people are asking deep theological questions trying to better understand God's love and forgiveness.*

And on the one hundred fifty third anniversary of our nation's end of slavery, the city of Charleston officially apologized for its role in regulating, supporting, and fostering slavery, recognizing with appreciation the free labor, technical expertise, and craftsmanship of enslaved black people.

As Charleston's Mayor Riley *witnessed firsthand the remark-able results of Biblical forgiveness, he stated: "A hateful person came to this community with some crazy idea he'd be able to divide. But all he did was unite us and make us love each other even more."*

So you see, Dylann, what you *meant for evil, destruction, and the ignition of a race war,* God *used to bring good to Charleston, the nation, and the world. And if you ask God to forgive you, He can take the evil you are harboring and bring good in your life. He can do that because nothing is impossible for the Lord.*

In closing this lengthy letter, let me tell you why I forgave you, Dylann. I want you to understand the reason for my deliberate decision. I forgave you because I am a believer in Christ, having repented of my sins and having been forgiven by my heavenly Father. Scripture states: ". . . all have sinned and fall short of the glory of God. . . ." That includes you and me and all humankind. Since I, myself, have been forgiven, I am obliged by God's Word to forgive you, the one who has so deeply hurt me. I can truthfully pray Jesus' prayer without pausing at the part that asks: "Forgive [me] my debts, as I also have forgiven [my] debtors" (Matthew 6:12). Scripture states clearly that if I fail to forgive you for Myra's murder, my heavenly Father will refuse to forgive me for my own sins (Matthew 6:14–15).

I forgave you, Dylann, because God called me to forgive you. My pardon also benefits me, for if I had refused to forgive you, the sin of unforgiveness forever would imprison me in my own self-made cell, forfeiting my good health, my ministry, and my future hope. By offering you my unconditional *forgiveness, I sev-ered any control you might have had on my life. Forgiveness has opened wide my own prison doors and allowed me freedom. It has provided healing for my soul, allowing me to move forward with my life, honoring my call from God to the ministry of seed sowing. My forgiveness may not affect you in any way, but it has been life-changing for me, allowing God's peace to flood my heart.*

Christ also implores me to love you, and to be merciful to you, and to do good to you even though you hate my black skin, curse my race, and take away my wife (Luke 6:27, 36). The "good" I now do for you comes within the words of this letter, though difficult and painful to write. For as I pen these words, I must journey back, facing again and remembering with much pain the tragedy that broke my heart. I reach out to you, speaking of God's Word and God's limitless love, the hope—the only hope to redeem your soul and to save it from eternal damnation.

Scripture promises us ". . . if anyone is in Christ, he is a new creation; the old has gone, the new has come! All this is from God, who reconciled us to Himself through Christ . . ." (2 Corinthians 5:17–18). You, too, can become a new creation, forgiven and redeemed. It's God's gift to you and to me.

Dylann, I am praying for you. I often think of you sitting in that small prison cell with only a sink, toilet, and bed. Sequestered in isolation, you must feel very much alone and forgotten. But I want you to know that you aren't alone within those four narrow, drab walls. Nor are you forgotten. God sits right beside you. He is always with you, Dylann, as David, the psalmist, discovered years ago when he wrote: "Where can I go from your Spirit? Where can I flee from your presence? If I go up to the heavens, you are there; if I make my bed in the depths, you are there. If I rise on the wings of the dawn, if I settle on the far side of the sea, even there your hand will guide me, your right hand will hold me fast" (Psalm 139:7–10). Even in your darkest most lonely hours, He is there, calling to you with His generous offer of love and salvation, yearning to adopt you within His own family.

Do you hear His voice, even now telling you: "I am the way and the truth and the life. No one comes to the Father except through me" (John 14:6).

Do you hear His voice, even now assuring you: "Trust in God; trust also in me. In my Father's house are many rooms . . . I am going there to prepare a place for you" (John 14:1–2).

Jesus waits for you to accept His amazing grace, and to know His peace—the peace that passes all human understanding.

The late Billy Graham writes: "None of us deserves God's forgiveness . . . we all have sinned . . . but the good news is this: God loves us, and Christ came into the world to save us. When we repent of our sins and receive Him into our hearts, God has promised to forgive us—completely and fully."

Dylann, I have recently written to your grandfather asking him to meet with me that we might talk together. I am also in the process of trying to arrange a visit with you at the prison in Terre Haute so that I might tell you in person of God's love and redemption. I pray you will accept my invitation and meet with me. I don't know at this point that either meeting will actually happen, but I won't give up trying to arrange them until every door slams shut.

Love always conquers hate, Dylann. Before it is too late, please choose love. It is my sincere hope, Dylann, that you will repent of your sins and give your heart and life to Christ, the One who loves you, the Savior who yearns to forgive you, the heavenly Father who can give you the gift of eternal life and an eternal home with Him. For one day in the distant future, I hope that you and I and Myra can stand together in the presence of Almighty God, His Word deeply sown in the good soil of our hearts, growing, thriving, and producing fruit that will last throughout eternity.

Sincerely yours,
Anthony Thompson

Bible Study Questions

Chapter 1: The Unthinkable Tragedy

1. Read chapter 1 and reflect upon these questions: "Must Christians be expected to forgive an extremely *heinous* crime? Are some crimes so horrific and evil that no forgiveness is required?" Record your reflections.

2. Have you ever experienced a tragedy similar to Anthony Thompson's? If so, describe. What was your immediate reaction? Did you choose to forgive the offender? Why or why not? What was the result of your forgiveness or unforgiveness?

3. What makes Dylann Roof's crimes almost impossible for society, and even some Christians, to forgive?

4. Read and contemplate the following Scripture verses on forgiveness and record your thoughts on the meaning of each:

   - "It is mine to avenge; I will repay" (Deuteronomy 32:35).
   - "Forgive us our debts, as we also have forgiven our debtors" (Matthew 6:12).

- "For if you forgive men when they sin against you, your heavenly Father will also forgive you. But if you do not forgive men their sins, your Father will not forgive your sins" (Matthew 6:14–15).

- "Love your enemies, do good to those who hate you, bless those who curse you, pray for those who mistreat you . . . Be merciful, just as your Father is merciful" (Luke 6:27, 36).

- "Bear with each other and forgive *whatever grievances* you may have against one another. Forgive as the Lord forgave you" (Colossians 3:13, emphasis added).

5. React to Anthony Thompson's statement: "As a Christian, a devoted follower of Jesus Christ, I choose to obey God's Word, and that means I make the decision to forgive the evil man who so wickedly and deliberately takes away my lovely wife." Do you agree? Why or why not?

6. Examine Anthony Thompson's question, "Can I, in the darkest remote closets of my all-too-human heart, forgive Dylann Storm Roof for the cold-blooded murder of my beloved companion?" Have you ever felt this way? Record your thoughts.

7. In your opinion, why did the bereaved Amish parents view their forgiveness of Charles Roberts as "the one good thing that can come out of this tragedy"?

8. Reflect on Corrie ten Boom's statement about forgiveness: "For I had to do it—I knew that. The message that God forgives has a prior condition: that we forgive those who have injured us. 'If you do not forgive men their trespasses,' Jesus says, 'neither will your Father in heaven forgive your trespasses.'"

9. Corrie learned that "forgiveness is not an emotion . . . forgiveness is an act of the will, and the will can function regardless of the temperature of the heart." Do you agree or disagree with the statement? Please explain.

10. Read Luke's account of Jesus' crucifixion and death in Luke 23:26–43. For what crimes did Jesus receive punishment and a death sentence? (See Luke 23:1–5.)

11. Reflect on parts of Jesus' life as recorded in the following Scriptures. Describe the event and record/discuss your thoughts.

    - Healing the sick: Matthew 4:23–25; 8:1–4; 8:14–17; 9:18–34; Mark 7:31–37; John 5:1–15
    - Feeding the hungry: Matthew 14:13–21; Mark 8:1–13
    - Casting out demons: Matthew 17:14–18; Mark 5:1–20
    - Restoring life to the deceased: Luke 7:11–17; John 11:38–44

12. How did Jesus, in His dying moments, express His forgiveness for those who so cruelly executed Him? (See Luke 23:34.) In your opinion, did the Roman soldiers who crucified Jesus receive His forgiveness? If so, how do you think Jesus' verbal forgiveness might have impacted their lives?

13. Reflect on this statement: "Jesus suffered a horrific crucifixion, and yet before He died, He forgave those who would torture and kill him. As Jesus is my Lord, Savior, and example to follow, I can do no less than to forgive the young white racist, Dylann Roof, for the heinous death of my dear wife, Myra."

14. In Isaiah 53:4–6, the prophet describes the suffering and pain Jesus willingly experienced so that we could be forgiven of our sins. In verse 5, Isaiah points out that because of Jesus' act of forgiveness, "by his wounds we are healed." What are we healed of? Who are the ones healed: us or the ones who offended us? Why?

15. Why is "the man-made catastrophe at Emanuel . . . among the most sorrowful and powerful stories in recent memory"? Please record/share your thoughts.

For Deeper Understanding

1. Read more about the life and work of Corrie ten Boom in her autobiography *The Hiding Place*.

2. Study Jesus' Parable of the Sower from Mark 4 and respond to these questions:

   - Verses 3–4: Why did Jesus use the farmer sowing seed as text for the story? What does the "seed" represent?
   - What did Jesus teach when He said that "some [seed] fell along the path, and the birds came and ate it up"? To what was He referring?
   - Verses 5–6: What did Jesus mean when He said some seed fell on rocky places, and it sprang up quickly because the soil was shallow? What happened to the seedlings when the sun came up? To what is He referring?
   - Verse 7: What does Jesus say about seeds planted among thorns? What happened to the plants? Why?
   - Verse 8: What does Jesus say about the seed that fell on good soil? To what is He referring?
   - Verses 10–20: Ponder the reason Jesus taught using parables. How did Jesus explain the Parable of the Sower to His disciples?

3. Read about the crucifixion and suffering of Jesus from a medical point of view at https://www1.cbn.com/medical-view-of-the-crucifixion-of-jesus-christ. What did you learn?

Your Notes

Chapter 2: The Aftermath

1. Must Anthony Thompson understand why Roof committed this crime in order to forgive him? Why or why not?

2. Contemplate Thompson's statement: "I must admit that I do not, in any way, understand the depth of darkness that must dwell so deeply in the young mind and heart of Dylann Storm Roof. It baffles me, completely eluding my most basic human understanding how and why Roof can plan such a deadly assault on Emanuel's members, people he does not know, but people he hates only because of their skin pigment." Record your thoughts.

3. What reasons did people give for Devin Patrick Kelley's shooting spree at First Baptist Church in Sutherland Springs, Texas?

4. In your opinion, why did Kelley kill the church members indiscriminately as they worshiped God?

5. Think about Pastor Pomeroy's statement in his message on forgiveness one week after the shooting: "We have the freedom to proclaim Christ. Folks, we have the freedom to choose, and rather than choose darkness as one young man did that day, I say we choose life." Record your thoughts.

6. Reflect on these four questions:

   - Are Christians required by God to forgive a mass shooter who kills their loved ones when they don't understand the reasons for the murder?

   - In order to forgive, does a believer deserve an acceptable motive for such a heinous act?

   - Can one truly and completely forgive what one doesn't understand, what one might never understand?

   - Does forgiveness come at different levels depending on the crime and the rationale behind the crime?

7. Express your opinion about the statement made by a Midwestern pastor: "Genocides and mass shootings are in a category all to themselves . . . but those who suffered loss because of these terrible crimes can extend the lowest level of forgiveness by simply not seeking vengeance and doing their best to cope with the loss and pain that will never go away." Do you agree or disagree? Why?

8. What is your opinion on the following:

   - Is "not seeking vengeance" and "doing their best to cope with the loss and pain" a form of genuine forgiveness? Is it enough? Why or why not?
   - Can partial forgiveness suffice as true biblical forgiveness? Explain.
   - Can partial forgiveness bring healing to the victim's loved one, removing the hatred and bitterness deeply rooted in the natural human heart and mind? Please explain.

9. Reflect on this analogy: "In its need to be total and complete, how is forgiveness like salvation in Christ?"

10. Explain what the Apostle Paul means in this Scripture verse: "Therefore, if anyone is in Christ, he is a new creation; the old has gone, the new has come! All this is from God, who reconciled us to himself through Christ" (2 Corinthians 5:17–18).

11. Explain the meaning of *reconciliation* as used here in Scripture: "All this is from God, who *reconciled us* to himself through Christ."

12. Express why you agree or disagree with this statement: "When we choose to forgive someone who has hurt us deeply, we cannot grasp how God can cleanse our hearts and minds of the desire to avenge, help us to completely cancel the debt owed to us, and even one day be able to pray and show compassionate love for the offender. But we

don't have to figure out the mystery of forgiveness in order to choose to forgive."

13. Pastor Frank Pomeroy, a heartbroken father and pastor, still reeling from the murder of his daughter and his church members, admitted to his congregation a week after the shooting that he couldn't understand why Kelley killed so many worshipers in his tiny church. But he goes on to explain the forgiveness enigma: "You lean in to what you don't understand, you lean in to the Lord. I don't understand, but I know my God does." What is your opinion of his statement?

14. What did the writer of Proverbs mean by his advice in Proverbs 3:5–6, "Trust in the Lord with all your heart and lean not on your own understanding; in all your ways acknowledge Him"?

15. Reflect on this statement: "Some people believe that if they forgive the offender, they are dismissing or condoning or excusing their crime. They fear it might appear as if they are shrugging off, overlooking, or even justifying a loved one's senseless murder at the hands of another."

16. Explain why you agree or disagree with this statement: Biblical forgiveness only applies to intentional, deliberate, and purposeful acts.

17. What is your opinion about this statement? "As believers in Christ, we have the ability to *choose* to forgive those who hurt us. And when we choose to forgive them completely, God produces the results, opening our prison door, and allowing us to walk out free and unhindered by hate and bitterness."

For Deeper Understanding

1. Ponder and record your thoughts on these powerful quotes:

- "As long as you live on earth, you won't see the end of injustices. Yet God desires for you to let go of injustices and hold on to His grace. Only He can give you the power to forgive those who have hurt you the deepest."[1]
- "To be a Christian means to forgive the inexcusable because God has forgiven the inexcusable in you."[2]
- "And you know, when you've experienced grace and you feel like you've been forgiven, you're a lot more forgiving of other people. You're a lot more gracious to others."[3]

2. Listen to Polly Sheppard's 9-1-1 call recording to better understand the terror of the shooting at Emanuel: https://www.wyff4.com/article/911-call-audio-from-inside-mother-emanuel-ame-church/8501434. (Warning: It contains graphic and disturbing content.) Record your thoughts.

Your Notes

Chapter 3: Dylann Storm Roof: A Homegrown American Terrorist

1. Dylann writes in his journal while waiting in jail: "I did what I thought would make the biggest wave, and now the fate of our race is in the hands of my brothers who continue to live freely. . . . I would rather live in prison knowing I took action for my race than live with the torture of sitting idle." Do you sense he feels any regret, remorse, or sorrow?

2. Record your reactions to Dylann's words about the crime: "I would like to make it crystal clear I do not regret what I did. I am not sorry. I have not shed a tear for the innocent people I killed."

3. People often ask Anthony Thompson, "How can you forgive Roof when he has not apologized for Myra's murder, and shows no pangs of conscience or contrition, lament or sorrow, no guilt or shame?" Do you understand why people might ask this question?

4. Do you agree with Anthony Thompson's statement, "Even premeditated murder can be forgiven. I'm not saying it's easy to forgive a person who has murdered your loved one, but murder is a sin just like any other sin. And, according to Scripture, a sin is a sin, and we are all guilty of sin"? Why or why not?

5. What does Romans 3:23, "For all have sinned and fall short of the glory of God," mean to you?

6. Ponder and react to this statement: "I believe we can be so quick to pass judgment when we catch people committing sin that we act as if *we* never sin. How can a sinner pass judgment on a sinner?! It isn't our role to judge others, but God's. Our job is to forgive."

7. Read Jesus' words in Luke 6:37 and reflect upon their meaning: "Do not judge, and you will not be judged. Do not condemn, and you will not be condemned. Forgive, and you will be forgiven."

8. Read the story of the adulterous woman in John 8:1–11. Why did the people drop their stones and turn away?

9. In your opinion, why did "the older ones" turn away first?

10. What did Jesus' words to the woman mean: "Woman, where are they? Has no one condemned you? . . . Then neither do I condemn you. Go now and leave your life of sin" (John 8:10–11)?

11. Read Stephen's story in Acts 6 and 7 and reflect on these questions:

    - Why was Stephen called "a man full of God's grace and power"?
    - Why was Stephen seized and taken to the high priest? What was his "crime"?
    - What is Stephen's prayer for his murderers (Acts 7:59–60)?
    - Why is Stephen's story such a powerful example of complete forgiveness?

12. Reflect on this statement: "I have long understood that biblical forgiveness does not rest on an offender's regret, remorse, or apology. I chose to forgive Dylann Roof with or without any response from him. I did not need an 'I'm sorry' in order to forgive him."

13. Have you ever been called by God to forgive someone who has hurt you or someone you love? If so, did the offender offer you an apology? Did you forgive without an apology? What led you to forgive?

14. Can you understand why Rwandan genocide survivor Immaculee Ilibagiza at first wished for weapons to avenge her loved ones' murders? "[I] wished for weapons—for guns and cannons to kill the Hutus—because I wanted vengeance so badly."

15. Read Jesus' prayer in Matthew 6:9–13. Why did Immaculee find it impossible to pray these words: "Forgive us our debts, as we also have forgiven our debtors" (Matthew 6:12)? Have these words ever been difficult for you to pray?

16. What changed Immaculee's heart and encouraged her to respond with forgiveness?

17. Read 1 John 1:8, 10: "If we claim to be without sin, we deceive ourselves and the truth is not in us. . . . If we claim we have not sinned, we make him out to be a liar and his word has no place in our lives." What do these verses mean to you?

18. Read 1 John 1:9: "If we confess our sins, he is faithful and just and will forgive us our sins and purify us from all unrighteousness." Please reflect on what this verse means to you?

For Deeper Understanding

1. Read Immaculee Ilibagiza's book, *Left to Tell: Discovering God Amidst the Rwandan Holocaust* (NYC: Hay House, Inc., 2006/2014), and record your thoughts about Immaculee's forgiveness.

2. Find out more about the Rwandan Holocaust at these websites and record your thoughts: Rwandan Genocide: https://www.history.com/topics/rwandan-genocide; United States Holocaust Memorial Museum: https://www.ushmm.org/confront-genocide/cases/rwanda; BBC News: http://www.bbc.com/news/world-africa-26875506.

3. Read Psalm 51:17, Scripture describing the heart of sin and regret: "My sacrifice, O God, is a broken spirit; a broken and contrite heart you, God, will not despise." Please respond in writing.

4. Write your own definitions of the three words:

   - **Repentance** is the action of repenting; expressing sincere regret or remorse.
   - **Remorse** is deep regret or guilt for a wrong committed.
   - An **apology** is a regretful acknowledgment of an offense or wrongdoing; expressing a genuine "I'm sorry" for a hurtful action.

Your Notes

Chapter 4: The Decision

1. Contemplate this statement: "Murder may be the hardest kind of death to process, and the emotional response is much more complicated because this unfathomable grief is coupled with anger." Do you agree or disagree? Why?

2. Describe the freedom Anthony Thompson felt in the courtroom when he decided to forgive Dylann Roof.

3. Ponder and respond to this statement: "Even atheists had to see divinity in these families built by love. God was there in that courtroom if He has ever been anywhere."

4. Think about and respond to President Obama's words: "Any death of this sort is a tragedy. There is something particularly heartbreaking about the death happening in a place in which we seek solace and we seek peace, in a place of worship."

5. Do you agree or disagree with one critic's statement that the "oversimplification of *I forgive* demonstrates a lack of understanding of the significance of the incident"? Explain.

6. Do you believe that "forgiveness alone can halt the cycle of blame and pain, breaking the chain of un-grace"? Why or why not?

7. Why does Anthony Thompson believe unforgiveness would "lock him forever into victimhood," and make him "a damaged slave to the evil deed of a depraved killer"?

8. What does author Lewis Smedes mean by the following statement? "Forgiving is a journey, sometimes a long one, and we may need some time before we get to the station of complete healing, but the nice thing is that we are being healed en route. When we genuinely forgive, we set a prisoner free and then discover that the prisoner we set free was us."

9. Anthony Thompson admits he didn't remember "feeling very forgiving" when he decided to forgive Roof. Do you believe a Christian must "feel forgiving" when he or she chooses to forgive another person? Why or why not?

10. When Peter asks Jesus how many times he must forgive sinful people who hurt him, how does Jesus respond? Why is the number seventy-seven so significant in the Emanuel Church shooting?

11. Contemplate the *Time* magazine reporter's statement about Thompson's courtroom call to Roof to seek God's mercy and forgiveness: "Thompson was calling on the killer to turn himself inside out, to inventory everything wrong about his thoughts and actions—the murders, of course, but also the willful ignorance and cultivated hatred that apparently fueled him, and the vanity that would make him think he was an instrument of history, and the hard-heartedness that made it possible for him to sit with his victims and know their humanity before he ever drew his gun. A true confession of his offenses would entail a wrenching calculation of the measureless grief and suffering his crimes caused in the lives of those who survived. It would comprehend the theft he committed of nine lives, and all the promise and love that lay in store for his victims. All stolen. And it would face up, as well, to the wastage of his own life and possibilities." Please put your thoughts into writing.

12. Do you believe that "forgiveness is a kind of purifier that absorbs injury and returns love"? Why or why not?

13. Jesus commands believers to "love your enemies, do good to those who hate you, bless those who curse you, pray for those who mistreat you" (Luke 6:27–28). Do you think Jesus' command can actually be accomplished?

14. Ponder this Scripture: "A man reaps what he sows. The one who sows to please his sinful nature, from that nature

will reap destruction" (Galatians 6:7–8). Do you agree? Why or why not?

For Deeper Understanding

1. Read Lewis B. Smedes's books on forgiveness, including *Forgive and Forget: Healing the Hurts We Don't Deserve* (2007); *The Art of Forgiving* (1997); and *Shame and Grace: Healing the Shame We Don't Deserve* (2009). What did you learn from these books?

2. Read Philip Yancey's book *What's So Amazing About Grace?* (1997). What did you learn about grace?

3. *Hope* might be defined as a wish or desire to believe that something good may happen. Biblical *hope*, however, is the certain expectation of God's promises based on His faithfulness. What is your personal definition of *hope*?

Your Notes

Chapter 5: A Mighty Long Journey

1. Define a "hate crime." In your opinion, how is it different from a general crime, and why?

2. After reading about Dylann Roof's crime, do you agree with the statement made by Assistant U.S. Attorney Nathan Williams, "You can see what kind of hatred he had. A vast hatred that was cold and calculated"? Why or why not? What is your definition of "hatred"?

3. Why is Emanuel AME Church called "a beacon and a bearer of the culture"? Research and describe its history and what the church means to African-Americans.

4. Evaluate this statement by Sarah Collins Rudolph, who lost a sister and an eye in the bombing of the Sixteenth Street Baptist Church in Birmingham, Alabama, in September 1963: "Being bitter won't bring the girls back, won't bring my sight back. So I had to forgive because it was what God wanted me to do."

5. Ponder and give your opinion about this statement: "Does biblical forgiveness require 'forgiving the debt' when the vicious crime is complicated by centuries of deep racial hate, violence, and cruel injustices? Does our heavenly Father really expect us to forgive such horrifying *hate crimes?*"

6. Contemplate the following statement: "How can someone possibly forgive somebody who would kill or maim in the name of white supremacy?" Do you believe "those are the people who are *irredeemable*"?

7. Why are hate crimes often huge obstacles to forgiveness?

8. Do you believe that the African-Americans' forgiveness of white racist crime is simply a way to eliminate anger from the black Christian's heart? Why or why not?

9. Anthony Thompson states he feels no anger toward Dylann Roof: "If I allow myself to feel intense anger, the

fiery rage inside me will complicate my decision to forgive Dylann, making me want to do something drastic about the murder, to seek revenge. If I focus on anger, the fury in my heart and mind will cloud my judgment about biblical forgiveness." Pen your thoughts.

10. Think about the difference between *cultural* and *biblical* forgiveness. Do you consider forgiveness a way for African-Americans "to move forward and acknowledge historic and recent racial pain"? Do you think this type of "ritual forgiveness and forgetfulness allows racism or white silence in the face of racism to continue to thrive"? Explain.

11. "Some argue that this type of cultural forgiveness is based on weakness, not strength, and that 'by forgiving racist crime so quickly and easily, black people cheapen their forgiveness.'" Do you agree or disagree? Why?

12. What did it cost Anthony Thompson to forgive Dylann Roof? What did Anthony Thompson gain?

13. Why is anger not always a negative emotion? Name circumstances in your life or throughout history in which righteous and constructive anger made a good difference.

14. Read John 2:13–16. What type of anger does Jesus show when He drives moneychangers out of His Father's house?

15. Ponder this statement: "It would be grossly unfair to the victim to be dependent on the whim of the perpetrator. It would make him or her a victim twice over. The gift has been given. It is up to the intended recipient to appropriate it." Please record your thoughts.

16. Desmond Tutu gives a formula for forgiveness, summarized here: "First and second, tell the story and name the hurt, that in order to forgive one must 'admit the wrong and acknowledge the harm.' Third and fourth, he encourages the victims to grant forgiveness and then either renew or release the relationship." Look at the value and reason

for each of the four forgiveness recommendations. Do you agree? Why or why not?

17. How does forgiveness "recognize that the love of God is more powerful than white racist hatred"?

18. Read Acts 22:20. If time allows, study the life of Paul, how God redeemed him, and Paul's future work for the Kingdom.

19. Ponder the following statement: "None of us deserves God's forgiveness . . . we all have sinned . . . but the good news is this: God loves us, and Christ came into the world to save us. When we repent of our sins and receive Him into our hearts, God has promised to forgive us—completely and fully."

For Deeper Understanding

[Note: The following material is given only to bring more understanding through suggested research and websites.]

1. **Sullivan's Island Pest Houses:** The plaque that greets tourists at Sullivan's Island reads: "This is Sullivan's Island, a place where . . . Africans were brought to this country under extreme conditions of human bondage and degradation. Tens of thousands of captives arrived on Sullivan's Island from the West African shores between 1700 and 1775." See https://loyaltytraveler.boardingarea.com/2014/06/09/sullivans-island-sc-is-perhaps-the-most-significant-historical-site-in-the-usa-you-never-heard-of/.

2. **The history of Charleston's slave trade:** During the Atlantic slave trade, the city processed nearly half of all incoming slaves from the African West Coast. Read more about the slave trade at https://iaamuseum.org/history/.

3. **South Carolina slave population:** In the late 1600s, some four-fifths of the state's population was white. But by the

mid-1700s, slaves accounted for more than 70 percent of South Carolina's population.[4] And by 1800, Charleston had 10,104 blacks—both slave and free—and only 8,820 whites.[5]

4. **Denmark Vesey:** Sick and tired of watching continuing horrors inflicted upon Charleston's slaves, Vesey, a freed slave, attempted to seize the city of Charleston in what was, at that time, the nation's largest slave revolt. Thousands of slaves prepared to follow Vesey's well-organized plan of 1822, willing and eager to kill every white person in sight, steal weapons and cash from banks, and escape by boat to Haiti. But just prior to the rebellion, some fearful followers betrayed him, rendering his uprising a disastrous failure. Seeking retribution for Vesey's planned revolution, the white citizens of Charleston sentenced Vesey to death, hanging him with about thirty-five of his black supporters, and imposing even stricter laws upon the city's African-Americans. See https://www.biography.com/people/denmark-vesey-9517932.

5. **Charleston's 1886 earthquake:** The Emanuel AME church is demolished when on August 31, 1886, the largest recorded earthquake in the history of the southeastern United States strikes South Carolina. Charleston takes the biggest hit, with more than one hundred townspeople killed, and most of the city's buildings destroyed. See https://www.history.com/this-day-in-history/earthquake-shakes-charleston-south-carolina.

6. **The Sixteenth Street Baptist Church:** The first black church in Birmingham, Sixteenth Street Baptist Church, was organized in 1873 as the First Colored Baptist Church of Birmingham, Alabama. The church moved to its current location in 1880, erecting a brick building four years later. When the city condemned the building, ordering it to be torn down, the members constructed the current

church, a mixture of Byzantine and Romanesque styles adorned with two impressive domed towers. Located in downtown Birmingham, it was completed in 1911 and served as headquarters for African-American activism, bringing in speakers like W. E. B. Du Bois, Mary McLeod Bethune, Paul Robeson, and others. See http://www.16thstreetbaptist.org/brief-history%2C-part-1.html.

7. **KKK church bombers:** It took almost four decades to charge all the Ku Klux Klan bombing suspects, known and named in 1965: Bobby Frank Cherry, Thomas Blanton, Robert Chambliss, and Herman Frank Cash. In 1977, Robert Chambliss was indicted by a Jefferson County grand jury on four counts of first-degree murder, and was sentenced to life imprisonment. Chambliss died in prison in 1985. Herman Frank Cash died in 1994, without being charged. In 2000, a grand jury in Alabama indicted Bobby Frank Cherry and Thomas Blanton with eight counts each of first-degree murder—four counts of intentional murder and four of murder with universal malice. Both men were sentenced to four life terms. Cherry died in prison in 2004. Blanton won't be eligible for parole until 2021.[6]

Your Notes

Chapter 6: Missing Myra

1. "Love Wins. Every. Single. Time." In light of the Mother Emanuel shooting, why is this slogan important? What does it mean?

2. Contemplate the meaning of Nikki Haley's comment: "Myra Thompson and those eight angels brought someone into a Bible study that did not look like them, that did not sound like them, and did not act like them, in the name of trying to love." Please share your thoughts.

3. Define what Myra's daughter, Denise, means by her comment, "I have finally accepted that your job here on earth is done. It's not a *good-bye*. It's a *see you later*."

4. How did Anthony Thompson react to Myra's death? How did he cope with his own states of grief?

5. Psychiatrists say that "grief is the inevitable process we experience as the result of a loss," claiming the universal five stages of grief are denial and isolation; anger; bargaining; depression; and finally acceptance and peace. Do you agree or disagree? Have you ever experienced these stages of grief?

6. Ponder this statement and respond: "I am told that in the cycle of grief, *peace* comes after *acceptance*, the fifth stage of grief. But for me, peace came after *forgiveness*, and only after forgiveness."

7. What did Charleston's Mayor Riley mean when he said about Myra: "Myra will always be here in the memory of this church. She was a martyr in the continuing fight to human dignity."

8. Why did Anthony Thompson question God when He called him to a new ministry?

9. Has God ever called you to do something that you questioned? If so, describe.

10. Read about Zacchaeus in Luke 19:1–9. Why did his fellow Jews hate him? How did he "make things right" for the people he robbed?

11. Ponder this quote and record your thoughts: "Does anyone really move on from such a tragedy? The short answer is no. . . . Even if the gunman is punished for his crimes, that will not bring back their loves ones."

12. Please respond to this statement: "Fortunately, my forgiveness of Dylann doesn't rest on his desire or ability to bring back my wife. I forgive him, fully knowing that the damage he has caused can never be undone. Surely, it is a myth to think forgiveness must depend on compensation and restoration. Myra is gone. She's not coming back."

13. "I am discovering that many people think they will find closure and peace only after their loved one's murderer is executed, with the killer getting what's coming to him— his just deserts." Why does Anthony Thompson believe "that is not necessarily so"?

14. Ponder and respond to this quote: "While it's easy to understand why people would seek the harshest punishment possible after a terrible crime, studies cast doubt on whether harsh punishment in general, and capital punishment in particular, actually brings the relief and peace of mind the victims deserve."

15. Do you believe God can forgive and redeem Dylann Roof? Why or why not? What needs to happen for salvation to take place in Dylann's life?

For Deeper Understanding

1. Research the life of slave trader John Newton. What happened in 1747 that turned his heart to God and changed his life forever?

2. Read the words of the hymn he wrote, "Amazing Grace." Contemplate their meaning and record your response.

3. Study the stages of grief found at this website: https:// psychcentral.com/lib/the-5-stages-of-loss-and-grief/. Give your opinion of each stage you have personally experienced:

- Denial anad isolation
- Anger
- Bargaining
- Depression
- Acceptance

Your Notes

Chapter 7: A Community and Nation React

1. Respond to Governor Nikki Haley's comment: "[Dylann Roof] was hoping to divide this state and this country. But what he doesn't know is what he did is going to bring us a whole lot closer."

   - What did she mean by this statement?
   - How did Roof's terrorist attack bring the community closer together?

2. Why did the city of Charleston fear violence and bloodshed after the shooting?

3. What happened in Ferguson, Missouri, after a white police officer shot and killed black teenager Michael Brown?

4. Describe what happened in Baltimore, Maryland, after six police officers arrested Freddie Gray, a twenty-five-year-old black man. Why did this incident cause city violence?

5. When New York City police officers in Staten Island arrested Eric Garner, why did the nation respond as it did? What happened in Berkeley, California, and why?

6. Why is Charleston called "the heart of the old Confederacy"?

7. Ponder this statement: "In many ways, Roof is 'not an anomaly but, in fact, a product of American history, a history shaped by a legacy of white supremacist thought dating back to the founding of the country. The 'heritage' of the Confederate States of America was of unabashed commitment to white supremacy and the perpetuation of chattel slavery.'"

8. Describe the city leaders' surprise when Charleston erupted in *grace* instead of violence. Why did this happen?

9. Why were newscasters, waiting to record street violence, so confused by Charleston's calm reaction to the shooting?

10. Contemplate Charleston Mayor Riley's comments after he witnessed the results of biblical forgiveness. "A hateful person came to this community with some crazy idea he'd be able to divide. But all he did was unite us and make us love each other even more."

11. What questions did reporters, talk-show hosts, and others ask upon watching biblical forgiveness in action in Charleston?

12. Dylann Roof hoped to start a race war. But it "has had the opposite effect, allowing the grieving families to put the Gospel's power on full display for not only Roof but for a watching television audience." Do you believe this statement by the *Christian Examiner* is profound and on target? Why or why not?

13. How did Charleston's black and white residents respond to each other after the shooting deaths, setting off a "godly chain of events"?

14. Ponder the meaning of this statement: "Linked together in the unity chain, each person bowed a head, honoring the fallen Emanuel Nine with five full minutes of silence. Their physical eyes may be closed during the quiet time of deep contemplation, *but the eyes of their hearts were wide open*, basking in the divine hope that came as a result of visible love and forgiveness openly shown one to another."

15. In your opinion, why was the Confederate flag removed from the South Carolina State House grounds? What happened to the flag?

16. Why did the nation's Jews join in the solidarity events after the Charleston shooting?

17. Read 1 Peter 1:24–25: What does "the grass withers and the flowers fall, but the word of the Lord endures forever" mean? Why is this so important to Christ-believers?

18. What did Jesus mean when He said, "Heaven and earth will pass away, but my words will never pass away" (Matthew 24:35)?

19. Describe *The Resolution to Recognize, Denounce and Apologize for the City's Involvement with Slavery.* What does it mean? Do you agree with it? Why or why not?

For Deeper Understanding

1. To learn more about *The Resolution to Recognize, Denounce and Apologize for the City's Involvement with Slavery,* read the full resolution in this book's appendices.

2. As you contemplate apologies and forgiveness, comment on the sections listed below (emphasis added), stating the need and potential results of each statement resolution:

   - "We hereby *denounce and apologize* for the wrongs committed against African-Americans by the *institution of slavery and Jim Crow,* with sincerest sympathies and regrets for the *deprivation of life, human dignity and constitutional protections* occasioned as a result thereof."

   - "A commitment is hereby made to promote in all City undertakings *tolerance and understanding and equal and fair opportunity for all citizens to prosper,* personally and economically, and to encourage others to treat all persons with *respect and to eliminate prejudice, injustice and discrimination* in our city."

   - "A commitment is hereby made to urge all businesses, institutions, organizations, and associations doing business or having activities in the City to *strive for racial equality and work for equity in wages, healthcare, housing,* and all other aspects of the lives of African-Americans."

   - "A pledge is hereby given to continue to work with the Charleston County School District to address the *quality*

203

of education for children in Charleston and in particular those who attend schools within the City of Charleston."

- "A pledge is hereby given to *promote an understanding of the contributions of African-Americans to the economic success, beauty, and culture of this City* by way of historic documentation in City art festivals, museums, public spaces, and monuments and to collaborate with other organizations to *memorialize the unmarked cemeteries of Africans* discovered throughout the City of Charleston and *to reinter* their remains."

- "An assurance is hereby provided that the City will seek to *promote racial harmony and acceptance* by way of initiatives, such as the creation of an office of *racial reconciliation*, measures designed to *educate and accommodate* the exchange of ideas among *all races and creeds*, and to assist in the ever-present process of *racial healing and transformation*."

3. In your opinion, what steps must be taken to promote the process of racial healing, transformation, and reconciliation in Charleston and in every U.S. city? How can biblical forgiveness aid in healing of racial wrongs?

Your Notes

Chapter 8: Honoring Myra's Wishes

1. "Dylann is not a part of my life or the lives of my children. That's why we forgave him, so that we can move on. We're through with him." What did Anthony Thompson mean when he made this statement? Why does he not want to have a relationship with Dylann?

2. Is reconciliation—a relationship—necessary in order to forgive? Why or why not?

3. Give your opinion of Roof's closing statement: "I felt like I had to do it. I *still* feel like I had to do it." What does his statement reveal about the state of his heart?

4. What did Anthony Thompson mean when he said, "I find healing for my grief in God's Word, my anchor in the storm that keeps me afloat, securely fastened, and focused on Christ's love. I fear that, like Peter seeking to walk on water, I will sink into the darkness if I take my eyes off Jesus"?

5. What is meant by this statement by Thompson: "With each tear that falls from my eyes, I feel an extraordinary connection, a close brotherhood, with the living Christ, who, in His life of flesh and blood also weeps, showing us His tears, His own broken heart"?

6. Read John 11:35 and ponder its significance.

7. What does Jesus show us in His tears?

8. What are Timothy McVeigh's final chosen words before his execution, and what do they say about the condition of his soul?

9. Ponder what C.S. Lewis meant when he wrote, "To be a Christian means to forgive the inexcusable, because God has forgiven the inexcusable" in me and that "to refuse is to refuse God's mercy for ourselves." Do you agree or disagree with this statement? Why or why not?

10. Think about the meaning of this statement: "If the offender has to respond, accepting the offered forgiveness, then he will dictate and control the victim's choice to forgive. Forgiveness will then depend on the offender's response, not the victim's decision to forgive him." Record your thoughts.

11. "The natural human response to deep hurt is retaliation, getting even. Not forgiveness." Do you agree or disagree with this statement? Why or why not?

12. Respond to this statement: "There are people who have wounded us to such a degree that it is not healthy for us to be in relationship with them. . . . We need to establish boundaries that create a safe buffer between our world and theirs. Yet, for the sake of our own spiritual and emotional health, it is critical that we forgive these people— even when relational reconciliation is not our goal." Do you agree or disagree? Why or why not?

13. Contemplate the meaning of this statement: "Forgiveness given does not automatically mean *trusting* the pain-causing individual. One can forgive an offender without putting her trust in him, the person who brutally violates that trust. Biblical forgiveness demands that we forgive, not that we become a doormat, a continual victim to the abuser." Do you agree or disagree?

14. Do you believe that society doesn't understand biblical forgiveness, that society instead desires eye-for-an-eye retaliation? Why or why not?

15. Contemplate this statement and respond: "Our human nature wants to keep alive the red-hot embers of bitterness, rejecting the peace of forgiveness, forever stoking the glowing coals that burn in our hearts, and embracing a new identify: victimhood."

16. What did a reporter mean when he referred to forgiveness in Charleston as "edifying, puzzling, or unnerving"?

17. How is forgiveness like "the writing off of a debt"?

18. List and describe other words and images that might define forgiveness.

19. Why do some people criticize a person who forgives?

20. Read Revelation 21:4. Do you believe this verse describes a believer's final reconciliation? Why or why not?

For Deeper Understanding

1. To learn more about the "And Jesus Wept" statue at the Oklahoma City memorial, see https://oklahomacity nationalmemorial.org. What other powerful monuments to the 168 people killed in the federal building are included?

2. Read William Ernest Henley's poem *Invictus* at https://www.theguardian.com/world/2001/jun/11/mcveigh.usa1. What does Henley mean when he claims, "I am the master of my fate; I am the captain of my soul"?

3. Read the story of forgiveness found in Genesis 37–45 and record your thoughts. Joseph, victimized by his older brothers, forgave them before they ever repented. How did God use the incidents in Joseph's life for good?

Your Notes

Chapter 9: The Deadly Dis-ease of Unforgiveness

1. Ponder the following and record your thoughts: "Hate and unforgiveness prove such powerful emotions, becoming states of mind and heart that destroy everything they touch." Do you believe this statement is true? Why or why not?

2. Why does Anthony Thompson write, "Now is the time to focus on God"? What does he mean?

3. Why is Simon Wiesenthal's story important for people today? Who was Karl, what did he do, and what did he want from Wiesenthal?

4. What would you have advised Wiesenthal to do with Karl's request?

5. Ponder this statement: "What happens to a lone man's mind, heart, body, and soul when he is so driven, so consumed, so burdened for an entire lifetime by unforgiveness, anger, hatred, and resentment?" What price did Wiesenthal pay in health and relationships when he hunted down Nazi criminals?

6. How is harboring hate and unforgiveness "like carrying a heavy burden—a burden that victims bring with them when they navigate the physical world"?

7. In what ways can refusal to forgive harm a person physically, emotionally, mentally? What happens to the health of those who hold grudges?

8. Contemplate this statement: "By requiring the offender's contrition, we're letting a person who harmed us decide if or when we can benefit from forgiveness. That's giving the wrongdoer a lot of control over our lives." Do you agree or disagree? Why or why not?

9. Describe the life of Eric Lomax. What did a life spent in hate cost Lomax?

10. Describe the type of forgiveness Eric Lomax extended to his enemy, Takashi Nagase. What was the condition of Lomax's forgiveness?

11. What did Lomax mean when he said, "Some time the hating has to stop"? Do you agree or disagree, and why?

12. Ponder this: "Scientific studies show that participants who believe God has forgiven them for their own sin and wrongdoings are more likely to offer others unconditional, unrestricted, and unqualified forgiveness." Do you believe this statement is true or false? Why?

13. What is *unconditional*, unrestricted, and unqualified forgiveness?

14. How is societal forgiveness different from biblical forgiveness?

15. Contemplate the meaning of this statement: "With biblical forgiveness, victims choose to forgive another person because they, themselves, have been completely forgiven by God. Their own sinful debt has been paid in full with no conditions—a grace gift from their heavenly Father." Do you agree or disagree with this statement? Why?

16. What did St. Augustine mean by this statement: "Thou hast made us for Thyself, O Lord, and our hearts are restless until they rest in Thee"?

17. What does Anthony Thompson mean when he says that "without God's direct divine intervention I don't expect Dylann to experience a positive change of heart and mind while inside the Terre Haute prison"? Why does he believe this? What happens to a human being shut up in isolation?

18. Why does Thompson believe that "Dylann's racist hate will only be nurtured in prison, not diminished, his tortured mind no longer able to make clear decisions—the choices that can change his eternal destination"?

19. Anthony Thompson states that "Dylann goes from court to prison still embracing hate, having issued the powerful emotion a *carte blanche* invitation to dictate his life, his actions, and his future." What does that mean?

20. According to Thompson, "To the slaughtered victims' family members and loved ones who chose *not* to forgive the young killer, Dylann has become the guard who now controls their lives, who holds the keys to their own personal prison cells, and who opens the door wide to allow hate, resentment, and bitterness to enter and take root in their hearts and minds." Do you agree with this statement? Why or why not?

21. Contemplate this Scripture and record your thoughts: "Search me, God, and know my heart; test me and know my anxious thoughts. See if there is any offensive way in me, and lead me in the way everlasting" (Psalm 139:23–24).

For Deeper Understanding

1. To learn more about Simon Wiesenthal, read his book *The Sunflower*. Please record your thoughts.

2. To learn more about the story of Eric Lomax and Takashi Nagase, read Lomax's book, *The Railway Man*. (The story has also been made into a film by the same name.) Please record your thoughts.

3. Read and contemplate the message in Psalm 139. Describe what this Scripture means to you personally.

Your Notes

Chapter 10: The Path to Healing and Peace

1. Ponder this statement made by Anthony Thompson: "When God speaks, *nothing* is transformed into *something*. And that's what the Word of God can do for our lives." Record your thoughts.

2. What did Dr. Robert Smith Jr. mean when he wrote, "There are some moments that are frozen in time"? What are some events in your own life that "are frozen in time"? Why are these events significant to you?

3. Why did Robert Smith choose to forgive his son's murderer?

4. In Smith's personal letter written to the killer, what is the main message Robert Smith shares with him? What does he want the young man to know?

5. Reflect on Smith's statement: "[God] is loving you through me. I want you to see that God is able to recycle, reclaim, and restore your broken life. God redeems pain. I cannot let *you* go because God will not let *me* go." What does this say to you?

6. Describe the murderer's possible reaction when he read Dr. Smith's words: "I only want you to know Tony's God and to serve Tony's Christ. My greatest hope is that one day you and Tony will bow side by side at the feet of our Lord in glory and worship the One who has redeemed you both by His blood!"

7. Do you believe that a "one-sided forgiveness" is invalid or valid? Must the offender accept it to make it complete and genuine? Please share your thoughts.

8. Think about Desmond Tutu's statements and respond to each:

   - "If forgiving depended on the culprit owning up, then the victim would always be at the mercy of the perpetrator. The victim would be bound in the shackles of victimhood." Do you agree or disagree? Why?

- "As the victim, you offer the gift of your forgiving to the perpetrator who may or may not appropriate the gift, but it has been offered and thereby it liberates the victim." Do you agree or disagree? Why?

9. Record your thoughts about this statement: "No amount of my unforgiveness will make Dylann Roof suffer or feel pain. My actions, my feelings, and my words have no control over him, none whatsoever. Whether he does or does not suffer the guilt of his crime is not in my hands."

10. Contemplate this statement and respond to it: "If I had decided *not* to forgive Dylann, *I* would be the one suffering, lingering in sorrow, living in despair each moment for the rest of my life. *I* would have no inner peace or productive future ministry. *I* would one day become a bitter old man, still living in hatred, yearning for revenge, and locking myself into a self-built prison. And *I* would live there in misery forever. My forgiveness, as I expressed it to the young racist, brings *me* God's peace, not necessarily Dylann. He must fall to his knees, repent, and deal with His heavenly Father himself."

11. Share your opinion about this statement by Anthony Thompson: "Some people tell me that my forgiving Dylann, striving to move beyond the tragedy, and trying to resume an active ministry, negates my love for Myra. They say that if I really love her, I cannot forgive her killer and move onward with my life."

12. Do you believe that "even those of us redeemed by Christ and adopted into God's family have within our hearts the capacity to hate, sin, betray, and even murder"? Why or why not?

13. Ponder this statement by Oswald Sanders and share your opinions: "A study of Bible characters reveals that most

of those who made history were men who failed at some point, and some of them drastically, but who refused to continue lying in the dust. Their very failure and repentance secured to them a more ample conception of the grace of God. They learned to know Him as the God of the second chance to His children who had failed Him— and the third chance, too."

14. What does the Apostle Paul mean when he writes, "I do not understand what I do. For what I want to do I do not do, but what I hate I do. . . . I know that nothing good lives in me, that is, in my sinful nature. For I have the desire to do what is good, but I cannot carry it out" (Romans 7:15–18)? Do you ever feel this way? If so, please describe.

15. What is your interpretation of this verse in Isaiah 43:25: "I, even I, am he who blots out your transgressions . . . and *remembers your sins no more*"?

16. What does it mean that God has purposely, deliberately chosen to remove our transgressions from us "as far as the east is from the west" (Psalm 103:12), and to hurl "all our iniquities into the depths of the sea" (Micah 7:19)?

17. What is the function of our God-given memory?

18. Share your opinion of this statement by Anthony Thompson: "We dare not forget what we suffer. For it is in our pain that we learn the great lessons we will never learn in frivolity and prosperity."

19. Ponder Desmond Tutu's words: "Forgiving is not forgetting. It's actually remembering—remembering and not using your right to hit back. It's a second chance for a new beginning. And the remembering part is particularly important. Especially if you don't want to repeat what happened."

20. Why is it important that we, as human beings, observe together the anniversaries of tragedies and painful happenings that bring sorrow to the world's people? What anniversaries and remembrances do you regularly observe in your life?

For Deeper Understanding

1. Read *The Oasis of God: From Mourning to Morning,* written by the Reverend Dr. Robert Smith Jr. about his son's murder and how he has trusted God, moving from mourning to morning. Dr. Smith is professor of Christian Preaching at Beeson Divinity School of Samford University, Birmingham, Alabama.

2. In your Bible, look up the references below, studying how the crowds Jesus forgives respond to His crucifixion. Please record your insights:

   - Luke 23:34   • Matthew 27:39
   - Luke 23:35   • Matthew 27:41
   - Luke 23:36

3. Read the entire story of the lost son, found in Luke 15:11–32, and record your thoughts. Ponder these questions:

   - The loving father forgives his prodigal son, who squandered his inheritance and crawled back home. What makes this story Jesus told so amazing?
   - Describe the reaction of the father upon the son's return. Does it surprise you? Why or why not?
   - How does the older son respond to his brother's unexpected return? What message did the father give to the elder brother, and why? Describe how you, as the loving father, might respond to the son.

4. Read the parable of the lost sheep in Luke 15:1–7 and the parable of the lost coin in Luke 15:8–10. Why did Luke group these two parables with the parable of the lost son? How are these stories similar? What do they each mean?

5. View the plans and designs for the Emanuel Nine Memorial at https://www.npr.org/2018/07/16/629424811 /architect-unveils-design-for-mother-emanuel-ame-church -memorial. Reflect on the design and its symbolism.

Your Notes

Appendix 1

A Call to Prayer from the Bishops in South Carolina

When the Anglican Church in North America received news that my wife, Myra, was one of the Emanuel Nine murdered by Dylann Roof on June 17, 2015, the Bishops in South Carolina responded with "A Call to Prayer." Below is their prayer in total:

To the Faithful across the Carolinas:

Greetings to you in the matchless Name of our Lord and Saviour Jesus Christ. As the eyes of the nation turn toward Charleston we commend her to your prayers. Our hearts are crushed by this violent act. Our minds reel as we consider the pain of our brothers and sisters who have lost loved ones—mothers and fathers, children and grandchildren, family and friends—as well as for those who have lost faith and hope from such a senseless act of hatred and insanity. Among those killed was one from our own Anglican family, Myra Thompson, the wife of The Rev'd Anthony Thompson, a priest in the Reformed Episcopal Church.

It is right that you feel sickened and angry. It is right that you struggle to know what to do. We all do. Scripture tells us that in the diminishment or suffering of one the whole church suffers. We are enjoined to weep with those who weep and to mourn with those who mourn. Today, we mourn and we weep with our brothers and sisters at Emanuel Church and all of Charleston.

Together we shall seek God's face on how he will have us respond as dioceses, as congregations, and as individual members of the Body of Christ—ambassadors of reconciliation—in this broken and fallen world for which His Son our Savior, Jesus Christ, has died that He might redeem.

Please join us in prayer as we remember:

The families of those killed
The members of Emanuel AME
The members of our law enforcement and first responders community
The members of the Charleston community

And pray that:

- *That there would be no further acts of violence*
- *There would be peace in our city*
- *That unity may overcome estrangement*
- *That joy might conquer despair*

Lastly, we commend the following prayer to our congregations across the Carolinas:

"O God, you have made of one blood all the peoples and races of the earth, and sent your blessed Son to preach peace to those who are far off and those who are near: Grant to those who have lost loved ones your hope, comfort and peace; grant to those members of Emanuel AME Church a sense of your presence; look with compassion on the whole human family here in Charleston and across our nation; show us how to respond to one another's hurt and suffering; shed abroad your Spirit on those who have lost faith, hope and trust in You and one another; break down the walls that separate us; unite us in bonds of love; and work through our struggle and confusion to accomplish your purposes on earth; that in your good time all peoples and races may serve you in harmony around your heavenly throne; through Jesus Christ our Lord. Amen."

Your faithful servants,

The Rt. Rev'd Al Gadsden,
Bishop of the Diocese of the Southeast (REC)

The Rt. Rev'd Mark Lawrence,
Bishop of the Diocese of South Carolina

The Rt. Rev'd Steve Wood,
Bishop of the Diocese of the Carolinas

The Rt. Rev'd David Bryan,
Bishop of the Diocese of the Southeast
(PEARUSA)

Appendix 2

Charleston Shooting, Trial, and Remembrance Timeline

April 3, 2015: Dylann Roof turns twenty-one years old, the legal age to purchase a gun from retailers and dealers.

April 11, 2015: Roof goes to Shooter's Choice in West Columbia and fills out an application to buy a Glock pistol.

April 16, 2015: Receiving no report (within the three-day waiting period) from the FBI, Roof is able to purchase the .45-caliber Glock pistol and five magazines at Shooter's Choice. In May and June, Roof bought additional ammunition.

June 17, 2015: Myra Thompson teaches the Wednesday night Bible study at Emanuel on Jesus' parable of the sower from Mark 4. When the group stands to pray, Dylann Storm Roof opens fire on the Bible study members. A survivor calls 9-1-1, and police respond.

June 18, 2015: Charleston Mayor Joseph P. Riley confirms that nine people are dead. Police apprehend and arrest Roof in Shelby, South Carolina.

June 19, 2015: Dylann makes his first appearance in court. Members of the victims' families attend his bond hearing. Some express forgiveness to Roof, including the Rev. Anthony Thompson.

June 26, 2015: President Obama delivers the eulogy at the Rev. Clementa Pinckney's funeral, singing the solo "Amazing Grace."

June 29, 2015: Myra Thompson's funeral is held at Mother Emanuel. She is laid to rest in the Carolina Memorial Gardens.

July 10, 2015: The Confederate flag is removed from State House grounds.

September 3, 2015: State prosecutor Scarlett Wilson announces she will seek the death penalty for Roof.

September 17, 2015: Joey Meek (Dylann's friend) is arrested on the charge that he lied to federal investigators.

May 24, 2016: U.S. Attorney General Loretta Lynch announces that federal prosecutors will seek the death penalty.

June 17, 2016: Charleston holds a twelve-day observance to remember the victims, the survivors, members of the church, and people in the community.

November 25, 2016: U.S. District Judge Richard Gergel rules Roof is mentally competent to stand trial.

December 15, 2016: Federal jury finds Roof guilty on all thirty-three counts, including hate crimes resulting in death and obstruction of exercise of religion resulting in death.

January 2, 2017: Judge holds a second competency hearing for Roof, ruling again that Roof is competent to stand trial for sentencing and to represent himself.

January 4, 2017: Roof's sentencing trial begins.

January 10, 2017: Dylann Roof is sentenced to death in the federal case. In Roof's closing statement, he admits, "I still feel like I had to do it."

April 10, 2017: Dylann Roof pleads guilty to nine counts of murder and three counts of attempted murder in the South Carolina state case. Joseph Roof, Dylann's grandfather, apologizes to the court for his grandson's murders. Roof is sent to death row to await execution at the United States Penitentiary, Terre Haute, Indiana.

June 2017: Charleston and other cities around the world hold events to remember the shooting tragedy at Mother Emanuel.

June 2018: Charleston events include the third anniversary remembrance of the shooting tragedy, and the two-hundredth anniversary of the founding of Emanuel AME Church. Plans are approved to build a $15 million white stone memorial in remembrance of the Emanuel Nine.

Appendix 3

The Ten Stages
of Biblical Forgiveness

1. **Shock and disbelief:** The shock of discovery, and the refusal to believe the crime or offense happened.
2. **Deep hurt, depression, tears, and sadness:** Realizing the magnitude of your loss and experiencing the inevitable human emotions.
3. **Placing the blame:** Blaming the offender for the pain he has caused you.
4. **Anger, hate, and disgust:** Hating the person who so deeply hurt you in such a senseless and tragic way. Anger, hate, and disgust are natural human reactions.
5. **Desire for revenge:** The desire to hurt the offender in the same way he hurt you, or worse.
6. **Prayer and Scripture study:** Taking your hurt, depression, tears, sadness, anger, hate, disgust, and desire for revenge to God in prayer, and asking Him for the strength to

forgive. Studying God's Word for the wisdom to take the needed steps toward *unconditional* forgiveness.

7. **Surrender:** Making the decision, with God's help, to let it go. Laying down your heavy burden of unforgiveness, and surrendering to God's will, allowing Him to help you let go of your anger, hate, and desire for revenge.

8. **Forgiveness:** Through an act of will, not emotion, forgiving the offender for the pain he has caused you.

9. **The journey:** Embarking upon the journey of forgiveness, keeping close to God in prayer and Scripture study, asking for His hourly guidance, and communing with others in Christian fellowship and wise counsel.

10. **Loving your enemy:** Knowing God's peace. In Christ's name, and in His strength, praying for and reaching out to the offender in good deeds.

Appendix 4

The Resolution to Recognize, Denounce and Apologize for the City's Involvement with Slavery

RESOLUTION

RECOGNIZING, DENOUNCING AND APOLOGIZING ON BEHALF OF THE CITY OF CHARLESTON FOR THE CITY'S ROLE IN REGULATING, SUPPORTING AND FOSTERING SLAVERY AND THE RESULTING ATROCITIES INFLICTED BY THE INSTITUTION OF SLAVERY AND FURTHER, COMMITTING TO CONTINUE TO PURSUE INITIATIVES THAT HONOR THE CONTRIBUTIONS OF THOSE WHO WERE ENSLAVED AND THAT ASSIST IN AMELIORATING REMAINING VESTIGES OF SLAVERY.

WHEREAS, Charleston (formerly Charles Town), founded in 1670, flourished in the 17th, 18th, 19th centuries from a robust economy, made possible by the labor of enslaved people, centering on the production of rice, indigo and other commodities; and

WHEREAS, as a result of the adoption and legalization of the institution of slavery from the 15th to the 19th centuries, more than 15.5 million Indigenous Peoples and Africans were subjected to enslavement to develop North America, South America and the Caribbean, with an estimated two million Africans not surviving the Middle Passage; and

WHEREAS, fundamental to the economy of colonial and antebellum Charleston was slave labor, Charleston prospering as it did due to the expertise, ingenuity and hard labor of enslaved Africans who were forced to endure inhumane working conditions that produced wealth for many, but which was denied to them; and

WHEREAS, approximately forty percent of enslaved Africans arrived in North America at the ports of Charleston, with hundreds of thousands of African-American citizens today being able to trace their ancestry to Africans arriving here; and

WHEREAS, the institution of slavery did not just involve physical confinement and mistreatment; it also sought to suppress, if not destroy, the cultural, religious and social values of Africans by stripping Africans of their ancestral names and customs, humiliating and brutalizing them through sexual exploitation, and selling African relatives apart from one another without regard to the connection of family, a human condition universal among all peoples of the world; and

WHEREAS, for a time, notwithstanding the Declaration of Independence tenet that all men are created equal, the federal law of the land as embodied in the Constitution did not recognize enslaved Africans as full-fledged humans, denying citizenship either in number or by way of access to basic rights of due process and equal protection of the law, a condition that persisted until 1865 with the enactment of the 13th amendment to the Constitution and 1868 with the enactment of the 14th amendment to the Constitution requiring State compliance with Constitutional mandates; and

WHEREAS, notwithstanding the 14th and 15th amendments to the Constitution, institutionalized discrimination continued in many parts of the country, with the enactment and enforcement of laws that would come to be known as Jim Crow that were designed to separate African-Americans from their fellow citizens, to suppress and intimidate their exercise of basic rights, as voting, and to frustrate educational opportunities that would create long-term loss of their personal and economic advancement; and

WHEREAS, basic decency requires an acknowledgment and apology for the City of Charleston's role in regulating, supporting and fostering the institution of slavery in the city and the past wrongs inflicted on African-Americans here in Charleston and elsewhere, and an acknowledgment and an expression of gratitude for the significant contributions made to our community by talented and skilled African-Americans that are reflected in the agriculture, architecture, artisanship, arts and cuisine of this City; and

WHEREAS, the City of Charleston has in recent times supported civil rights and social justice, and has taken measures to promote racial tolerance, such as the passage of the City of Charleston Public Accommodations Ordinance which provides for equal enjoyment and privileges to public accommodations; the City of Charleston Fair Housing Practices Ordinance which makes discrimination in housing illegal; the creation of the City of Charleston's Minority and Women Business Enterprise Development office; partnering with the Charleston County School District and education-focused organizations and programs to improve the quality of education in our schools and to encourage children to stay in school; and supporting the efforts of institutions and churches, including in a variety of ways the church members and community of the Mother Emanuel AME Church following the tragedy of June 2015; and

WHEREAS, the story of enslavement, discrimination and segregation of African-Americans and the dehumanizing atrocities committed against them should not be purged from, or minimized in the telling of Charleston's history; moreover, the faith, perseverance, hope, and triumphs of African-Americans and significant contributions to the development of this State and the nation should be embraced, celebrated, and retold for generations to come; and

WHEREAS, the City of Charleston acknowledges that these efforts to strive for equality and equity and opportunity in all areas of life for African-Americans in Charleston must persist and therefore commits to the necessity of continuing to undertake and promote effective measures to assist in the amelioration of remaining vestiges of slavery.

NOW, THEREFORE, BE IT RESOLVED by the Mayor and Council members of Charleston, in City Council assembled, that:

a) We hereby denounce and apologize for the wrongs committed against African-Americans by the institution of slavery and Jim Crow, with sincerest sympathies and regrets for the deprivation of life, human dignity and constitutional protections occasioned as a result thereof.

b) A commitment is hereby made to promote in all City undertakings tolerance and understanding and equal and fair opportunity for all citizens to prosper, personally and economically, and to encourage others to treat all persons with respect and to eliminate prejudice, injustice and discrimination in our city.

c) A commitment is hereby made to urge all businesses, institutions, organizations, and associations doing business or having activities in the City to strive for racial equality and work for equity in wages, healthcare, housing, and all other aspects of the lives of African-Americans.

d) A pledge is hereby given to continue to work with the Charleston County School District to address the quality of education for children in Charleston and in particular those who attend schools within the City of Charleston.

e) A pledge is hereby given to promote an understanding of the contributions of African-Americans to the economic success, beauty, and culture of this City by way of historic documentation in City art festivals, museums, public spaces, and monuments and to collaborate with other organizations to memorialize the unmarked cemeteries of Africans discovered throughout the City of Charleston and to reinter their remains.

f) An assurance is hereby provided that the City will seek to promote racial harmony and acceptance by way of initiatives, such as the creation of an office of racial reconciliation, measures designed to educate and accommodate the exchange of ideas among all races and creeds, and to assist in the ever-present process of racial healing and transformation.

ATTEST:
John J. Tecklenburg, Mayor City of Charleston
Vanessa Turner Maybank Clerk of Council[1]

Appendix 5

Myra's Bible Study on Jesus' Parable of the Sower (from Mark 4)

Myra's original Bible study notes were handwritten, not typed. Their presentation here is as close as possible to the original.

Studying Mark's Gospel: Preparing Our Heart's Soil

Lesson 5: Preparing Our Heart's Soil

Mark 4:1–25

DAY 1: Parables and Mysteries

1. (v. 1) The crowd that gathered around Him was so large that He got into a boat and sat out on the lake, while all the people were along the shore at the water's edge.

2. (v. 2) Jesus used parables to instruct the crowds.
3. Some of the reactions Jesus got from those who heard His parables and teachings in the following passages were:
   - Matthew 13:36–57

       His disciples asked Jesus to explain the parables.
   - Luke 13:7

       All His opponents were humiliated, but the people were delighted with all the wonderful things He was doing.
   - Luke 18:31–34

       (This is sometimes referred to as the 3rd prediction of Jesus' death. The first prediction is in Luke 9:22 and the second prediction is in 9:43–45. The disciples did not understand any of this (what Jesus told them). Its meaning was hidden from them, and they did not know what He was talking about.
   - Matthew 21:45–46

       45When the chief priests and the Pharisees heard Jesus' parables they knew he was talking about them. 46They looked for a way to arrest him, but they were afraid of the crowd because the people held that he was a prophet.
   - Luke 11:53–54

       53When Jesus left there, the Pharisees and the teachers of the law began to oppose him fiercely and to besiege him with questions, 54waiting to catch him in something he might say.

       NOTE (53) The Pharisees and the teachers of the law should have opened the people's minds concerning the law [but] obscured their understanding by faulty interpretation and an erroneous system of theology.
       - They kept themselves and the people in ignorance of the way of salvation, or as Matthew's account puts it,

they shut the kingdom of heaven in men's faces (Matt. 23:13). (54) They were determined to trap Jesus.

Scripture Memory: Mark 4:24–25 (NKJV): Then He said to them, "Take heed what you hear. With the same measures you use, it will be measured to you; and to you who hear, more will be given. For whosoever has, to him more will be given; but whoever does not have, even what he has will be taken away from him."

Lesson 5: DAY 2—Parable of the Soils

Read Mark 4:3–9

1. Jesus told them a parable about a sower, some seed and the soil. How did Jesus begin and end His parables to assure the audience's attention?

   Jesus emphasized that they should listen to what He was about to say and that they should have heard what He had said.

2. What are some of the things He promised for those who truly listen and apply what He tells them in Rev. 2:7–29?

   - To the Church in Smyrna—The crown of life
   - To the Church in Pergamum—Some of the hidden Manna
   - To the Church in Thyatira
   - To those who do not hold to her teaching and have not learned Satan's so-called deep secrets:
     - No other burden will be imposed upon them; to him who overcomes and does His will to the end
     - Authority over the nations and the morning star

Where it was sown	verse	What happened	Why
By the Wayside	(v. 4)	Birds ate them	
Stony ground	(v. 5)	Scorched & Withered	Had no root b/c of lack of soil
Among thorns	(v. 7)	Choked the plants	
Good soil	(v. 8)	Produced crop multiplying 30, 60, or 100 times	

June 10, 2015

DAY 3: Perceiving Hearts

Mark 4:10–13

1. The twelve and others wanted to know more about the parables (v. 10).

2. Jesus responded to their request by rebuking them, "Don't you understand this parable? How then will you understand any parable?" Then He explained it to them.

3. (Most directly relate to us) Isaiah 6:9–10 is in relation to the sower hearing and listening for understanding. Sacred truths not only shed a bright light but cast a shadow. [There's a shadow that overshadows most of our days.]

   • God's infinite holiness: Holy, Holy, Holy—The holy Trinity (Father, Son, Holy Spirit).

   1. He who created us.

   2. He who redeemed us.

   3. He who sanctifies us.

   • The worldwide glory of God is linked with His miraculous signs.

235

- We must have a desire to hear.
  - We must walk in the WORD—Hear the WORD.
  - 1 Corinthians 1:18–29
  - 1 Corinthians 2:12–14
- Jesus met a lot of people who did not want to hear. The Corinthians were worldly—infant believers and the proof of their immaturity was their division over human leaders.
  1. (v. 12) These are people whose eyes are opened but don't see a thing.
  2. Their ears are opened but they don't understand a word.
  3. They avoid making an about-face to be forgiven.
- The only way we can be forgiven is to accept Jesus as our Lord and Savior.
- Once we accept Him we will receive the Holy Spirit and the Holy Spirit will give understanding of the Word of God.

Mark 4:13

(v. 13) Don't be afraid to ask when you don't understand. The disciples asked about the parable of the sower, and Jesus explained it in Mark 4:14–20.

June 17, 2015

DAY 4: Parable of the Soils Explained

Let's read Mark 4:14–20 and look at the chart before we answer the questions. The chart will help us to see the events clearer.

- v. 15—By the Wayside (the path). Read Pulpit Commentary Mark 4:15

  What happened?

  They heard it but it fell on deaf ears, because they do not accept what they hear.

  What was the result?

  Satan came and took the Word away.

- vv. 16–17—Stony Ground. A step up from those who do not accept the Word; those with shallow character. Read pulpit commentary Mark 4:16–17.

  What happened?

  They heard and received it with joy. They got excited about the Word but do not apply it to their daily living.

  What was the result?

  The Word lasted a short time and quickly fell away.

  > Examples: 1) When trouble comes
  > 2) When faced with hardships

We must prioritize the Lord's Word so we can fight off deceitfulness. Satan is very powerful with deceitfulness.

- v. 18–19—Among Thorns. Read pulpit commentary Mark 4:18–19. The love of riches versus the love for God. Those who are overwhelmed with all they want to do and what they want to have. The stress from this strangles the Word and nothing becomes of it.

  What happened?

  They heard the Word but lost focus by their own desires.

  - For what does it profit a man to gain the whole world and lose his soul? (Matthew 16:26).

What was the result?

The Word was choked by their desires, making it
unfruitful.

- Wealth gives a false sense of self-sufficiency, security and
  well-being.
- Our first priority is in God, so the devil will not be able
  to encourage deceit further.
- Satan makes things look better than they are.

- v. 20—Good Soil. Read pulpit commentary Mark 4:20.
  Those who trust in the Lord and leaned not on their own
  understanding (Proverbs 3:5).

  What happened?

  They heard the Word and embraced (accepted) it, and ap-
  plied it to their life by depending on God.

  What was the result?

  They produced a harvest beyond their wildest dreams by
  applying the Word to their lives.

What does the soil represent?

The soil represents the human heart; the way we respond to
the Word.

What does the seed represent?

The seed represents the Word of God.

1. Jesus didn't tell us who the sower is. What are some possibilities you can think of? In other words, who do you think
   can be a sower?

   - Examples: Preacher, church school, teacher, missionary,
     lay members, spiritual leaders. Anyone who is obedient
     to the Word of God.

- The sower is all those God uses in establishing His kingdom within the hearts of men and in the world. He uses all those redeemed by the blood to fulfill His redemptive work.

2. Do you consider yourself a sower? If so, why?
   Encourage people to remain faithful when things are not going well. Allow God to use me to help others and let them know that it is not me but God.

3. What is the impact of the seed (the Gospels and God's Word) being implanted in any of the four soils?

Let's read Isaiah 55:10–11 and then Hebrews 4:12–13.

CONCLUSION: Hebrews 4:12–13 sums up the whole matter because God's Word will do what God wants it to no matter how we initially respond to it. In other words, every knee shall bow and every tongue shall confess that Jesus Christ is LORD.

Therefore, we must pray to be delivered from Satan when we do not accept the Word of God, because a person's reception of God's Word is determined by the condition of his heart. Our faith and the way we live our lives will show what type of soil relates to us.

MEMORY VERSE: "Then He said to them, 'Take heed what you *hear*. With the same measure you use, it will be *measured* to you; and to you who hear, more will be *given*. For whoever has, to him *more* will be given; but whoever does not *have*, even what he has will be *taken* away from him'" (Mark 4:24–25 NKJV, Myra's emphasis).

Notes

Chapter 1: The Unthinkable Tragedy

1. David Von Drehle with Jay Newton-Small and Maya Rhodan, "How Do You Forgive a Murder?" *Time*, November 12, 2015, http://time.com/time-maga zine-charleston-shooting-cover-story/.

2. Janell Ross, "Dylann Roof reportedly wanted a race war. How many Americans sympathize?" *Washington Post*, June 19, 2015, https://www.washingtonpost .com/news/the-fix/wp/2015/06/19/dylann-roof-reportedly-wanted-a-race-war -how-many-americans-feel-like-he-supposedly-does/?utm_term=.a1a9fc8edb6a.

3. The nine slain were: the Reverend Clementa Pinckney (Emanuel's pastor), Cynthia Hurd, the Reverend Sharonda Coleman-Singleton, Tywanza Sanders, Ethel Lance, Susie Jackson, Depayne Middleton Doctor, the Reverend Daniel Simmons, and Myra Thompson.

4. David Kocieniewski and Gary Gately, "Man Shoots 11, Killing 5 Girls, in Amish School," *New York Times*, October 3, 2006, http://www.nytimes.com/20 06/10/03/us/03amish.html.

5. "School Shooting in an Amish One-Room School," *LancasterPA.com*, October 2, 2006, https://lancasterpa.com/amish/amish-school-shooting/.

6. Joanna Walters, "The Happening: 10 Years After the Amish Shooting," *The Guardian*, October 2, 2016, https://www.theguardian.com/us-news/2016/oct/02 /amish-shooting-10-year-anniversary-pennsylvania-the-happening.

7. Brian Hicks, "Slavery in Charleston: A Chronicle of Human Bondage in the Holy City," *The Post and Courier*, April 9, 2011, https://www.postandcourier .com/news/special_reports/slavery-in-charleston-a-chronicle-of-human-bondage -in-the/article_54334e04-4834-50b7-990b-f81fa3c2804a.html.

8. Corrie ten Boom, "Guideposts Classics: Corrie ten Boom on Forgiveness," *Guideposts*, July 24, 2014, https://www.guideposts.org/better-living/positive-liv ing/guideposts-classics-corrie-ten-boom-on-forgiveness.

9. Walters, "The Happening: 10 Years After the Amish Shooting."

10. H. R. Jerajani, Bhagyashri Jaju, M. M. Phiske, and Nitin Lade, "Hematohidrosis: A Rare Clinical Phenomenon," *Indian Journal of Dermatology*, July–September 2009, https://www.ncbi.nlm.nih.gov/pmc/articles/PMC2810702/.

Chapter 2: The Aftermath

1. Reuven Blau, Sasha Goldstein, and Corky Siemaszko, "Remembering the Victims: Stories of the nine senselessly killed in Charleston," *New York Daily News*, June 19, 2015, http://www.nydailynews.com/news/national/victims-charleston -church-shooting-diverse-group-article-1.2263187.

2. Blau, Goldstein, and Siemaszko, "Remembering the Victims."

3. "Winchester USA Ammunition 38 Special +P 125 Grain Jacketed Hollow Point Box of 50," *USA Midway*, n.d., https://www.midwayusa.com/product/29 00642685/winchester-usa-ammunition-38-special-p-125-grain-jacketed-hollow -point.

4. David Von Drehle with Jay Newton-Small and Maya Rhodan, "How Do You Forgive a Murder?" *Time*, November 12, 2015, http://time.com/time-maga zine-charleston-shooting-cover-story/.

5. Tim Stelloh, Caitlin Fichtel, and Tracy Connor, "Who Is Devin Kelley, the Texas Church Shooter?" *NBC News*, November 5, 2017, https://www.nbcnews .com/storyline/texas-church-shooting/who-devin-kelley-alleged-texas-church -shooter-n817806.

6. Stoyan Zaimov, "Pastor Preaches Forgiveness After Texas Church Shooting Says Victims Are 'Dancing with Jesus,'" *The Christian Post*, November 13, 2017, https://www.christianpost.com/news/pastor-preaches-forgiveness-after-texas -church-shooting-says-victims-are-dancing-with-jesus-206398/.

7. James Macintyre, "Amazing Grace: Family that Lost 9 in Sutherland Springs Shooting Encourages Forgiveness at Tearful Funeral," *Christian Today*, November 16, 2017, https://www.christiantoday.com/article/amazing-grace-family-that-lost -9-in-sutherland-springs-shooting-encourages-forgiveness-at-tearful-funeral/11 8829.htm.

8. Zaimov, "Pastor Preaches Forgiveness."

9. Zaimov, "Pastor Preaches Forgiveness."

10. Tara Isabella Burton, "Christians Are Supposed to Practice Forgiveness. What About After Mass Shootings?" *Vox*, November 9, 2017, https://www.vox .com/identities/2017/11/9/16619438/christians-forgiveness-mass-shootings-turn -cheek-religion-tragedy.

11. "Sutherland Springs Slaughter: 'We Are People Whose Faith in God Even Transcends the Viciousness of Death," *CBN News*, November 6, 2017, https:// www1.cbn.com/cbnnews/us/2017/november/sutherland-springs-slaughter-we-are -people-whose-faith-in-god-even-transcends-the-viciousness-of-death.

Chapter 3: Dylann Storm Roof: A Homegrown American Terrorist

1. Lydia Warren, "I Forgive You," *Daily Mail.com*, June 19, 2015, http://www.da ilymail.co.uk/news/article-3131874/Repent-Relatives-Charleston-killer-s-victims

-confront-court-heart-wrenching-speeches-FORGIVENESS-adopts-vacant-re morseless-stare.html.

2. Harriet McLeod, "Charleston Gunman Dylann Roof Bought His Pistol at a Gun Store 25 Miles from His Home," *Business Insider*, June 23, 2015, https:// www.businessinsider.com/r-charleston-church-gunman-bought-pistol-near -home-nbc-2015-6.

3. Mark Follman, "9 Killed in Mass Shooting at Historic Black Church in South Carolina," *Mother Jones*, June 18, 2015, http://www.motherjones.com/poli tics/2015/06/9-people-dead-mass-shooting-south-carolina-church/.

4. Follman, "9 Killed in Mass Shooting at Historic Black Church in South Carolina."

5. Doyle Murphy, "Dylann Roof Taken Down by Tip from North Carolina Florist Who Followed the Suspected Church Shooter for 35 Miles," *New York Daily News*, June 19, 2015, http://www.nydailynews.com/news/national/dylann -roof-north-carolina-florist-tip-article-1.2263256.

6. Murphy, "Dylann Roof Taken Down."

7. Emily Shapiro, "Key Moments in Charleston Church Shooting Case as Dylann Roof Pleads Guilty to State Charges," *ABC World News Tonight*, April 10, 2017, http://abcnews.go.com/US/key-moments-charleston-church-shooting -case-dylann-roof/story?id=46701033.

8. Jeffrey Collins, "Dylann Roof Cold to Victims But Apologized to His Parents," *Associated Press*, January 6, 2017, https://www.yahoo.com/news/dylann -roof-cold-victims-apologized-parents-085328645.html.

9. Timothy M. Phelps, Christopher Goffard, and Richard A. Serrano, "Mass Shooting at Church in Charleston Resonates Far Beyond," *Los Angeles Times*, June 19, 2015, http://www.latimes.com/nation/la-na-charleston-church-shooting -roof-20150619-story.html, and "Dylann Roof's and Michael Slager's cells are right next to each other," *USA Today*, June 19, 2015, https://www.usatoday.com /story/news/nation/2015/06/19/dylann-roof-michael-slager-jail-cell/28995939/.

10. "Coroner Identifies Nine Victims in Emanuel AME Church Shooting," *Live 5 News*, June 18, 2015, http://www.live5news.com/story/29352185/coroner -identifies-nine-victims-in-emanuel-ame-church-shooting/.

11. Ray Sanchez and Keith O'Shea, "Mass Shooter Dylann Roof, with a Laugh, Confesses, 'I Did It'," *CNN*, December 10, 2016, https://www.cnn.com/2016/12 /09/us/dylann-roof-trial-charleston-video/index.html.

12. Lydia Warren, "I Forgive You," *Daily Mail.com*, June 19, 2015, http:// www.dailymail.co.uk/news/article-3131874/Repent-Relatives-Charleston-killer -s-victims-confront-court-heart-wrenching-speeches-FORGIVENESS-adopts -vacant-remorseless-stare.html.

13. Tonya Maxwell, "Dylann Roof Showed No Remorse in Writings While in Jail," *Citizen Times*, updated January 5, 2017, http://www.citizen-times.com /story/news/local/2017/01/04/dylann-roof-showed-no-remorse-writings-while -jail/96145438/.

14. Harriet McLeod, "U.S. Sued over Flawed Gun Background Check in Charleston Church Shooting," *Reuters*, July 1, 2016, http://www.reuters.com/arti cle/us-south-carolina-shooting/u-s-sued-over-flawed-gun-background-check-in -charleston-church-shooting-idUSKCN0ZH5GA.

15. Frances Robles and Nikita Stewart, "Dylann Roof's Past Reveals Trouble at Home and School, *New York Times*, July 16, 2015, https://www.nytimes.com /2015/07/17/us/charleston-shooting-dylann-roof-troubled-past.html, and Ray Sanchez and Ed Payne, "Charleston Church Shooting: Who Is Dylann Roof?" *CNN*, December 16, 2016, http://www.cnn.com/2015/06/19/us/charleston-church -shooting-suspect/index.html.

16. Robles and Stewart, "Dylann Roof's Past," and Sanchez and Payne, "Who Is Dylann Roof?"

17. Lydia Warren, "I Forgive You."

18. Lydia Warren, "I Forgive You."

19. Dan Kedmey, "Dylann Roof's Family Breaks Silence on Shooting," *Time*, June 19, 2015, http://time.com/3929115/roof-family-statement-church-shootings/.

20. Jennifer Rash, "Walking the Lonely Path of Regret," *The Alabama Baptist*, May 25, 2018, https://rashionalthoughts.wordpress.com/2018/05/25/walking-the -lonely-path-of-regret/psalm-51_17-4/.

21. Rash, "Walking the Lonely Path of Regret."

22. "Rwanda Genocide: 100 Days of Slaughter," *BBC News*, April 7, 2014, http://www.bbc.com/news/world-africa-26875506.

23. Immaculee Ilibagiza, *Left to Tell: Discovering God Amidst the Rwandan Holocaust* (NYC: Hay House, Inc., 2006/2014), 158.

24. Quoted in Ilibagiza, *Left to Tell*, 173.

25. Quoted in Ilibagiza, *Left to Tell*, 93.

26. Ilibagiza, *Left to Tell*, 178.

27. Ilibagiza, *Left to Tell*, 158.

28. Kevin Sack, "Grandfather Apologizes After Dylann Roof's Guilty Pleas Add to Sentence," *New York Times*, April 10, 2017, https://www.nytimes.com /2017/04/10/us/dylann-roof-grandfather-charleston-shooting.html.

Chapter 4: The Decision

1. Herb Frazier, Bernard Edward Powers Jr., Marjory Wentworth, *We Are Charleston: Tragedy and Triumph at Mother Emanuel* (Nashville: W Publishing Group, 2016), 166.

2. Michael McLaughlin, "Judge at Dylann Roof's Hearing, James Gosnell, Used Racial Epithet in Charleston Court," *Huffington Post*, June 20, 2015, https:// www.huffingtonpost.com/2015/06/20/james-gosnell-racist-word_n_7628398 .html.

3. McLaughlin, "Judge at Dylann Roof's Hearing."

4. Tara Fowler, "Gracious Relatives of Shooting Victims Offer Forgiveness for Accused Charleston Gunman as They Confront Him in Court: 'Hate Won't Win,'" *People*, June 19, 2015, http://people.com/crime/gracious-relatives-of-shoot ing-victims-offer-forgiveness-for-accused-charleston-gunman-as-they-confront -him-in-court-hate-wont-win/.

5. David Von Drehle with Jay Newton-Small and Maya Rhodan, "How Do You Forgive a Murder?" *Time*, November 12, 2015, http://time.com/time-maga zine-charleston-shooting-cover-story/.

6. Von Drehle, Newton-Small, and Rhodan, "How Do You Forgive a Murder?"

7. Michele Gorman, "Granddaughter of Charleston Shooting Victim to Suspect: 'Hate Won't Win'," *Newsweek*, June 19, 2015, http://www.newsweek.com /charleston-shooter-appears-court-bond-hearing-345063.

8. Michael Daly, "Turning the Other Cheek: Charleston Shooting Families Proved Grace Wins Out Over Hate," *Daily Beast*, June 20, 2015, https://www.the dailybeast.com/charleston-shooting-families-proved-grace-wins-out-over-hate.

9. Daly, "Turning the Other Cheek."

10. Daly, "Turning the Other Cheek."

11. Frazier, Edward Powers Jr., Wentworth, *We Are Charleston*.

12. Philip Yancey, *What's So Amazing About Grace?* (Grand Rapids, MI: Zondervan, 1997), 96.

13. Yancey, *What's So Amazing About Grace?*

14. Lewis B. Smedes, *Shame and Grace: Healing the Shame We Don't Deserve* (San Francisco: HarperCollins, 1993), 141.

15. Many versions render this "seventy times seven" (490), an even stronger case for limitless forgiveness.

16. Frazier, Edward Powers Jr., and Wentworth, *We Are Charleston*, 167.

17. Von Drehle, Newton-Small, and Rhodan, "How Do You Forgive a Murder?"

18. Von Drehle, Newton-Small, and Rhodan, "How Do You Forgive a Murder?"

19. Lisa Weismann and Patrick Phillips, "SC Supreme Court Replaces Charleston Co. Chief Magistrate," *Live 5 News*, June 24, 2015, http://www.foxcarolina .com/story/29400161/sc-supreme-court-replaces-charleston-co-chief-magistrate.

Chapter 5: A Mighty Long Journey

1. Andrew Buncombe, "Remembering Obama's 2015 Speech at the Charleston Shooting Service, Where He Sang 'Amazing Grace,'" *Independent*, https://www .independent.co.uk/news/world/americas/barack-obama-charleston-church -shooting-speech-in-full-victoms-funeral-2015-amazing-grace-dylann-a75296 41.html.

2. Jeffrey Collins, "Dylann Roof Cold to Victims, But Apologized to His Parents," *Associated Press*, January 6, 2017, https://www.yahoo.com/news/dyl ann-roof-cold-victims-apologized-parents-085328645.html.

3. Kevin Sack and Alan Blinder, "No Regrets from Dylann Roof in Jailhouse Manifesto," *New York Times*, January 5, 2017, https://www.nytimes.com/2017 /01/05/us/no-regrets-from-dylann-roof-in-jailhouse-manifesto.html.

4. Desmond Tutu, AZ Quotes, n.d., https://www.azquotes.com/quote/1290714.

5. "Charleston relatives 'forgive' shooting suspect in court," *BBC News*, June 20, 2015, http://www.bbc.com/news/world-us-canada-33206084.

6. Lydia Warren, "I Forgive You," *Daily Mail.com*, June 19, 2015, http://www .dailymail.co.uk/news/article-3131874/Repent-Relatives-Charleston-killer-s -victims-confront-court-heart-wrenching-speeches-FORGIVENESS-adopts-vac ant-remorseless-stare.html.

7. Ray Sanchez and Ed Payne, "Charleston Church Shooting: Who Is Dylann Roof?" *CNN*, December 16, 2016, https://www.cnn.com/2015/06/19/us/charles ton-church-shooting-suspect/index.html.

8. Sanchez and Payne, "Who is Dylann Roof?"

9. Brendan O'Connor, "Here Is What Appears to Be Dylann Roof's Racist Manifesto," *Gawker*, June 20, 2015, http://gawker.com/here-is-what-appears -to-be-dylann-roofs-racist-manifest-1712767241.

10. O'Connor, "Roof's Racist Manifesto."

11. Greg Lacour, "White Supremacist Found Guilty on All Counts in Charleston Church Massacre," *Reuters*, December 15, 2016, https://www.reuters.com/arti cle/us-south-carolina-shooting-roof/white-supremacist-found-guilty-on-all -counts-in-charleston-church-massacre-idUSKBN14418R.

12. "Dylann Roof Cold To Victims, But Apologized to His Parents," *Associated Press*, January 6, 2017, http://foxnews.com/us/2017/01/06/dylann-roof-cold -to-victims-but-apologized-to-his-parents.html.

13. Glenn Smith, Jennifer Berry Hawes, and Abigail Darlington, "Dylann Roof Says He Chose Charleston, Emanuel AME for Massacre Because They Were Historic, Meaningful," *The Post and Courier*, December 9, 2016, https://www.post andcourier.com/church_shooting/dylann-roof-says-he-chose-charleston-emanuel -ame-for-massacre/article_6fab532c-be05-11e6-ab05-575a173993ee.html.

14. Jonathan Greenblatt, "The Resurgent Threat of White-Supremacist Violence," *The Atlantic*, January 17, 2018, https://www.theatlantic.com/politics/arch ive/2018/01/the-resurgent-threat-of-white-supremacist-violence/550634/.

15. Kevin Sack, "Congregants' Quiet Agony at the Dylann Roof Trial," *New York Times*, December 15, 2016, https://www.nytimes.com/2016/12/15/us/dylann -roof-trial-charleston-church-killings.html?emc=eta1&_r=0.

16. Harriet McLeod, "Dylann Roof Stopped at Second Church After 2015 Massacre - Prosecutors," *Reuters*, February 22, 2017, https://www.reuters.com /article/us-south-carolina-shooting-roof/dylann-roof-stopped-at-second-church -after-2015-massacre-prosecutors-idUSKBN1612HQ.

17. Adam Woznikowski, "Bond Set at $1 Million for Charleston Shooting Suspect," *WWLP-22News*, http://wwlp.com/2015/06/19/first-hearing-for-charles ton-shooter-expected-this-friday-afternoon/.

18. Woznikowski, "Bond Set at $1 Million."

19. Timothy Egan, "Apologize for Slavery," *New York Times*, June 19, 2015, https://www.nytimes.com/2015/06/19/opinion/an-apology-for-slavery.html.

20. "Charleston's African-American History," *IAAM*, n.d., https://iaamuseum .org/history/.

21. Lilly Workneh and Sebastian Murdock, "A Year After the Charleston Massacre, the Only Thing Gone from South Carolina's Racism Is a Flag," *Huffpost*, June 17, 2016, https://www.huffingtonpost.com/entry/charleston-massacre-racism -south-carolina_us_576364f0e4b0853f8bf05d5e.

22. Smith, Berry Hawes, and Darlington, "Dylann Roof Says He Chose Charleston, Emanuel AME for Massacre Because They Were Historic, Meaningful."

23. Tribune news services, "Dylann Roof's Confession, Journal Details Racist Motivation for Church Killings," *Chicago Tribune*, December 10, 2016, http:// www.chicagotribune.com/news/nationworld/ct-dylann-roof-charleston-shooting -20161209-story.html, and Kevin Sack and Alan Blinder, "Jurors Hear Dylann Roof Explain Shooting in Video: 'I Had to Do It,'" *New York Times*, December 9, 2016, https://www.nytimes.com/2016/12/09/us/dylann-roof-shooting-charleston -south-carolina-church-video.html?_r=0.

24. "FBI Agent Testifies that Dylann Roof Chose Emanuel AME Church Because It Would 'Make the Biggest Wave,'" *BCNN1*, January 6, 2017, http://black christiannews.com/2017/01/fbi-agent-testifies-that-dylann-roof-chose-emanuel -ame-church-because-it-would-make-the-biggest-wave/.

25. "A Brief History of 16th Street Baptist Church," *16th Street Church*, n.d., http://www.16thstreetbaptist.org/brief-history%2C-part-1.html.

26. CNN Library, "1963 Birmingham Church Bombing Fast Facts," *CNN*, September 7, 2018, updated, https://www.cnn.com/2013/06/13/us/1963-birming ham-church-bombing-fast-facts/index.html; Solomon Crenshaw Jr., "Restoring Faith in Birmingham Decades After Deadly Church Bombing," *Alabama Newscenter*, September 15, 2016, http://alabamanewscenter.com/2016/09/15/re storing-faith-birmingham-decades-deadly-church-bombing/, and F. Erik Brooks, "Sixteenth Street Baptist Church," *Encyclopedia of Alabama*, n.d., http://www .encyclopediaofalabama.org/article/h-1744.

27. CNN Library, "1963 Birmingham Church Bombing Fast Facts."

28. To read more about the Sixteenth Street Church bombing from a survivor's perspective, read Carolyn Maull McKinstry's book, *While the World Watched* (Tyndale House, 2011).

29. Bill Plante, "Survivor of KKK Baptist Church Bombing: 'I Had to Forgive,'" *CBS News*, May 24, 2013, https://www.cbsnews.com/news/survivor-of-kkk-bap tist-church-bombing-i-had-to-forgive/.

30. The Matthew Shepard and James Byrd Jr. Hate Crimes Prevention Act of 2009 makes it a federal crime to "willfully cause bodily injury, or attempt to do so using a dangerous weapon, because of the victim's actual or perceived race, color, religion, or national origin. . . . The Shepard-Byrd Act is the first statute allowing federal criminal prosecution of hate crimes motivated by the victim's actual or perceived sexual orientation or gender identity." "Hate Crime Laws," The United States Department of Justice, n.d., https://www.justice.gov/crt/hate-crime-laws.

31. "The Psychology of Hate Crimes," Public Interest Government Relations Office, n.d., https://www.apa.org/advocacy/civil-rights/hate-crimes.pdf.

32. "Finding Forgiveness for a Racist," *60 Minutes Overtime*, December 17, 2017, https://www.cbs.com/shows/60_minutes/video/ga05XnY1qJcHIDG6liXie do5HGQBkUhd/finding-forgiveness-for-a-racist/.

33. Roxane Gay, "Why I Can't Forgive Dylann Roof," *New York Times*, June 23, 2015, https://www.nytimes.com/2015/06/24/opinion/why-i-cant-forgive-dyl ann-roof.html.

34. "Psychological Effects of Hate Crime—Individual Experience and Impact on Community," Latvian Centre for Human Rights, 2008, http://cilvektiesibas .org.lv/site/attachments/30/01/2012/Naida_noziegums_ENG_cietusajiem_Inte rnetam.pdf.

35. "Psychological Effects of Hate Crime," Latvian Centre for Human Rights.

36. "Psychological Effects of Hate Crime," Latvian Centre for Human Rights.

37. "How the Legacy of Slavery Affects the Mental Health of Black Americans Today," *The Conversation*, July 27, 2015, http://theconversation.com/how-the -legacy-of-slavery-affects-the-mental-health-of-black-americans-today-44642.

38. Victoria M. Massie, "Forgiveness in the Wake of the Charleston Shooting Does Not Absolve America of Racism," *Vox*, June 17, 2016, https://www.vox.com/2016/6/17/11962622/charleston-shooting-forgiveness.

39. Anthea Butler, "The Decision to Forgive Is Rooted in Faith. The Desire to Forget Is Rooted in Racism," *The Guardian*, June 24, 2015, https://www.theguardian.com/commentisfree/2015/jun/24/charleston-shooting-church-faith-forgiveness-racism.

40. Massie, "Forgiveness in the Wake of the Charleston Shooting."

41. Butler, "The Decision to Forgive is Rooted in Faith."

42. Stacey Patton, "Black America Should Stop Forgiving White Racists," *Washington Post*, June 22, 2015, https://www.washingtonpost.com/posteverything/wp/2015/06/22/black-america-should-stop-forgiving-white-racists/?utm_term=.c6602913eaad.

43. Vermon Pierre, "Forgiveness Is a Marathon," *The Gospel Coalition*, August 12, 2015, https://www.thegospelcoalition.org/article/forgiveness-is-a-marathon/.

44. Becky Little, "How Doug Jones Brought KKK Church Bombers to Justice," *History*, December 13, 2017, https://www.history.com/news/how-doug-jones-brought-kkk-church-bombers-to-justice.

45. "Desmond Tutu Biography," *Biography*, n.d., https://www.biography.com/people/desmond-tutu-9512516.

46. Janice Harper, "A Lesson from Nelson Mandela on Forgiveness," *Psychology Today*, June 10, 2013, https://www.psychologytoday.com/us/blog/beyond-bullying/201306/lesson-nelson-mandela-forgiveness, and Barbara Mutch, "Mandela Taught the Power of Forgiveness: Column," *USA Today*, December 8, 2013, https://www.usatoday.com/story/opinion/2013/12/08/nelson-mandela-remember-column/3896245/.

47. Jonathan Merritt, "Desmond Tutu's four steps to forgiving others: An RNS interview," *RNS Religion News*, August 25, 2014, https://religionnews.com/2014/08/25/desmond-tutu-forgiveness-apartheid/.

48. Merritt, "Desmond Tutu's Four Steps to Forgiving Others."

49. Merritt, "Desmond Tutu's Four Steps to Forgiving Others."

50. Kelly Brown Douglas, "Why the Black Church Forgives Dylann Roof," *The Nation*, July 2, 2015, https://www.thenation.com/article/why-the-black-church-forgives-dylann-roof/.

51. Patton, "Black America Should Stop Forgiving White Racists."

52. "On Tuesday, July 29, 2008, the US House of Representatives issued an unprecedented apology to black Americans for the institution of slavery, and the subsequent Jim Crow laws that for years discriminated against blacks as second-class citizens in American society. Rep. Steve Cohen, a Democrat from Tennessee, drafted the resolution. Cohen explains the apology's long journey for Congressional approval and the significance of its timing.

"This country had an institution of slavery for 246 years and followed it with Jim Crow laws that denied people equal opportunity under the law. There was segregation in the south and other places in this country, at least through the year 1965 when civil rights laws were passed. The fact is, slavery and Jim Crow are stains upon what is the greatest nation on the face of the earth and the greatest government ever conceived by man.

"But the fact that this government has not apologized to its own citizens, African-Americans, for the institution of slavery and for the Jim Crow laws that followed and accepted that fact and encouraged changes in our dialogue and understanding in the actions of this country to rectify that is certainly a mistake. And today we rectify that mistake." "Congress Apologizes for Slavery, Jim Crow," *NPR*, July 30, 2008, https://www.npr.org/templates/story/story.php?story Id=93059465.

53. "Can God Forgive Serial Killers?" *Billy Graham Evangelistic Association UK*, n.d., https://billygraham.org.uk/answer/can-god-forgive-serial-killers/.

Chapter 6: Missing Myra

1. Alan Blinder, "Charleston Church Mourns One More Beloved," *New York Times*, June 29, 2015, https://www.nytimes.com/2015/06/30/us/emanuel-ame -church-mourns-myra-thompson.html.

2. Blinder, "Charleston Church Mourns."

3. "John Newton, Reformed Slave Trader," *Christian History*, n.d., https:// www.christianitytoday.com/history/people/pastorsandpreachers/john-newton .html.

4. Born and raised in Charleston, Myra Thompson graduated from Burke High School and received a bachelor's degree from Benedict College in Columbia. She returned to the Lowcountry, teaching reading and language arts at both Cathedral Catholic and Brentwood Middle School before becoming a guidance counselor at Brentwood. "Funeral Held for Myra Thompson Whose Husband Forgave Dylann Roof," *BCNN1 WP*, June 28, 2015, http://wspa.com/2015/06/29/funeral-for-myra -thompson-whose-husband-forgave-suspect/.

5. Corky Siemaszko, "Hundreds Attend Funeral of Myra Thompson, Emanuel AME Church Massacre Victim," *Daily News*, June 29, 2015, http://www.nydaily news.com/news/national/hundreds-attend-funeral-church-victim-myra-thomp son-article-1.2275265.

6. Cleveland L. Sellers Jr., "Segregation," *South Carolina Encyclopedia*, n.d., http://www.scencyclopedia.org/sce/entries/segregation/, and Jeremy Richards, "Gressette Committee," *South Carolina Encyclopedia*, n.d., http://www.scencyc lopedia.org/sce/entries/gressette-committee/.

7. "Flashback: Dr. King Visited Charleston in 1962, July 1967," January 15, 2018, *Live 5 news*, http://www.live5news.com/story/37266288/flashback-dr-king -visited-charleston-in-1962-july-1967.

8. Paul Bowers, "Mother Emanuel Shooting Was a Loss for the Gullah/ Geechee," *Charleston City Paper*, June 22, 2015, https://www.charlestoncity paper.com/charleston/mother-emanuel-shooting-was-a-loss-for-the-gullah-gee chee/Content?oid=5260131.

9. Anthony Thompson graduated from Bishop England High School in 1970 and attended Benedict College in Columbia, South Carolina. After six years of military duty in the US Navy, he resumed his studies at Benedict College where he received a bachelor of arts degree in secondary education. He graduated from

Cummins Theological Seminary of Summerville, S.C., in 1995 with a masters of divinity degree.

10. "Zacchaeus," *Bible History Online*, n.d., https://www.bible-history.com/sketches/ancient/tax-collector.html.

11. James O. Cunningham, "Commentary: Parkland Tragedy: Forgiveness Might Free Survivors from Hatred," *Orlando Sentinel*, February 23, 2018, http://www.orlandosentinel.com/opinion/os-ed-parkland-shooting-history-of-forgiveness-moving-on-20180223-story.html.

12. Jason Marsh, "Is Vengeance Better for Victims than Forgiveness?," *Greater Good Magazine*, July 29, 2015, https://greatergood.berkeley.edu/article/item/is_vengeance_better_for_victims_than_forgiveness.

Chapter 7: A Community and Nation React

1. Timothy M. Phelps, "Mass Shooting at Church in Charleston Resonates Far Beyond," *Los Angeles Times*, June 19, 2015, http://www.latimes.com/nation/la-na-charleston-shooting-20150619-story.html.

2. Lee Powell, video: "Four Years After Riots in Ferguson, MO, This Part of the City Is Still Reeling," *Washington Post*, June 21, 2018, https://www.washingtonpost.com/video/business/segments/four-years-after-riots-in-ferguson-mo-this-part-of-the-city-is-still-reeling/2018/06/21/849535d8-70be-11e8-b4d8-eaf78d4c544c_video.html?utm_term=.105ddbcc94c6.

3. "Timeline: Freddie Gray's arrest, death and the aftermath," *The Baltimore Sun*, April 12, 2015, http://data.baltimoresun.com/news/freddie-gray/, and Jean Marbella, "Six Baltimore Police Officers Charged in Freddie Gray's Death," *The Baltimore Sun*, May 2, 2015, http://www.baltimoresun.com/news/maryland/freddie-gray/bs-md-freddie-gray-mainbar-20150501-story.html.

4. Christina Tkacik, "Remembering the Baltimore Riots After Freddie Gray's Death, 3 Years Later," *The Baltimore Sun*, April 27, 2018, http://www.baltimoresun.com/news/maryland/baltimore-city/bs-md-ci-riots-three-years-later-20180426-story.html.

5. Terry Gross, "'I Can't Breathe' Examines Modern Policing and the Life and Death of Eric Garner," *National Public Radio*, October 23, 2017, https://www.npr.org/2017/10/23/559498678/i-can-t-breathe-explores-life-and-death-at-the-hands-of-police.

6. Gross, "'I Can't Breathe' Examines Modern Policing."

7. Chad Williams, Kidada E. Williams, and Keisha N. Blain, eds., *Charleston Syllabus: Readings on Race, Racism, and Racial Violence* (Georgia: University of Georgia Press, 2016), 2.

8. Jeffrey Collins, "'No Room for Hate' As Families of Charleston Church Shooting Victims Confront Suspect," *Star Tribune*, June 19, 2015, http://www.startribune.com/gunman-feared-blacks-were-taking-over-the-world/308369381/.

9. Mark Berman, "'I forgive you.' Relatives of Charleston Church Shooting Victims Address Dylann Roof," *Washington Post*, June 19, 2015, https://www.washingtonpost.com/news/post-nation/wp/2015/06/19/i-forgive-you-relatives-of-charleston-church-victims-address-dylann-roof/?utm_term=.7669106f08e8.

10. Robert Greene II, "Racism Can't Destroy This Charleston Church," *POLITICO Magazine*, June 29, 2015, https://www.politico.com/magazine/story/2015/06/charleston-shooting-emanuel-african-methodist-episcopal-church-119205.

11. Sebastian Murdock, "Thousands Walk Hand In Hand Across Ravenel Bridge to Show Support for Mother Emanuel Church," *Huffpost*, updated December, 6, 2017, https://www.huffingtonpost.com/2015/06/21/charelston-shooting-bridg_n_7633190.html.

12. Michael Foust, "Charleston Families Forgive Killer; Media & Others in 'Awe'," *The Christian Examiner*, June 23, 2015, https://www.christianexaminer.com/article/media-awed-when-charleston-families-forgive-killer/49143.htm.

13. Benge Nsenduluka, "'Repent, Give Your Life to Christ,' Relatives of Charleston Church Massacre Victims Forgive Dylann Roof at Bond Hearing," *The Christian Post*, June 19, 2015, http://www.christianpost.com/news/repent-give-your-life-to-christ-relatives-of-charleston-church-massacre-victims-forgive-dylann-roof-at-bond-hearing-140633/.

14. Lauren Markoe, "A Year After the Charleston Church Shooting, What Has Changed?" *National Catholic Reporter*, June 8, 2016, https://www.ncronline.org/news/people/year-after-charleston-church-shooting-what-has-changed.

15. Oliver Laughland, Paul Lewis, and Raya Jalabi, "'I Forgive You': Charleston Church Victims' Families Confront Suspect," *The Guardian*, June 19, 2015, https://www.theguardian.com/world/2015/jun/19/i-forgive-you-charleston-church-victims-families-confront-suspect.

16. Amanda Borschel-Dan, "Charleston Shooting Sets Off Chain Reaction in Faith Communities," *The Times of Israel*, June 22, 2015, https://www.timesofisrael.com/charleston-shooting-sets-off-chain-reaction-in-faith-communities/.

17. Kevin Liptak, "Obama's Charleston Eulogy: 'Amazing Grace'," *CNN Politics*, June 29, 2015, https://www.cnn.com/2015/06/26/politics/obama-charleston-eulogy-pastor/index.html.

18. Robert Barron, "Forgiving Dylann Roof," *First Things*, March 2017, https://www.firstthings.com/article/2017/03/forgiving-dylann-roof.

19. Barbara Kelley-Duncan, Carolyn Rivers, and Melissa Maddox-Evans, "City's Apology for Slavery Helps Usher in Healing," *Post and Courier*, June 18, 2018, https://www.postandcourier.com/opinion/commentary/city-s-apology-for-slavery-helps-usher-in-healing/article_1003566a-7324-11e8-ad05-6f5931bdfdd5.html.

20. Hannah Alani and Abigail Darlington, "Debate Emerges Around Charleston's Apology for Slavery: Too Much or Not Enough?" *Post and Courier*, June 18, 2018, https://www.postandcourier.com/news/debate-emerges-around-charleston-s-apology-for-slavery-too-much/article_99b2d1ac-7319-11e8-9b4e-8b9569df6fdb.html.

Chapter 8: Honoring Myra's Wishes

1. Ann O'Neill, Aaron Cooper, and Ray Sanchez, "Boston Marathon bomber Dzhokhar Tsarnaev sentenced to death," *CNN*, May 17, 2015, https://www.cnn.com/2015/05/15/us/boston-bombing-tsarnaev-sentence/index.html.

2. Edward Ball, "United States v. Dylann Roof," *The New York Review of Books*, March 9, 2017, http://www.nybooks.com/articles/2017/03/09/united -states-versus-dylann-roof/.

3. Associated Press, "Charleston Massacre: Dylann Roof's Mom Had Heart Attack During Trial, Attorney Says," *NBC News*, updated December 9, 2016, https://www.nbcnews.com/storyline/charleston-church-shooting/charleston -massacre-dylann-roof-s-mom-had-heart-attack-during-n693776.

4. Khushbu Shah and Eliott C. McLaughlin, "Victim's Dad Warns Dylann Roof: 'Your Creator . . . He's Coming for You,'" *CNN*, January 11, 2017, https:// www.cnn.com/2017/01/11/us/dylann-roof-sentencing/index.html.

5. Jennifer Berry Hawes, "Calling Attorneys His 'Political and Biological Enemies,' Dylann Roof Seeks New Ones for Federal Appeal," *Post and Courier*, September 18, 2017, http://www.postandcourier.com/church_shooting/calling -attorneys-his-political-and-biological-enemies-dylann-roof-seeks/article_591c 3de4-9c97-11e7-a4b1-0bd8f75abd5a.html.

6. Abigail Darlington, "Dylann Roof Threatened to Kill His Capital Defense Attorney David Bruck 'If He Gets Out of Jail,'" *Post and Courier*, April 12, 2017, https://www.postandcourier.com/charleston_sc/dylann-roof-threatene d-to-kill-his-capital-defense-attorney-david/article_2912d8de-1fc8-11e7-b5b8 -47447277e2dd.html.

7. Kevin Sullivan, "Jury Sentences Dylann Roof to Death for Charleston Church Slayings," *Washington Post*, January 10, 2017, https://www.washington post.com/news/post-nation/wp/2017/01/10/i-still-feel-like-i-had-to-do-it-dylann -roof-tells-jury-deliberating-his-fate-in-church-slayings/?utm_term=.2268fa91 8756.

8. Sullivan, "Jury Sentences Dylann Roof to Death."

9. Jelani Cobb, "Inside the Trial of Dylann Roof," *The New Yorker*, February 6, 2017, https://www.newyorker.com/magazine/2017/02/06/inside-the-trial -of-dylann-roof.

10. Mike James, "Parkland's Nikolas Cruz Made Chilling Videos Before Shooting: 'You're All Going to Die,'" *USA Today*, updated May 31, 2018, https://www .usatoday.com/story/news/2018/05/30/parkland-killer-video-im-going-next -school-shooter/657774002/.

11. James, "Parkland's Nikolas Cruz Made Chilling Videos," and Elizabeth Chuck, Alex Johnson, and Corky Siemaszko, "17 Killed in Mass Shooting at High School in Parkland, Florida," *NBC News*, updated February 15, 2018, https:// www.nbcnews.com/news/us-news/police-respond-shooting-parkland-florida -high-school-n848101.

12. F. Wesley Shortridge, "Tears: Towards a Biblical Theology," *The Pneuma Review*, September 18, 2017, http://pneumareview.com/tears-towards-a-biblical -theology/.

13. The Right Reverend Al Gadsden, et al., "A Call to Prayer from the Bishops in South Carolina," Anglican Church in North America website, n.d., http:// anglicanchurch.net/?/main/page/1053.

14. Associated Press, "McVeigh Labels Young Victims 'Collateral Damage,'" *Los Angeles Times*, March 29, 2001, http://articles.latimes.com/2001/mar/29/news /mn-44250.

15. Sylvia Moreno, "Nichols Seeks Forgiveness for Okla. City Bombing," *Washington Post*, August 10, 2004, http://www.washingtonpost.com/wp-dyn/articles/A52840-2004Aug9.html.

16. Associated Press,"McVeigh Labels Young Victims."

17. "McVeigh's final statement," *The Guardian*, June 11, 2001, https://www.theguardian.com/world/2001/jun/11/mcveigh.usa1.

18. Oklahoma City National Memorial Museum, n.d., https://oklahomacity nationalmemorial.org.

19. "And Jesus Wept—Oklahoma City, OK," *Waymarking.com*, n.d., http://www.waymarking.com/waymarks/WMB4R3_And_Jesus_Wept_Oklahoma_City_OK; Simon Jeffery, "The Execution of Timothy McVeigh," *The Guardian*, June 11, 2001, https://www.theguardian.com/world/2001/jun/11/qanda.terrorism; and "Timothy McVeigh Biography," *Biography*, n.d., https://www.biography.com/people/timothy-mcveigh-507562.

20. Charles Montaldo, "Profile of Child Killer Susan Smith," *ThoughtCo.*, updated April 1, 2018, https://www.thoughtco.com/susan-smith-profile-of-child-killer-972686.

21. Harrison Cahill, "Exclusive: Sincerely, Susan: Union Mother Convicted of Murder 20 Years Ago Defends Herself," *The State*, July 21, 2015, https://www.thestate.com/news/local/article28050157.html.

22. HLN Staff, "Where Is Susan Smith's Ex-Husband Now?" *HLNTV.com*, August 14, 2015, http://www.hlntv.com/slideshow/2013/10/09/david-smith-susan-smith-killed-sons-where-are-they-now/.

23. Nicole Weisensee Egan, "The Susan Smith Murders 15 Years Later 'It Haunts Me Every Day'," *People*, April 5, 2010, https://people.com/archive/the-susan-smith-murders-15-years-later-it-haunts-me-every-day-vol-73-no-13/.

24. "Interview with David Smith," *CNN Larry King Live*, March 6, 2002, http://transcripts.cnn.com/TRANSCRIPTS/0203/06/lkl.00.html.

25. Steve Helling, "Sex, Drugs and Infractions: Inside Susan Smith's Life in Prison for Drowning Her Two Sons," *People*, September 26, 2017, https://people.com/crime/susan-smith-drowning-sons-inside-life-prison/.

26. Michael Johnson, "C.S. Lewis on the Problem of Forgiveness," *Desiring God*, May 26, 2011, https://www.desiringgod.org/articles/c-s-lewis-on-the-problem-of-forgiveness.

27. MSNBC.com staff and wire reports, "15 Years Later, Hear McVeigh's Confession," *NBC News*, n.d., http://www.nbcnews.com/id/36633900/ns/msnbc-documentaries/t/years-later-hear-mcveighs-confession/#.W0suMC2ZPUI.

28. Jim Ryan, "Some Bombing Survivors Offer Forgiveness," *ABC News*, June 8, 2001, https://abcnews.go.com/US/story?id=93148&page=1.

29. Ryan, "Some Bombing Survivors Offer Forgiveness."

30. MSNBC.com staff and wire reports, "15 Years Later, Hear McVeigh's Confession."

31. Todd Morrison, "The Real Danger of Unforgiveness," *Relevant*, October 2, 2014, https://relevantmagazine.com/life/real-danger-unforgiveness.

32. Amy Viteri, "'I Forgive Him,' Parkland School Shooting Survivor Says," *Local10.com*, February 15, 2018, https://www.local10.com/news/parkland-school-shooting/i-forgive-him-parkland-school-shooting-survivor-says-.

33. Robert Barron, "Forgiving Dylann Roof," *First Things*, March 2017, https://www.firstthings.com/article/2017/03/forgiving-dylann-roof.

34. Barron, "Forgiving Dylann Roof."

Chapter 9: The Deadly Dis-ease of Unforgiveness

1. "Simon Wiesenthal Quotes," AZQuotes, n.d., https://www.azquotes.com/author/15628-Simon_Wiesenthal.

2. Lecia Bushak, "How Forgiveness Benefits Your Health: Forgiving Wrongdoers Can Expand Physical Fitness," *Medical Daily*, January 7, 2015, https://www.medicaldaily.com/how-forgiveness-benefits-your-health-forgiving-wrongdoers-can-expand-physical-fitness-316902.

3. "Biography," Simon Wiesenthal Center, n.d., http://www.wiesenthal.com/site/pp.asp?c=lsKWLbPJLnF&b=4441351, and "The Sunflower Synopsis," Facing history.org, n.d., https://www.facinghistory.org/sunflower-synopsis.

4. Lorie Johnson, "The Deadly Consequences of Unforgiveness," *CBN News*, June 22, 2015, http://www1.cbn.com/cbnnews/healthscience/2015/june/the-deadly-consequences-of-unforgiveness.

5. David B. Feldman and Lee Daniel Kravetz, "Grudge Match: Can Unforgiveness Be Bad for Our Health?" *Psychology Today*, September 17, 2013, https://www.psychologytoday.com/us/blog/supersurvivors/201309/grudge-match-can-unforgiveness-be-bad-our-health.

6. Paul Vallely, "The Ultimate Heroism Is Forgiving the Enemy," *Independent*, October 14, 2012, https://www.independent.co.uk/voices/comment/the-ultimate-heroism-is-forgiving-the-enemy-8210307.html; "The Railway Man," *History vs. Hollywood*, 2014, http://www.historyvshollywood.com/reelfaces/railway-man/, and "Stories," The Forgiveness Project, n.d., http://theforgivenessproject.com/stories/eric-lomax-scotland.

7. Feldman and Kravetz, "Grudge Match."

8. Kevin Sack and Alan Blinder, "No Regrets from Dylann Roof in Jailhouse Manifesto," *New York Times*, January 5, 2017, https://www.nytimes.com/2017/01/05/us/no-regrets-from-dylann-roof-in-jailhouse-manifesto.html.

9. Taylor Marshall, "Top Ten Paradise Lost Quotes," *TaylorMarshall.com*, n.d., http://taylormarshall.com/2008/03/top-ten-paradise-lost-quotes.html.

10. Jason M. Breslow, "What Does Solitary Confinement Do to Your Mind?" *Frontline*, April 22, 2014, https://www.pbs.org/wgbh/frontline/article/what-does-solitary-confinement-do-to-your-mind/.

11. George Dvorsky, "Why Solitary Confinement Is the Worst Kind of Psychological Torture," *Daily Explainer*, July 1, 2014, https://io9.gizmodo.com/why-solitary-confinement-is-the-worst-kind-of-psycholog-1598543595.

12. "St. Augustine, God shaped void," *Catholic Answers Forums*, September 2007, https://forums.catholic.com/t/st-augustine-god-shaped-void/85175.

13. "Charleston Shooter Dylann Roof Moved to Death Row in Terre Haute Federal Prison," *Death Penalty News*, April 23, 2017, https://deathpenaltynews.blogspot.com/2017/04/charleston-shooter-dylann-roof-moved-to.html; Alexis Simmons, "Dylann Roof After the Death Penalty Verdict, the Process to Execution," *Live5News.com*, updated July 10, 2017, http://www.live5news.com/story

/34231742/dylann-roof-after-the-death-penalty-verdict-the-process-to-execution; Avalon Zoppo, "Charleston Shooter Dylann Roof Moved to Death Row in Terre Haute Federal Prison," *NBC News*, April 22, 2017, https://www.nbcnews .com/storyline/charleston-church-shooting/charleston-shooter-dylann-roof -moved-death-row-terre-haute-federal-n749671; Harrison Jacobs, "What It's Like Inside the Terrifying Super-Max Prison Where the Boston Bomber Will Be Executed," *Business Insider*, June 24, 2015, http://www.businessinsider.com/what -its-like-inside-terre-haute-2015-6, and Breslow, "What Does Solitary Confine-ment Do To Your Mind?"

Chapter 10: The Path to Healing and Peace

1. Robert Smith Jr., *The Oasis of God: From Mourning to Morning* (Mountain Home, AR: BorderStone Press, 2014), 11.

2. Michael Wear, "Stop Explaining Away Black Christian Forgiveness," *Christianity Today*, June 24, 2015, http://www.christianitytoday.com/ct/2015/june-web -only/stop-explaining-away-black-christian-forgiveness.html.

3. Jonathan Merritt, "Desmond Tutu's Four Steps to Forgiving Others: An RNS Interview," *RNS*, August 25, 2014, https://religionnews.com/2014/08/25 /desmond-tutu-forgiveness-apartheid/.

4. Merritt, "Desmond Tutu's Four Steps to Forgiving Others."

5. As quoted in Christina Walker, "When Failure Isn't an Option: How to Press Forward in Sharing Jesus Even When We Stumble," *Christianity Today*, April 2017, https://www.christianitytoday.com/edstetzer/2017/april/when-failure -isnt-option-how-to-press-forward-in-sharing-je.html.

6. "Simon Wiesenthal Quotes," AZ Quotes, n.d., https://www.azquotes.com /author/15628-Simon_Wiesenthal.

7. "Apartheid," *History*, n.d., https://www.history.com/topics/apartheid.

8. "Desmond Tutu," AZ Quotes, n.d., https://www.azquotes.com/author/14881 -Desmond_Tutu?p=2.

9. "Desmond Tutu," AZ Quotes.

10. Dustin Waters, "Events Commemorating Emanuel AME Tragedy Promote Public Service, Discourse on Race," *Charleston City Paper*, June 1, 2017, https:// www.charlestoncitypaper.com/TheBattery/archives/2017/06/01/events-commem orating-emanuel-ame-tragedy-promote-public-service-discourse-on-race.

11. Adam Parker, "Emanuel AME Church Celebrates 200th Anniversary with Events, Unveiling of Memorial," *Post and Courier*, July 10, 2018, https://www.post andcourier.com/church_shooting/emanuel-ame-church-celebrates-th-anniver sary-with-events-unveiling-of/article_cb1179b8-83bf-11e8-8709-5b007e8f9189 .html.

12. Parker, "Emanuel AME Church Celebrates."

13. Natalie Price, "Celebration of Emanuel Nine Held for 3rd Shooting An-niversary," *News 2*, June 18, 2018, https://www.counton2.com/news/local-news /celebration-of-emanuel-nine-held-for-3rd-shooting-anniversary/1245415769.

14. Camila Domonoske, "Architect Unveils Design for Emanuel AME Church Memorial," *NPR*, July 1, 2018, https://www.npr.org/2018/07/16/629424811/archi tect-unveils-design-for-mother-emanuel-ame-church-memorial.

15. Domonoske, "Architect Unveils Design."

16. Domonoske, "Architect Unveils Design."

Bible Study Questions

1. Paul Chappell, "20 Powerful Quotes About Anger and Forgiveness," Christian Quotes, https://www.christianquotes.info/top-quotes/20-powerful-quotes-about-anger-and-forgiveness/#axzz5BSdY92qc.

2. C. S. Lewis, "20 Powerful Quotes About Anger and Forgiveness," Christian Quotes, https://www.christianquotes.info/top-quotes/20-powerful-quotes-about-anger-and-forgiveness/#axzz5BSdY92qc.

3. Rick Warren, "20 Powerful Quotes About Anger and Forgiveness," Christian Quotes, https://www.christianquotes.info/top-quotes/20-powerful-quotes-about-anger-and-forgiveness/#axzz5BSdY92qc.

4. Ron Stodghill, "In Charleston, Coming to Terms with the Past," *New York Times*, November 15, 2016, https://www.nytimes.com/2016/11/20/travel/charleston-south-carolina-past-slave-trade-history.html.

5. "Charleston," *South Carolina Encyclopedia*, n.d., http://www.scencyclopedia.org/sce/entries/charleston/.

6. CNN Library, "1963 Birmingham Church Bombing Fast Facts," *CNN*, September 7, 2018, https://www.cnn.com/2013/06/13/us/1963-birmingham-church-bombing-fast-facts/index.html.

Appendix 4: The Resolution to Recognize, Denounce and Apologize for the City's Involvement with Slavery

1. "Resolution," June 2018, https://thesophiainstitute.org/wp-content/uploads/2018/06/Final-Draft-Slavery-Resolution-pdf-version-6.15.2018-1-pm.pdf.

The Reverend Anthony Batiste Thompson served six years in the US Navy before receiving a BA in secondary education from Benedict College and an MDiv from Cummins Theological Seminary of Summerville, S.C.

He spent twenty-seven years as an adult probation parole agent for the South Carolina Department of Probation, Parole and Pardon Services, but presently he is the pastor of Holy Trinity Reformed Episcopal Church of Charleston.

Rev. Thompson and Myra Singleton have three children and six grandchildren. Since the murder of his wife, Thompson has spoken at many churches and organizations across the U.S. and has been featured in major newspapers and magazines, as well as in television documentaries.

Denise George is author/coauthor of thirty-one books. She has served as church administrator at the historic Old South Church in Boston, Massachusetts; was founding director of LifeWay's denomination-wide Women's Ministry program; was an adjunct professor at Beeson Divinity School; and has traveled the world speaking and teaching at universities, seminaries, churches, and libraries, and for pastors and community groups.

She is married to Dr. Timothy George, founding dean of Beeson Divinity School, Samford University, Birmingham, Alabama. The Georges have two grown children and a grandson.